KU-200-984

A Reversal of Fortunes?

Women, Work and Change in East Germany

Rachel Alsop

U.W.E.L.
LEARNING RESOURCES

ACC. N. 2260484 CLASS 124

CONTROL
1571819657

331.
409431

DATE 17. JUL 2002 SITE WV ALS

Berghahn Books
New York • Oxford

First published in 2000 by
Berghahn Books

Editorial offices:
604 West 115th Street New York, NY 10025, USA
3 New Tec Place, Magdalen Road, Oxford OX4 1RE, UK

©2000 Rachel Alsop

All rights reserved.
No part of this publication may be reproduced in any form or by
any means without the written permission of Berghahn Books.

Library of Congress Cataloging-in-Publication Data
Alsop, Rachel.
A reversal of fortunes? : women, work and change in East
Germany / Rachel Alsop.
p. cm.
Includes bibliographical references and index.
ISBN 1-57181-965-7 (alk. paper). — ISBN 1-57181-771-9
(alk. paper)
1. Women—Employment—Germany (East) 2. Sex discrimi-
nation in employment—Germany (East) 3. Sex role—Germany
(East) I. Title.
HD6150.5.A47 2000   99-35019
331.4'0943'1—dc21

British Library Cataloguing in Publication Data
A catalogue record for this book is available
from the British Library

Printed in the United States on acid-free paper

Contents

List of Tables

List of Figures

Acknowledgements

Many thanks to the Economic and Social Research Council for financing my doctoral work and to the Haddenham Education trust, which gave me financial help on numerous occasions during my studies. I owe a debt of gratitude to my supervisors at Bradford University, Kenneth Dyson and Jenny Pearce for their support, encouragement and guidance during my Ph.D.; to Barbara Einhorn for all her help; and to Kathleen Lennon and Jenny Pearce for their comments on sections of the final draft. I would also like to extend my thanks to the many people in Germany who so willingly and cheerfully gave me their time and help during my field trips; and to my family and all my friends in Britain and Germany who have helped me out in so many ways. Special thanks to Chris.

Abbreviations

ABM	Arbeitsbeschaffungsmassnahmen – Work-creation schemes
CDU	Christian Democratic Union
CSU	Christian Social Union
DFD	Demokratische Frauenbund Deutschlands – Democratic Women's Union of Germany
DM	Deutschmark
EC	European Community
FDP	Free Democratic Party
FRG	Federal Republic of Germany
GDR	German Democratic Republic
GTB	Gewerkschaft Textil-Bekleidung – Textile and Clothing Trade Union
IGBE	IG Bergbau und Energie – Trade Union for Energy and Mining
LDC	Less-developed country
MASGF	Ministerium für Arbeit, Soziales, Gesundheit und Frauen – Ministry for Work, Social Affairs, Health and Women.
NIC	Newly industrialising country
OECD	Organisation for Economic Co-operation and Development
SED	Sozialistische Einheitspartei – Socialist Unity Party
SPD	Social Democratic Party
THA	Treuhandanstalt – agency for the privatisation of nationalised industries
TKC	Textilkombinat Cottbus

Glossary

Arbeitsgesetzbuch	Labour Code
Ausbildungsberufe	Occupations requiring training
Bundestag	Parliament of West Germany
Erziehungsurlaub	Baby leave
Frauensonderstudien	Women's study courses
Frauenpolitik	Women's policies
Hochschulen	Colleges
Kitagesetz	Childcare law
Kombinat	Combine
Kurzarbeit	Short-time working
Kurzarbeit Null	Workers employed but not working
Land, Länder	State, states
Muttipolitik	Mummy policies
Volkskammer	Parliament of East Germany
Wende	Turning point

1

Introduction

The fall of the Berlin Wall in November 1989 heralded the beginning of a new era in East German history. It also symbolised more generally the collapse of state socialism in Central and Eastern Europe, the dismantling of the Cold War divide and the advent of post-communism as a global phenomenon. Although the nature and the pace of post-communist change has varied across the region, economic uncertainty has been a by-product of reconstruction. In many quarters of the old Soviet bloc, East Germany included, economic restructuring has resulted in widespread firm closures, job loss and unemployment. Whilst in East Germany no section of the workforce has been immune to job loss, women workers have born the brunt of unemployment. Under state socialism the high level of female employment was flaunted as a marker of women's social progress, of their improved social status and the eradication of gendered inequalities. But when the wall came tumbling down so did the myth of equality. Women's greater vulnerability to unemployment exposed not only the fragility of women's place within the labour market, despite their previously high level of participation, but also the fiction of gender equality more generally.

Gender, Employment and Post-Communism

This book draws together issues relating to three fields of study – gender, employment and post-communism – and examines their intersection in the particular context of women's employment in East Germany in the period immediately following the *Wende*.[1] At its basis is a concern not just to describe how women's working lives have changed during the reconstruction of East Germany, but also

1

to understand how gender relations are restructured during such periods of enormous social, economic and political change, in this instance in the particular arena of employment. Underpinning the book is an engagement with feminism as a transformative politics. What can we learn from the East German experience about how gender inequalities are maintained, transformed, challenged or undermined? To what extent does the economic and political framework in which we operate influence the construction of gender relations and hierarchies? Will women lose or gain from the collapse of state socialism?

Theorising Gender

Over the past two decades feminist accounts of gender have paid increasing attention to issues of diversity and difference, shifting away from the hitherto dominant conceptualisation of women as a united, homogenous group. Mainstream feminist thought had come under enormous criticism for privileging the experiences of white, Western, middle-class, heterosexual women, constituting them as 'a "normative referent" against which women of other races, classes and especially third world nations seemed lacking or "underdeveloped"' (Holmgren 1995: 18). By constructing general 'truths' from the experiences of this small (and in many ways socially privileged) group of women, mainstream feminist theory had been culpable of creating the type of theoretical partiality that it had set out to oppose in traditional 'man-made' theory.

Acknowledgement of and attention to the diversity of gendered experiences underpin much of the current theoretical literature on women and gender. The politics of difference has replaced the politics of commonality, with feminist writings increasingly centred on 'in-gender' as opposed to 'between-gender' differences. Yet despite endeavours to address diversity and to confront and rectify the ethnic, sexual and class biases of feminist thought, dominant feminist discourses in the West have given far less recognition to the previous (and continuing) exclusion from mainstream feminist theory of women from the so-called Second World – women who were living in 'real existing socialism' and now in post-communist societies. This is not to say that Western feminists have not for some time researched, documented and analysed the lives of women living in state socialist societies. And, since the collapse of the Soviet bloc, a profusion of texts has appeared detailing the impact of change on women's lives. But, with some notable exceptions (Molyneux 1981,

1991; Holmgren 1995), the analysis of women's lives under state socialism has tended to remain within its own academic ghetto and has infrequently been taken on board, at least in any extensive or critical way, by those academics working in more mainstream or other areas of feminist research. As Berry (1995: 2) points out in relation to feminist analyses of national and sexual identities, 'for a number of reasons, not least of which has been the relative unavailability of information from and about the Second World, most discussions have tended to focus almost exclusively on postcolonial contexts or a first–third world nexus'.

Much Western feminist literature had been (and, to some extent still is) concerned either implicitly or explicitly with gender relations within a capitalist mode of production. The domestic labour debate, which raged in the 1970s in Western academic circles, situated its discussion almost exclusively within the context of capitalism, concerned overwhelmingly with the relationship between women's domestic labour and capitalist accumulation. Feminist theorists exploring the family as a key site of women's oppression centred their discussion mainly on the experience of white women in Western capitalist societies. They thereby ignored not only the particular position of black women for whom the family was often a site of resistance to racism, but also the experiences of women in state socialist societies where the family often provided a haven of respite and privacy away from the long arm of the state (Einhorn 1995; Holmgren 1995). Even socialist and Marxist feminists who, to varying degrees, saw the eradication of gendered inequalities as entwined with the removal of capitalist relations of production have at times been reticent to theorise the persistence of inequalities within socialist societies.

Now the Cold War is over the opportunities for exchange between scholars on both sides of the former divide are far greater than before. However, a continued lack of attention and sensitivity on the part of Western feminist scholars to the specificity of women's position in the 'Second World' and to the particular manifestations of gender inequalities within state socialist and post-communist societies has been exemplified by the tensions, even hostility, between Western and Eastern European women since the end of the Cold War (Einhorn 1995; Holmgren 1995). Despite the increased emphasis on difference within academic feminism, Western feminists have once again been culpable of seeing the world through 'Western-tinted' glasses, guilty, in this instance, of 'the critical appropriation of 'second world' realities by 'first world' formulations' (Anne Snitow cited in Einhorn 1995: 23). Eastern European women have found women in the West arrogant, intolerant and dogmatic (Einhorn 1995: 23), irritated by their 'we know best' approach. Western women, on the other hand, have been exasperated by what they see as Eastern European women's passivity and conformity (Einhorn 1995: 23), at times failing to understand the different place that family and work took in their lives under state socialism. In the new united Germany East–West relations have been equally acicular. Despite unification and their shared German identity women on each side of the former divide have spoken of a continuing gulf, of the persistence of 'the Wall in our heads' (Einhorn 1995: 23).

Accompanying the emerging recognition of the diversity of women's experiences (albeit with observable limitations) has been a shift in the *mode* of theorising gender within feminist thought (Fraser and Nicholson 1990). There has, as Barrett (1992: 201) comments, been a 'turn to culture' within feminist thought: a shift of focus from 'things' to 'words'. Whereas earlier feminist work was concerned primarily with the material indications of inequality – gendered pay differentials, domestic division of labour, sexual violence – more recent feminist theories have been more preoccupied with language, signification, text and discourse (Ebert 1996). Drawing on poststructuralism, 'woman' has come to be seen as a 'constantly shifting signifier of multiple meanings' (Stacey 1993). Thus the notion of diversity has been re-mapped to include the discursive variability of the signifiers 'woman', 'man', and no longer merely takes account of structural inequalities arising from the intersection of gender with other axes of social inequality, such as 'race' or class. Poststructuralist feminist theory suggests that what it is to be a woman or a man varies according to discursive location. Thus, in any particular society at any given time contradictory and conflicting versions of femininity may coexist. Poststructuralist theory suggests that we make sense of ourselves and our relationship with the rest of the world via the discourses available to us (Weedon 1987). Subjectivity is seen as discursively constructed and, given the diversity of discourses, as fragmented, disjointed and contradictory.

This brief discussion does not attempt to, nor can it in any way, do justice to the diversity and complexity of contemporary feminist thought. It does, however, attempt to draw attention to the general shift of mood within academic feminism over the past three decades. Soper (1991: 103 104) draws a contrast between

> an earlier phase of feminist campaigning which pursued its ends in the
> name of 'liberation' of women and directed its energies primarily to the

4

analysis and removal of the material – economic and social conditions – responsible for female subordination, and a later more 'culturalist' orientation which has focused more on the symbolic negation of the feminine and on the need for a general re- or de-gendering at the level of language and conceptualisation. ... What is needed now we are asked to believe, is not 'simply' changes at the material level since these, even if quite radical (a transformation of the mode of production) are consistent with the maintenance of a masculine Symbolic or cultural order and its binary gender system. What is needed, rather, is a cultural revolution which delivers us from the very modes of conceptualization within which we have hitherto constructed gender identities.

However, a straightforward shift of attention from the material to the cultural is problematic. The relationship between the material and the cultural is dialectical. Thus, to understand how gender roles and relations are constructed and reconstructed, attention to both material and cultural factors, and the interrelationship between the two, is vital. As this study of women's employment in East Germany shows, the transition to a state socialist economic and political system after the Second World War, as Soper implies, did not eradicate gendered inequalities and did not undermine 'the binary gender system'. However, changes at the material level during this period – the restructuring of the distribution and organisation of resources and power, both economically and politically – did impact upon the ways in which gender was constructed and conceptualised. A gender hierarchy did survive the transition to socialism. But at the same time the social construction of 'womanhood' was, to some extent at least, transformed under state socialism. In stark contrast to the Nazi period beforehand in which involvement in public life was regarded as an essentially male pursuit, being a worker became a central part of the adult feminine identity in the state socialist period. Discontinuities as well as continuities in the cultural construction of gender have been observable during the periods of immense economic and political change in East Germany's history. To lose sight of such change and to focus entirely on the continuity of a binary gender system would be to miss key shifts in the ways in which both femininity and masculinity have been constructed. Thus, to understand and explore the *cultural* reconstruction of gender requires an engagement with *material* changes.

Ironically, academic feminism in the West has shifted its focus to culture at a point when many women in the newly emerging post-communist states are facing mounting material hardship. How we make sense of gender and the priority academic feminism places on the material conditions that construct gender are thus of crucial *political* importance. I am not suggesting for one moment that feminist academics should abandon attention to language and discourse when theorising gender. I am definitely not suggesting that poststructuralist discourse theory is not useful in analysing gender relations in post-communist societies. Indeed, the growth of nationalist discourses in many corners of Eastern Europe is playing a central role in the reconstruction of women's social roles and has on-going implications for the ways in which women make sense of their place within society. Nationalist discourses tend to define women primarily as mothers, as reproducers of the 'nation', and are mobilised not only by politicians to justify and promote women's marginalisation within the workforce but also by the anti-abortion lobby to argue against women's right to self-determination in reproductive matters. What I am advocating, however, is a greater attention to the interconnections between 'words' and 'things' and a more detailed analysis of the dialectical relationship between the discursive and the nondiscursive. To what extent, for example, can the growth of nationalism in Eastern Europe be regarded as symptomatic of conflict over economic resources during a period of massive and rapid socioeconomic and political change? How then do the material conditions of gendered inequality feed into the construction of gendered subjectivities and identities?

The question of how to reconcile structural and cultural analyses of gender is, as Coole points out, an 'enduring problem for feminism' (Coole 1994). Many feminists, she argues, are 'wary of going so far into the merely discursive'. Barrett (1992), for instance, whilst arguing that the traditional social sciences have 'lost their purchase' within the feminist movement also warns against a 'wholesale abandonment of the areas of study traditionally denoted by the academic disciplines of sociology, political economy, economics and politics.' Yet as Ebert (1996) points out, feminist and postmodern theory, in all its many guises, has been 'preoccupied with distancing itself from issues of economics, labor, production and exploitation', leading, she argues, to feminist studies of economics, sociology and labour relations being 'relegated to the terrain of specialist knowledges and excluded from any integrated transdisciplinary inquiry into gender and sexuality, thus marginalising these issues in feminist theory' (Ebert 1996: 23).

Yet social life cannot be equated solely with language, discourse and cultural practice (Hennessy 1993; Ingraham 1996). Although we make sense of the material via discourses this does not mean we can fully understand how the world around us operates merely by attention to language, signification and discourse. As Hennessy (1993:149) points out, all aspects of social life are

> discursively mediated and regulated, but at the same time their materiality is not simply discursive [...] While political and economic practices are always made intelligible and shaped by our ways of making sense of them, reducing materiality to discourse alone has the effect of obscuring much of social life.

In East Germany therefore, to understand the shifting construction of womanhood, say, in state discourses, attention needs to be paid to changes in the material world, for example the shortage of labour, falling birth rate, to the state apparatus and so on. In many ways it is hard to disentangle the discursive from the nondiscursive because of the mediation of the 'real' by the discursive. But whilst sense is made of economic shortage, demographic trends and so on via discourse their existence is not purely discursive. As Coole (1996: 23) points out, the reality of economic inequality exists 'regardless of our discursive ability to articulate it'.

Gender and Employment: Global Change

The recognition of diversity and the incorporation of 'difference' into feminist analyses of gender have been crucial and important moves within the development of feminist thought. In a bid to avoid generalisations and the construction of false universals, feminist analyses have in recent years paid more attention to the position of women and men within specific contexts, taking into account difference according to time-period, geographical location, social context and so on. Accompanying, and to a large extent, underpinning this shift has been the postmodern challenge to the modernist tradition of ahistorical, generalising and totalising theories. In particular, the poststructuralist emphasis on the diffuse nature of power (Harstock 1990) has helped cement the shift of inquiry within feminist theory from macro- to micro-level analyses. In a Foucauldian poststructural framework 'social life comes to be a network of power relations – relations which should be analyzed not at the level of large-scale social structures but rather at very local, individual levels' (Harstock 1990:170).

Whilst more studies of the cultural and historical specificity of capitalism, of the particularity of local economies and the construction of gendered relations within such contexts are vital to understand the diversity of gendered economic relations (see for example Walby 1997), when looking at questions relating to gender, production and consumption attention to the global as well as to the regional and the local and the interrelationship of all such sites is crucial. In analyses of gender and employment, given the increasingly globalised nature of capitalist relations, attention purely to the particular, the specific or the local without consideration of 'the bigger picture' 'cannot explain the relationship between the social construction of difference and power in any *systemic* way' (Hennessy 1993: 21 – my italics – RA). What is needed instead is the linking of 'the local to the macro level of analysis' (Ingraham 1996: 171) without the construction of totalising meta-theories. A blanket analysis of gender and capitalism would miss the varied, multiple and dynamic interconnections of gender and capitalist relations. Likewise a totally blinkered focus on a specific form of capitalist accumulation, region or time-period would miss broader patterns and the possibility of interconnections on a larger scale. In the postwar period capitalist relations of production and consumption have become increasingly globalised, fuelled by advances in information technology and the industrialisation of developing (postcolonial) countries amongst other factors. A computer, a car, even a pair of jeans may be 'worked on' in a number of different locations across the world before ready for sale. In the same vein the decision to locate production in a certain area or to shut down a particular production site will be determined by local and global considerations. Patterns of production and thus the profile of employment within any one area cannot be divorced from wider social relations and structures. As Massey (1994: 9) points out, it is difficult to maintain a distinction between the global and the local 'if each is part of the construction of the other'. In sum, the local, the regional and the global are inextricably linked. Any analysis of female employment has therefore to be aware and take account of these interrelationships.

In terms of labour distribution and production within the world capitalist economy, two key trends have been evident globally in the postwar period: firstly, a shift of manufacturing, particularly labour-intensive production, from the advanced capitalist economies to newly industrialising capitalist economies, most notably countries in Southeast Asia and the Latin Rim; and, secondly, within advanced capitalist economies there has been a shift, albeit to varying degrees, from manufacturing to service sector employment. In both instances gender has been a crucial dynamic in the restructuring process. Economic transformation in both the first and the third worlds has been dependent, to some extent at least, upon the increased use of women in waged employment.

However, the suggestion that is sometimes made that the industrialisation of the developing world 'in the post-war period has been as much female led as export led' (Susan Joekes cited in Moghadam 1993: 331; Pearson 1992: 234) needs to be treated with a certain degree of caution. In both the developed and developing world, we should not overestimate the extent to which labour has been feminised during this restructuring process. Looking at the particular case of newly industrialising countries, Ruth Pearson (1992) argues that the recruitment of women has been central to the expansion of export processing industries. Yet she warns against equating women's employment in export processing factories with all industrial activity in developing countries. Not only does women's employment extend beyond export processing – they are also employed in the informal sector of sweatshops and homeworking – but also an exaggerated focus upon female employment in manufacturing geared for the external markets ignores production for the home markets and the many areas in which industrial workforces remain predominantly male, for example shipbuilding. In the advanced capitalist West the extent to which women have been drawn into the workforce varies between countries and within individual countries between different regions and localities (Esping-Andersen 1990; Lane 1993). Moreover the expansion of female employment has not benefited all groups of women to the same extent. Women's place in the labour market is constituted by more than their gender. In the labour markets of the Western world ethnicity, able-bodiedness, domestic labour arrangements and locality can all influence men's and women's access to employment and their experiences in work. Furthermore, an increase in the quantity of women employed does not signify improvements across the board in the quality of women's employment. World-wide, the occupational segregation of men and women both horizontally and vertically persists despite the seemingly greater inclusion of women within the formal paid labour market. In Britain, for example, despite increasing numbers of women in employment in the past thirty years, the number of women in senior positions remains particularly low. At the end of the 1990s fewer than four in every 100 directors of British companies are women, signifying only a 2 percent increase in the past twenty years.

We also need to guard against making any general statements about the feminisation of waged labour internationally, in view of the disproportional 'de-feminisation' of waged labour in most quarters of the former Soviet bloc engendered by the process of post-communist reconstruction (Einhorn 1993a; Fong and Paull 1993; Millard 1995). Propelled by ideological concern and, most significantly, by economic need the state socialist countries of Central and Eastern Europe had mobilised women into the waged labour force in the early postwar years. The later collapse of state socialism and the ensuing economic crises that have engulfed many parts of the region have led to job loss, firm closures and unemployment. Although levels and patterns of unemployment vary, overall it has been women who have been hardest hit by labour rationalisation and unemployment.

Aslanbeigui et al (1994: 1–2), surveying the contributions to their edited collection on women and economic transformation in developing and post-communist countries, state that:

> regardless of the country examined and regardless of whether per capita income has increased, stagnated or decreased, women have been over-represented among the losers or under-represented amongst the winners. Women's relative losses have been manifested in different ways, but in every country examined in this volume, economic transformation has led to fewer gains or greater losses for women. *The outcome of economic transformation, therefore, does not appear to be random* [my italics – RA].

Although at first glance the trends in the first and third world towards women's greater involvement in waged labour may appear at odds with the displacement of women from waged labour in post-communist Central and Eastern Europe, the two trends have inter-connections. To look at either in isolation by adopting an exclusively micro-level approach would be to miss points of interrelation. The expansion of female employment should not be taken as an immediate indicator of greater gender equality or women's improved social status. Looking at the West, clearly some women have made considerable social advances and have penetrated the professional strata of employment. Yet the expansion of women's employment in many parts of the Western world has been mostly in 'low-skilled' areas of the service sector, often in part-time jobs with fixed-term contracts, which command, on average, lower rates of pay and in some countries much less employment protection. In the developing world similar patterns are evident. Women are recruited into labour-intensive manufacturing because of the relative cheapness of their labour, their supposedly nimble fingers, their perceived passivity and pliability. Women have been drawn into areas of employment that are 'immediate and temporary' and have 'no permanent status, no statutory protection against dismissal, is subject to short-time working or retrenchment, and cannot demand a wage above what is competitive in the market' (Pearson 1992: 237). Looking at the first and third worlds, in certain economic contexts at least, women's disadvantaged status in society generally and their greater vulnerability economically has made them a preferred source of labour.

As the following chapters explore in more detail, women's weaker socioeconomic position manifested itself in their disproportional vulnerability to unemployment. In post-unification East Germany, as this book demonstrates, gender inequalities persisted both in the labour market and beyond, despite women's previously near full employment under state socialism. Whilst women had entered the labour market in near equal numbers to men prior to the collapse of the GDR, they had not entered the labour market on an equal footing nor did they enjoy equal status. The male worker was still defined as the 'norm' and the female worker as 'other', different and by comparison deficient and lacking. During the economic uncertainties of post-communism women's relatively disadvantaged status has been intensified. What is interesting in the global context is why at certain junctures gender inequalities make women a more attractive source of labour and while at other junctures the hierarchical relationship between men and women serves to marginalise women within the workforce. In the post-communist context what forces are at work to displace women from the labour market? Are there some instances, even within the overall context of disproportionally high female unemployment, where women do constitute a preferred source of labour?

Despite varying patterns of female employment worldwide a global analysis reveals similarities as well as differences. Throughout the world women have a greater tendency to find themselves in a relatively disadvantaged position economically. This disadvantage, however, does not necessarily signify women's greater vulnerability to unemployment. Indeed, as studies of developed and developing countries reveal, women's weaker position vis-à-vis the labour market can make them a more attractive source of labour (Bruegel 1979; Pearson 1992). Yet within the context of post-unification East Germany gender inequalities in the labour market result broadly in women's increased susceptibility to unemployment. However, as the analysis of the clothing sector suggests, in certain contexts at least women remain a favoured source of labour. The interconnections between the growing inclusion of women in the workforces of the West and the developing world and the growing exclusion of women from the workforces of post-communist Central and Eastern Europe can only be satisfactorily understood and theorised if global as well as local and regional analyses are conducted. In this sense 'global' must be extended beyond the first world–third world nexus to also include the second world. The opening up of former centrally-planned state socialist economies fully to world trade has and will continue to have specific consequences for the share of global trade held by both the advanced and more recent capitalist economies, as well as for the distribution of labour, production and wealth globally. Women's experiences of employment in the so-called 'second' world, like those of women elsewhere, need to be viewed against the backdrop of a dynamic global economy.

Post-Communist Transformations

The balance between local and global, between the particular and the general needs to be carefully balanced and constantly monitored. I have so far used post-communism as an umbrella term to capture the processes of political, economic and social transformation in Central and Eastern Europe after the fall of state socialism at the end of the 1980s. Common to post-communist societies, it could be argued, are three broad transformational processes: the creation of a more pluralist political system; the retreat of the state from the economy; and the closer integration of former state socialist states into the global economy (Hettne 1994: 50). However, care should be taken neither to universalise nor homogenise the processes of transformation underway in Eastern and Central Europe, but instead to recognise the specificities and complexities of post-communist change on national, regional and local levels. As Hettne (1994: 47) comments, 'The meaning of post-communism is elusive since we are dealing with an emerging reality with different national manifestations'. Post-communism is both plural and diverse. The pace, nature and consequences of reform are varied, making it unwise, in fact quite fallacious, to assume that each country in question will follow the same course of transition.

Indeed as time unfolds it becomes ever clearer that the neo-liberal, universalist approach adopted to manage the process of transformation in societies emerging from 'communism' is problematic. Western advisers and Eastern governments have worked on the assumption that the introduction of policies ensuring the liberalisation and marketisation of the economy and the democratisation of the political sphere would be sufficient to secure the successful and rapid transition to Western-style capitalism evenly throughout the region. This universalist approach to reform has failed to take fully into account the heterogeneity of the region and thus the extent to which 'the legacies of institutional frameworks and existing social relations' (Smith and Pickles 1998: 2) would influence the outcome of reform strategies. Soviet-style socialism, despite the push towards a certain degree of uniformity, did not eradicate the cultural, economic and political diversity of the region. As Miall (1993: 63) poetically puts it, the cultivation of 'the flower of democracy' takes place 'not only in the acid topsoil of post-communist societies, but also on the subsoil of older historical and cultural traditions, which continue[d] to exert a powerful and subtle influence'.

Integral to the ethos of reform in the initial post-communist period has been the notion that 'West is best'; that the introduction of western-style institutions and modes of practice into Eastern Europe would ensure the speedy approximation of East with West. The flaws in this judgement are seen no more clearly than in East Germany. The unification of East and West Germany was a one-way process, based upon the rapid introduction of West German systems, standards and practices into East Germany. What the case of East Germany exhibits is that 'the overnight introduction of a fully developed set of social market institutions will fail because there is a reciprocal inter-dependence between economic structures, institutions and learned rules of behaviour' (Dunford 1998: 107). Whilst the case of East Germany is unique in that it was the only former Eastern bloc country to go through such a process of unification, the analysis can also be applied more generally to Eastern Europe. The belief held by key economic and political agencies in the initial period of post-communist reconstruction that the marketisation and democratisation of the region could be successfully and uniformly ensured by mimicking Western institutions and traditions has been shown to be severely misguided. Interestingly the case of post-communist transformation in East Germany is often ignored or marginalised in studies of post-communism (Henderson 1994) because of its presumed peculiarity and particularity within the region. Indeed, looking at its state socialist heritage – with its particularly high levels of female employment, relatively prosperous standards of living and developed system of social care – as well as the unique nature of its post-communist transformation engendered by unification, the specificity of its position becomes apparent. However, the fundamental dissimilarities should not be

13

stressed without an accompanying recognition of points of commonality. The 'West is best' approach prevailed not just in post-unification East Germany but elsewhere in the Eastern bloc. Economic and political reconstruction in Eastern Europe has not taken place in a vacuum but has been influenced both ideologically and financially by Western agencies and advisers. As West Germany has been used as a yardstick to measure and guide the transformation of East Germany, so more generally has the Western world acted as the model for Eastern Europe to imitate. Thus, whilst the position of the former GDR within the post-communist landscape may be fundamentally different in so many key ways, this does not make it any less worthy of the label 'post-communist' nor of its inclusion within accounts of transformation within Eastern Europe.

A Reversal of Fortunes?

This study of women's employment in East Germany examines women's changing relationship to the labour market during two periods of economic and political restructuring in East Germany's postwar history. Chapter 2 considers the implications of the transition to a state socialist system after the Second World War for women's socioeconomic status in East Germany. The remaining chapters of the book are concerned primarily with the period after the collapse of state socialism in 1989 and the implications of capitalist restructuring and the democratisation of the political sphere for women's labour. When posing the question 'A Reversal of Fortunes?', this study is concerned with two main issues. Firstly, what have women lost and gained during the transition from state socialism to capitalist, liberal democracy? Secondly, what processes of continuity and change can be identified over the two periods? Did the collapse of state socialism rupture the entire fabric of gender relations or can lines of continuity be identified?

Millard (1995), writing on women's employment in post-communist Poland, argues that the economic and political transformation of Poland has resulted in both losses and gains for women. The process of transformation and its implications for the citizens of Poland are, she argues, 'complex, contradictory and replete with paradox' (Millard 1995: 60). In East Germany post-communist transformation has granted East Germany citizens certain fundamental rights previously denied to them under state socialism. The freedom of speech, of organisation and of movement is guaranteed to all by law. Within the democratic system free elections are held giving East Germans the first chance of real suffrage since the Weimar Republic, for most the first time in their lives. Women can now organise autonomously and independently from the state without fear of reprisals, censorship or imprisonment by the state. East German citizens are now able to travel freely beyond their national borders, notwithstanding visa and entry restrictions to specific countries. Shortages in goods and foodstuffs are no longer everyday occurrences. Instead East Germans have on offer a far greater variety of shops stocking a far wider range of goods.

Yet at the same time the transition to the market has had its costs and these costs have not been borne equally by all. The collapse of state socialism has brought to an end the situation where workers had a job for life. East Germans may now, in principle, buy what they wish and travel where they want, but growing unemployment and economic insecurity inhibits the extent to which many can take advantage of these new-found freedoms. In the new market economy the potential to have a higher standard of living may be greater but so is the potential for greater relative poverty, unemployment and homelessness. Whilst it is sometimes difficult to talk of gains and losses, Millard (1995: 73) concludes in her analysis of Poland that '[o]n balance, however, the losses outweighed the gains'. Her conclusions reinforce Aslanbeigui et al.'s claim that women are overrepresented amongst the losers and underrepresented amongst the winners during periods of economic transformation (see above). Similar conclusions can be drawn from the East German experience. Whilst the new system offers the possibility of greater prosperity and more individual freedom, it also offers the possibility of greater economic insecurity. As women have been more vulnerable to unemployment and are often more tied to the home through caring responsibilities they are often less likely to be able to reap the potential rewards of capitalism.

To a certain extent women's employment experiences before and after the Wende stand in marked contrast to each other. The full employment of the state socialist period has been replaced by economic insecurity and, in the initial post-Wende period at least, high levels of unemployment. Under state socialism the state intervened to secure the high level of female employment. Women's full-time employment became the social norm throughout the life-course, even during the years of childrearing. Post-unification welfare reform has drastically altered the state's involvement in welfare provision. Women wishing to combine full-time work with the care of young children can no longer rely on the same degree of state support in the new system. Yet changes are not all for the worse. The greater availability of goods and services in the new market system has unleashed the potential for the dramatic reorganisation of domestic-related work. The greater availability of labour-saving household appliances, of constantly rather than sporadically available fresh produce, of time-saving frozen foods, and of better quality goods all transform the content of domestic labour.

Yet clear lines of continuity are also evident. Regardless of the greater availability of goods and services after the Wende women continue to perform the majority of domestic labour. In fact research suggests that women are taking on an even greater share of domestic work after the Wende. The welfare systems of the GDR and the new united Germany may be organised fundamentally differently in certain ways (particularly in relation to the state's role in the public provision of services), but both systems rest on the idea that caring is primarily a woman's job. Neither before the Wende nor after did male and female workers enter the labour force on equal terms. Although the boundaries of male and female employment were redrawn in the two periods of economic restructuring, both before and after the Wende occupational segregation according to sex existed within the labour force. In short, although the manifestation of gendered inequalities varied between the two systems, in both periods women were disadvantaged in terms of their socioeconomic status. The extent to which post-communist change heralded a 'Reversal of Fortunes' for women is, as Millard suggests, 'complex' and 'contradictory'.

The Research Project

The research that forms the basis of this book was originally conducted for a doctoral thesis, funded by the Economic and Social Research Council (ESRC). The book is concerned with the initial impact of post-communist change on women's employment. The initial research took place between 1990 and 1994; the main fieldwork was undertaken between October 1991 and September 1992 with additional shorter visits in April 1991 and April 1994. Followup research was conducted in the summer of 1998 to assess the medium-term implications of post-communist change.

Women's employment is examined from both a regional and a sectoral perspective. The book looks in particular at women's employment within Land Brandenburg, one of the five new federal states constructed in East Germany after unification, and at the fate of female labour within the textile and clothing sector. As a means of narrowing and deepening the analysis the research pulls together the regional and sectoral studies to produce a case study of a particular textile and clothing enterprise (TKC) in Cottbus, a town in southeast Brandenburg. This part of the project was undertaken between 1991 and 1994 and is thus confined to the initial post-unification period. The study of the East German textile and clothing industry endeavours to link the local with the global by exploring the impact of East Germany's changing economic position globally on its domestic textile and clothing industry, and more specifically on the gendered division of labour within the sector.

To complement and supplement the vast array of quantitative data chapter 7 explores women's subjective responses to economic and political restructuring. This chapter is based primarily on the results of thirty-two interviews with women who had worked at TKC prior to the Wende. The interviews were conducted in May 1992. At this point twenty-seven of the women participating were midway through a two-year retraining course in office skills at a further education establishment in Cottbus. Three women were unemployed and two were still working at TKC but had received their redundancy notices. The objective of the interviews was to gather information on women's subjective interpretation of their social and labour roles. The interviews were semi-structured in that broad questions were asked on particular topics, relating to both their public and private lives. The discussion focused upon the women's work histories, their experiences and expectations of the labour market both before and after the Wende, the division of labour at home and their thoughts on the general process of social, economic and political change underway in East Germany.

Note

1. Wende means turning point. It is used to describe the general process of change in East Germany following the collapse of state socialism.

2

Rhetoric and Reality: Women's Employment in the GDR

State socialism in the GDR achieved the near full employment of both men and women. By 1989 over 90 percent of all East German women were employed, in training or in education, constituting one of the highest levels of female employment internationally (Winkler 1990: 63). Of the 8.5 million GDR citizens involved in paid labour by the end of the 1980s virtually half (49 percent) were women (Winkler 1990: 62). High levels of female employment were both ideologically desirable and economically imperative in the GDR. Solving the 'Woman Question' – as outlined in Marxist–Leninism, the official ideology of the GDR – was one of the stated aims of the Socialist Unity Party (SED), the ruling party in the GDR (Einhorn 1989). Ideologically, the mass mobilisation of women into paid labour was regarded as a prerequisite of female emancipation. In addition, the endemic shortage of labour made the full employment of all indigenous labour supplies, including women, economically vital. Casualties sustained in the Second World War, the later exodus of mainly young, skilled workers to the West prior to the border closures in 1961 (Jeffries 1987: 6–7) together with a falling birth rate, reaching its nadir in the mid-1970s (Winkler 1990: 24–25), all curbed labour supply.[1] In a labour-intensive economy characterised by low levels of technology, a burgeoning bureaucracy and inefficient employment practices, women became essential constituents of the labour force.

This chapter begins by examining the status and relevance of Marxist–Leninist theory to the formulation of *Frauenpolitik* (women's policies) in the GDR. The discussion suggests that Marxist–Leninist ideology was not only inadequate as an emancipatory strategy but also that ideological principles were only selectively implemented in the policy-making process. The SED only partially adhered to the principles of Marxism–Leninism, at times subordinating ideology to economic and demographic concerns. As a result certain distinct phases can be identified in the history of GDR Frauenpolitik, most notably the shift towards a more pro-natal agenda in the 1970s in response to the falling birth rate. Yet despite the fluctuations of policy making, this chapter also argues that a certain degree of underlying continuity was evident in the state's handling of women's issues. Firstly, throughout the state socialist period policy initiatives were concerned primarily with the position of women and did not engage with the broader notion of gender. Implicit within socialist policy (as with Marxist–Leninist ideology) was the assumption that equality between men and women could be achieved by focusing on women in isolation rather than at the complex and multiple interconnections of gender. Secondly, throughout the state socialist policy focused on the economic position of women to the exclusion of other (noneconomic) aspects of gender relations. Indeed, women's employment became the central focus of the state's campaign to eradicate inequalities between men and women.

The reality of women's lives was far removed from socialist rhetoric, which went as far as to proclaim that equality between men and women had already been achieved. This is not to say that state socialism did not alter women's life-chances in many key ways. Despite the inadequacies of both ideology and policy, women's working lives were transformed under state socialism. Levels of female employment hit record heights with women more visible in traditionally male areas of the economy and in more senior positions. Yet, as the later sections of this chapter record, gendered inequalities persisted both in the labour market and beyond. The majority of women workers remained clustered in a relatively small number of traditionally female occupations and sectors, working often at lower levels of employment hierarchies and commanding lower rates of pay than their male counterparts. Within the home women continued to shoulder the vast majority of domestic labour, which in turn impacted upon both their employment aspirations and possibilities. Women were more likely to avoid additional responsibilities and duties within the workplace, to desire shorter working hours, to avoid overtime and to be more cautious about undertaking shift employment than their male colleagues. A broad overview of the impact of state socialism on women's employment in East Germany thus indicates continuity as well as change in women's relationship to paid labour, signalling gains as well as persisting disadvantage.

Socialist Rhetoric: Defining Women's Position

Ideological Limitations

Marx himself gave little time and space to the particular position of women.[2] It was left to fellow socialists, most significantly perhaps in the East German context, Engels, Bebel and Lenin, to devote more attention to the specificity of the 'Woman Question'. Marxism–Leninism offers an economically deterministic analysis of women's position (Delmar 1976; Landes 1989), seeing women's social position as derivative of the particular mode of production. Engels (1972), for example, argued that women's oppression was rooted in the emergence of capitalist relations of production, the rise of private property, the economic isolation of the family and monogamous marriage, which secured the inheritance of private property. The key to women's emancipation, according to Engels' thesis, was the transition to socialism. Female emancipation would be achieved through the overthrow of private property, the mass participation of women in paid labour and the socialisation of domestic tasks (Buckley 1989; Delmar 1976; Einhorn 1993a; Heitlinger 1979). Lenin, focusing more on the practical implications of theory implementation (Buckley 1989: 25), also stressed the need to remove domestic chores from the private into the public sphere. He emphasised the liberation of women from domestic slavery as a prerequisite of attaining equality between the sexes, attacking housework as 'barbarously unproductive, petty, nerve-racking, stultifying and crushing drudgery' (Kuusinen 1961: 819).

The use of Marxist–Leninist theory as a strategy for women's emancipation or liberation is deeply problematic on many levels. The works of Engels, Lenin and Bebel as well as Marx, whilst stressing the importance of women's involvement in the public sphere, all took for granted the continuation of a division of labour between men and women (Landes 1989: 21–22; Penrose 1990: 61). At the heart of Marxist–Leninist theory was an acceptance and a perpetuation of sexual dimorphism. Both Lenin and Engels stressed the socialisation of domestic labour as a key force in liberating women from sexual oppression, yet gave no clear indication that once such tasks were removed from the private into the public sphere they would not continue to be performed by women. Whilst endorsing the public provision of nurseries, kindergartens and communal eating areas (Heitlinger 1979:17), Lenin, for example, still believed that a woman should remain 'a woman with all her distinctive characteristics, and with the great social mission of motherhood' (Kuusinen 1961: 821). The implications for women and the hierarchical relationship between men and women of a continuing sexual division of labour remained largely unchallenged. A central theoretical problem was that Marxist–Leninism looked to solve the 'Woman Question' and not the 'Gender Question'. It aimed to make women equal with men, but on male terms. Women's roles and status were to be transformed by entering the sphere of production, whilst male gender roles were to undergo minimal change in terms of the redistribution of their labour between the public and private spheres. The position of women rather than male–female relations constituted the central subject of analysis in socialist theory (Buckley 1989: 48/49).

Classical Marxist theory placed the eradication of gender inequalities firmly within the framework of the proletarian struggle, prioritising the issue of class over gender and 'thereby obscuring other sources of social divisiveness, including sexual antagonism' (Landes 1989: 22). Private property and the emergence of capitalist social relations rather than male–female power relations were identified as the primary sources of women's oppression. Orthodox socialist doctrine thus neglected the evaluation of nonmaterial factors shaping women's position, instead emphasising the economic determinants of inequality between men and women. Early Soviet theorists, such as Alexandra Kollantai and Inessa Armand, had tried to open up the analysis of class struggle and women's particular position to incorporate the issues of sexuality and sexual relations but had been effectively silenced during the early years of the Soviet Union (Holt 1977). Kollantai's argument that relationships between men and women should be founded on genuine friendship and 'free love' were rejected in the early years of the USSR. In the difficult years of war communism 'free love' became synonymous with moral and social disintegration (Heitlinger 1979).

Within the GDR, as throughout the former Soviet bloc, the ruling elite did not allow the public space to fully discuss the ideological foundations of the state, to dispute official doctrine and to develop alternative ideas. Debate equalled dissent and was therefore actively discouraged. The result was the 'ossification' of ideology. Ideology acted as a 'mechanism of control which depended on the coercive enforcement of conformity at whatever cost to the development of knowledge and practice' (Walker 1990: 76). Whilst Marxist–Leninist theory was the product of a specific era, its validity and applicability remained very much unchallenged by the state throughout the communist period, late into the latter part of the twentieth century. As Walker (1990: 82) notes:

> the Stalinist desire to master all change locked the CPSU, and its East European counterparts, into a time-warp that stunted their ability to change by constantly returning them to a revolutionary heritage which the system had either long since outgrown or which had never belonged to them in the first place.

The ideological foundations of state socialism therefore became, as in Gorbachev's words, 'unquestionable truths that could only be commented upon' (Walker 1990: 88).

As a Czech writer commented; 'Communism acted on women's behalf – they were never active participants' (Einhorn 1993a: 174). Within East Germany policy decisions were made by an elite group from which women were largely excluded. In comparison with West Germany, where until 1983 women constituted less than 10 percent of representatives sitting in the *Bundestag* (parliament)(Kolinsky 1993: 222), the level of women's representation in the GDR parliament appeared on first glance quite favourable. In 1976 one-third of the *Volkskammer*, the parliament in the GDR, was female (Childs 1988: 251). But, in the vastly dissimilar political regimes of the GDR and the FRG the parliaments played quite different roles in the process of decision making and policy formation. In the GDR the Volkskammer was a token parliament, a gesture towards a democracy which did not exist. Likewise, the female members sitting in the Volkskammer were in effect token women. The relatively high level of women's representation was a sham of greater sexual equality that in fact carried no real political weight. In the Volkskammer the DFD, the official women's organisation in the GDR, was accorded block representation as part of the façade of interest group representation (Childs 1988: 23,131). But, as an agency of the state rather than an autonomously formed movement, the DFD uncritically accepted the dictate from above (Einhorn 1989; Teschner 1994). Instead of providing a forum for women to develop their own ideas and define their own needs it toed the party line, following rather than forming state policy on women. The true power base in the GDR was the *Politburo* – a near exclusively male domain. In the entire history of the GDR no woman was ever a full member of this organ. Just two attained nonvoting membership (Einhorn 1993a: 152).

This is not to say that women were not active politically in opposing the regime. In the 1980s the political group 'Women for Peace' emerged in opposition initially to the imprisonment of conscientious objectors and later to the state's declaration that women could be drafted into the armed forces in times of emergency (Einhorn 1991; Einhorn 1993a). But the state combated the establishment of truly oppositional interest and pressure groups, including an independent women's movement. The 'Women for Peace' group, its aims and motives were considered subversive and dangerous and thus attracted a significant amount of attention from the security forces. Because of the nonhierarchical nature of the group, the state had difficulty pinning down the key figures in the organisation. However, two of its most prominent members were eventually imprisoned for a short period in 1983, following close surveillance of its members by the authorities and the acquisition of information from a 'mole' within the group (Einhorn 1991; Einhorn 1993a).

Changing Priorities

As suggested above, initiatives within the framework of Frauenpolitik came in waves, reflecting the varying priorities of the state. Although Marxist–Leninist theory officially formed the basis of women's policies in state socialist systems, the priority of ideological aims in the formulation of policy initiatives is questionable (Buckley 1985; Einhorn 1993a; Molyneux 1981; Molyneux 1990). Although both Engels and Lenin had outlined the socialisation of domestic labour as well as women's inclusion in the production process as prerequisites of women's liberation, in practice women's entry to production came to be regarded as the single, sufficient rather than just one necessary precondition of women's emancipation (Einhorn 1993a: 20; Einhorn 1994: 20). Looking broadly at state socialist systems, Molyneux (1990: 26) argues that; ' the policies of Communist states towards women and the family were kept subservient to broader economic goals, and changed in accordance with them'. Policies were, she argued, 'the effect of both principle and necessity' (1981: 55).

In the GDR economic and demographic needs were instrumental in defining the particular content and direction of Frauenpolitik.

Ideological aims were hence only patchily translated into measures. Although from the outset the leadership of the SED had placed the 'Woman Question' on the political agenda, throughout the forty-year history of the GDR distinct policy phases are identifiable. (Marx Ferree 1993; Penrose 1990). The period directly after the establishment of the GDR was devoted primarily to bringing women into the production process (Penrose 1990: 64–66). In the immediate postwar period the shortage of (male) labour engendered by the casualties of war demanded the mobilisation of all potential sources of labour, of which women provided the most abundant supply. Legislation was enacted to grant women legal parity with men (Einhorn 1993a: 22) and to increase the number of women, including those with children, in paid employment. Firms and administrative bodies were instructed to recruit women and to facilitate women's employment by setting up childcare and other social facilities (Penrose 1990: 65).

From about the early to mid-1960s a new emphasis in the women's policy agenda was observable (Penrose 1990: 66 67). At the 6th Party Conference in 1963 SED leaders placed even greater stress on the need to improve women's qualification and training levels. Between 1964 and 1970 the Volkskammer introduced a whole raft of resolutions and pieces of legislation aimed at promoting the education and vocational training of women, the equalisation of qualification levels between men and women and thus enabling women's access to middle and higher levels of management. Special study courses for women were to be established in order to give women the opportunity to gain technical and higher level qualifications (Penrose 1990: 67).

On the one hand, the aim of improving the representation of women in training can be seen as part of an overall strategy to improve women's status and was therefore in line with the state's ideological principles to create greater equality between men and women. On the other hand, the increased emphasis upon women's training also satisfied economic need. Migration from the GDR up until 1961 had resulted in a deficit of appropriately trained workers (Jeffries 1987: 6 7). Thus, the state's endeavours to improve women's qualification levels constituted a key element in the general drive to improve the skill levels of a dwindling workforce.

Yet it was from the 1970s onwards that the most distinct shift in the women's policy agenda was evident; policy entered a phase defined by some as a period of *Muttipolitik* (Mummy Policies) (Marx Ferree 1993). From this point onwards the SED's policies

25

were increasingly pro-natal, fuelled by growing alarm over the falling birth rate (Penrose 1990: 68). In 1950 16.5 births per thousand persons of the population were recorded. By 1975 the number of births had fallen to 10.5 per thousand persons (Winkler 1990:24). A package of measures introduced in 1976 aimed to make the conditions surrounding motherhood more appealing and to ease the reconciliation of family and work responsibilities. Of particular importance was the introduction of the 'Baby Year'. Initially women were able to take one year's paid leave from work after the birth of the second or third child. From 1984 the leave was lengthened to 18 months for the third or subsequent children and from 1986 the entitlement was extended to include twelve months' paid leave for the first child and to men as well as women (Penrose 1990: 68–73). Additionally, in a bid to reverse the trend towards smaller families (Winkler 1990: 28) the state introduced incentives to encourage children earlier in life and larger families. Extra financial help and preferential treatment in the allocation of childcare places and housing were offered to student families, the parents of large families and single-parent families. Mothers with three or more children under 16 years of age, together with shift-working mothers of two or more children, were eligible to work just 40 hours per week with no reduction in wages. Large families also received concessions on leisure activities and were awarded priority in housing and childcare (Winkler 1990: 150).

The shift in policy emphasis was reflected in the state-controlled media. Up until the end of the 1960s the dominant female image was that of the career woman. Family, children and household were relegated to a position of secondary importance. From the 1970s the three-child family was depicted as the norm. Women were still portrayed as career-minded but now they were equally as oriented towards family and motherhood as to employment. By this point, the childless career woman had disappeared from official propaganda (Enders 1986; Penrose 1990: 73).

Unlike in many other Eastern bloc countries (for further information see Einhorn 1993a; Molyneux 1981), the new pro-natal edge in women's policies was not accompanied by an erosion of women's rights to abortion. On the contrary, the 1970s saw the liberalisation of abortion policy in the GDR. In 1972 women were given the right to terminate their pregnancies in the first three months. Although this move on the surface appears to contradict the state's desire to increase the number of children born, the prior, stricter regulations on abortion had not prevented the birth rate from falling (Interview with Dr Edith Ockel, Berlin 1991). Moreover, the introduction of the more pro-natal legislation, such as the extended baby leave, was intended to make motherhood a more attractive possibility, to ease the reconciliation of work and motherhood and thereby offset the need to terminate pregnancies because of social difficulties or economic hardship.

Towards the end of the 1980s, I would argue, a new period of policy was beginning to emerge. Attention was being diverted more and more to the issue of education, particularly to the question of 'qualificationally-correct' employment. Honecker noted in 1981 that 20 percent of all skilled workers were employed in semi- or unskilled occupations (*EIU Country Profile 1988–1989 East Germany*: 16). Given the financial resources invested in training and education this underutilisation of skilled workers amounted to a clear waste of both time and money. The relationship between qualifications and employment was gendered. The employment of workers below their qualification level was particularly striking amongst female workers (Röth 1988). Thus, it is plausible to assume that any measures introduced to bring jobs in line with training would have had especial repercussions for women. This remains purely speculative, as the collapse of state socialism at the end of the 1980s precluded the introduction of any concrete policy measures to combat this problem. However, the growing attention to the issue of qualificationally-correct employment during the 1980s supports the contention made in the following section that the pro-natal turn in policy from the 1970s did not signify a complete abandonment of the state's desire (whether economically or ideologically driven) to improve women's access to employment and education.

Policy Continuity

Although at different historical points certain aspects of policy were emphasised – in the early years the inclusion of women in the workforce, later the promotion of women's education and training levels and from the 1970s the desire to create better conditions for women to combine work and motherhood – policy continuity was also evident. For example, when policy makers turned their attention to women's education levels in the 1960s they did not abandon their commitment to maintain a high level of women's employment. Instead, the next stage built upon the success of the first.

Although from the 1970s onwards a clearly pro-natal agenda underpinned the new package of policy measures, the extent to which it is accurate to describe the Frauenpolitik solely as a Muttipolitik needs to be clarified. From this point onwards working mothers became the focal recipients of new policy measures. It was hoped that by making the reconciliation of work and family easier women would opt to have more children but continue working, thereby solving the problem of a falling birth rate and maintaining workforce numbers. As a result, younger women and mothers received more public recognition and attention than other groups of women in the new set of policies after the 1970s. Nonetheless, the state retained its general commitment to the promotion of women's life-long involvement in paid labour and the maintenance of education and training standards for all women.

Throughout, the primary aim of women's policy in the GDR was to enable women to take part in paid labour, in line with the requirements of the economy, whilst at the same time continuing to fulfil their roles as mothers and housewives. Women's employment was to be assisted by the state through its provision of an array of childcare and welfare provisions and the promotion of women in education and training. The falling birth rate had prompted the state to reassess the policy pertaining to mothers, but not at the expense of losing their labour from the workforce, hence the increasing number of measures introduced into welfare policy from the 1970s onwards to positively discriminate in favour of working mothers.

Like Marxist–Leninist theory the SED's treatment of the 'Woman Question' failed to address the 'Gender Question', most notably the gendered division of labour at home and the parallel need for male roles to be reassessed. It was a one-sided approach to gender equality. As East German writer Christa Wolf commented, the GDR gave women the chance to do what men wanted to do (Woods 1985: 93). Paradoxically, the legislation that sought to liberate women actually perpetuated their inequality. Women were generally the sole targets of family and domestic legislation, thereby cementing women's links to housework and childcare. The provision of a housework day – one day off each month to catch up on household chores – for all full-time working women illustrates the inconsistency that existed within SED policy on women. Men were only eligible for the housework day if they were single parents or if their spouse was sick: in other words, if there was not a woman available in the household to perform the domestic tasks. Not only did the introduction of the provision clearly show how policy, under the guise of equality legislation, strengthened women's tie to domestic labour; it also reinforced the state's backing of the private nature of domestic labour, thereby undermining one of the basic preconditions of female emancipation in Marxist–Leninist theory – the socialisation of domestic tasks.

In comparison with other state socialist countries the GDR had a high level of childcare provision. By 1989 the state was able to cover virtually all demand for childcare places (Winkler 1990: 141–145). Yet, the socialisation of housework received little practical support. Often hot meals were available to workers, pupils or children. However, the communal living arrangements as envisaged by Lenin were destined to reside in textbook socialism. Most people lived within a family unit – in 1981 over 90 percent of households consisted of either parent(s) with children or a cohabiting couple (Winkler 1990: 101) and most housework remained performed within the private family sphere. Despite the emphasis on the importance of socialising domestic labour in Marxist–Leninist theory, even the more developed socialist states, such as the GDR, were less advanced in terms of consumer-based technologies than their capitalist counterparts. The prioritisation of heavy industries over consumer industries (Breitenacher 1991: 7) reflected a long-standing disregard of consumer needs. The resulting lack of labour-saving devices for the home and prepared foods together with inconsistent food supplies all exacerbated the problems women already faced trying to juggle work and family commitments.

Although SED women's policy prioritised the emancipating effects of women's employment, it would be misleading to assert that the SED never identified the problems arising from the unequal division of labour in the household. As Einhorn (1993a: 28–29) points out, the state did at times publicly call for men to take their equal share of housework. However, such declarations were not backed by material incentives or practical provisions and were made only half-heartedly and unconvincingly. The proof of the pudding, as it were, was definitely in the eating. Such statements made no decisive impact on the focus of policy; women continued to be targeted in family legislation. The measures introduced by the state aimed to ease the reconciliation of work and *mother*hood rather than work and *parent*hood, thereby maintaining and reinforcing the sexual division of labour. If there was a 'Mummy policy' there was no accompanying 'Daddy policy'.

Haug (1991: 41) asks whether the demise of socialism in the Eastern bloc has led us to dismiss ' a model of women's emancipation whose fruits we have yet to harvest?' The sexual revolution has been described as the longest revolution. Is it just the case that more time was needed for women's equality to be achieved? Looking at the historical record of women's policy in the GDR and the ideological foundations of policy formulation, there is no evidence to indicate that all that was needed was a bit more time. Both the ideology on which state policy rested and the policies implemented by the state failed to fully conceptualise the complexities of gender inequalities. The state overlooked the multidimensional character of women's oppression, instead equating women's high level of employment with equality. Issues such as the sexual division of labour, domestic violence and rape remained to varying degrees unchallenged. Without fully confronting the plural and complex character of male–female power relations, inequalities based on sex were able to persist. Instead, the state merely added to women's roles by creating the conditions to enable women to work. Full-time employment was tacked on to their many other social roles. The architects of state socialism had seen 'equality as something that can be given to women without affecting the position of men' (Scott cited in Einhorn 1993a: 32). For women workers this attitude was to prove to have crucial and devastating implications in the aftermath of state socialism. In a climate of economic uncertainty, job loss and mounting unemployment, what had been added on to women's roles – employment – proved all too easy to subtract.

The Reality of Women's Working Lives

This following section offers an introduction to the position of women workers within the labour market of the GDR. In doing so the discussion indicates the extent to which, in terms of paid employment, the state was unable to meet its promise of eradicating inequalities between men and women. It also provides the basis to analyse in later chapters the impact of the collapse of state socialism on women's employment. Thus many of the issues raised in this section, such as sex segregation at work, gendered pay differentials, working hours, are brought up again in subsequent chapters.

Much was achieved under state socialism. By 1989 women made up nearly half of the East German workforce. Aside from the generally high level of female employment, perhaps the most striking features of women's employment in the GDR was the high employment rate of women with young children and the high number of women engaged in full-time employment. At the end of the 1980s around 90 percent of all women had at least one child. The average

age of the mother at the time of a first birth was at this point 22.9 years. Yet nearly all women were engaged in employment, training or education. The female employment quota was an indicator of the success of the SED's programme to bring women into paid work. In 1955 only slightly more than half of women had been employed (Winkler 1990: 63), compared to around 90 percent in 1989. Likewise, the introduction of measures aimed at improving women's qualification levels had also born fruit. By October 1989 both male and female qualification levels had improved considerably and the gap between male and female qualification rates had closed significantly. Nearly 90 percent of female workers and virtually 93 percent of male workers held some form of qualification (Winkler 1990: 38). For younger male and female workers the gap had closed completely. By the middle of the 1980s women constituted half of all students at universities or *Hochschulen* (colleges), although the number dipped just slightly towards the end of the 1980s (Winkler 1990: 42). In the latter years of state socialism, the overwhelming number of unqualified women were in the older age ranges of the workforce (Winkler 1990: 40). But, as the following discussion indicates, glaring divisions in men's and women's positions within the workforce persisted under state socialism, despite the quantitative improvement in their workforce representation.

Horizontal and Vertical Segregation

Women workers were needed not only in traditionally female occupations and sectors but also in hitherto male enclaves of employment. The prioritisation of heavy industry over consumer industries created a vast need for blue-collar workers in customarily male areas of industrial employment. A third of all workers in the mining and energy sector, for example, was female (IG Bergbau und Energie 1991). Although women filled the majority of white-collar jobs in traditionally male areas, they were also employed in blue-collar, manual work – work historically performed by men. In contrast to their West German neighbours, the majority of East German women were allowed by law to work through the night (and therefore in a three-shift system) and in open caste mining. Restrictions usually only applied to pregnant and nursing women.[3] Women were excluded formally from just thirty of the 355 skilled jobs in which one could train at the end of the 1980s (Winkler 1990: 47–48).

But the lack of formal restrictions to women's employment aside, the vast majority of women was still employed in a quite narrow band of jobs (Winkler 1990: 47–48). The majority of young women leaving school found employment within around forty to fifty professions. In certain regions the choice was even more restricted because of the concentration of economic sectors in a particular area (Winkler 1990:48). Despite the increased presence of women in the workforce and at all levels of education, the occupational segregation of men and women, both horizontally and vertically, persisted. Overall within the economy women had a greater tendency to be employed in white-collar work, and men in blue-collar work. Whilst 40 percent of all industrial workers were female in 1989 – a third of all women workers were engaged in industrial production – 30 percent of the women working in the industrial sector were employed in administrative or management tasks compared to less than one in five male workers (Winkler 1990: 58). Those women who did work in blue-collar industrial jobs were overrepresented in job areas with low levels of technology and unfavourable work conditions. In industry women performed around 60 percent of industrial work defined as semi- or unskilled.

Thus women's increased presence within male bastions of employment did not automatically signify an upgrading of their employment status nor did it indicate improved individual employment choice. As Heinen (1990: 45) points out:

> even if women enter jobs and professions traditionally dominated by men, there is no guarantee that gender equality will increase. … Nor does the employment of Soviet, Bulgarian or East German women in 'typically masculine' but unskilled, exhausting, and poorly paid jobs in construction, agriculture or the postal service mark an improvement in their social situation.

The extent to which the greater inclusion of women in employment, and in traditionally male areas of employment, failed to improve women's status is indicated by the shortage of women in management. In terms of employment seniority women made up a third of all management staff in the GDR. Whilst far outstripping the number of women in senior positions in West Germany, in comparison with their male colleagues East German women were vastly underrepresented at higher levels of employment (Winkler 1990: 93). Women's access to senior levels varied between economic sectors. In industry overall four out of five managers were male. In the male-dominated areas of mining, metallurgy and potash women made up just one-tenth of bosses (Winkler 1990: 95). In female-dominated spheres the proportion of women managers was higher, but still lower than their share of the workforce overall. Women made up 55 percent of workers in light industry and 47 percent of workers in the food stuff industry; but when it came to management they constituted just 44 percent of management personnel in the former branch, and a mere 28 percent in the latter (Winkler 1990: 67, 95).

Internal mechanisms operated within the labour market to maintain and reinforce a sexual division of labour. Despite the state's public commitment to women's employment, certain firms were still reluctant to employ or to promote women workers. Although the practice was unlawful, firms sometimes tried to reduce the number of female apprentices they took on (Winkler 1990: 48). Despite state-provided childcare women shouldered the majority of domestic labour within the home, carrying the double burden of work and family. As a result, women were often regarded as less flexible and less reliable than their male colleagues (Winkler 1990: 68), which culminated at times in a preference for less skilled male workers over appropriately qualified female workers. Thus despite the increased presence of women in all areas of the workforce, their greater numbers did not engender a levelling of opportunity and reward for male and female workers.

Working Hours

Working life for the vast majority of women was full-time. The need to maximise labour resources necessitated the maximum participation of as many workers as possible. As a result, part-time work was discouraged. However, around a quarter of all female labour worked less than the state prescribed hours (Winkler 1990: 81).[4] By comparison fewer than 2 percent of male employees worked shortened hours, in the majority of cases for health reasons (Rudolph 1990b: 476). In contrast to trends in many major Western nations, including West Germany, the vast majority of part-time workers in the GDR were not women with young children but, instead, older women. Part-time work was not used in the main as a means of combining work and family as in the West but usually acted instead as a prelude to retirement. In addition part-time workers in East Germany tended to work longer hours than their counterparts in countries such as West Germany; the majority between 25 and 35 hours a week.

In another effort to maximise scarce labour resources, as many industrial workers as possible were organised into shift working. By 1989 30 percent of employed women were working in shifts, the numbers highest in the textile industry, followed by the food and

33

chemical industries. But the proportion of workers employed in shifts and, as importantly, the desire or inclination to work shifts was lower amongst women than men (Winkler 1990: 82). In part this can be explained by the higher concentration of men in the production process where there was more opportunity for male labour to be employed in a multi-shift system. But, as will be discussed in more detail below, women, particularly women with caring commitments, also had a greater tendency to avoid working in shifts than their male colleagues.

Education

As indicated above, gaps between male and female education levels were closed during the state socialist period, with women making up half of the university student population by 1985. In 1960 only a quarter of students at university had been female. However, improved educational opportunities in this sense did not break down gender divisions and discrimination within the education system overall. In schools this was perhaps most visibly evident in the use of texts still portraying men and women in conventional gender roles, performing traditional masculine and feminine occupations, despite the state's official commitment to gender-neutral schooling (Einhorn 1993a: 48–49). In universities women remained predominantly in certain subject areas, making up the majority of students in economics, education, literature and languages as well as in medicine, maths and natural sciences. To be fair, women did make progress in traditionally male areas of study. Although less than a third of all engineering students were women, as engineering students constituted the largest body of students, women studying engineering in fact made up one in five of all female students, second in size only to the education faculty (Rudolph 1990a: 4–5; Winkler 1990: 42–43). However, higher education continued to be divided along gender lines, with areas such as engineering still dominated by men. Access to apprenticeship schemes was also gendered. Of the ten most common *Ausbildungsberufe* (occupations requiring training) that women entered six were exclusively female domains (Rudolph 1990a: 4)

Pay Differentials

In terms of relative income women made some clear gains. The wage gap between men and women in the GDR narrowed slightly and was narrower than in West Germany by 1989. Women earned between 76 and 84 percent of male incomes in the GDR compared to just 65 to 70 percent in the old Federal Republic (Einhorn 1993a: 122). But clearly, gender-based wage differentials endured despite the state's formal commitment to equal pay for men and women (Röth 1988). Women were disadvantaged in the wage structure, with female workers making up the majority of lower-income workers. Women constituted two-thirds and men just one-third of workers who earned one thousand marks or less in 1988 (Winkler 1990: 88). In part, women's lower earning power was attributable to their lesser likelihood of taking on overtime or being employed at a more senior level. However, the areas of employment in which women predominated continued to command lower rates of pay than male-dominated spheres. In 1988 female production workers earned around 80 percent of their male counterparts (Winkler 1990: 92).

In the GDR the state subsidisation of basic costs such as rent and utilities meant that single-parent households could survive on one income. However, the low rates of pay overall meant that two wages were preferable, even necessary to provide an acceptable standard of living. From the 1970s single-parenthood was becoming increasingly common. By 1989 a third of babies were born to unmarried mothers (Winkler 1990: 28). By the 1980s around 20 percent of families were headed by a single parent (Winkler 1990: 112). As women made up the majority of single parents it was therefore single mothers (along with the children of single parents) who were most affected by the relative poverty arising from one income. The comparatively lower level of female wages exacerbated the situation.

Reconciliation of Work and Motherhood

Under state socialism 'womanhood' was reconstructed in state discourses to encompass the dual roles of worker and mother. Whilst women added paid employment on to their domestic labour roles, there was no concurrent reconstruction of the male social identity. Despite the high rate of both male and female employment in the GDR, women retained primary responsibility for domestic labour and childcare within the home. Men did not extend their roles to include a significantly higher amount of work within the household or to take a more active role in parenting to compensate for women's increased participation in paid labour. Sixty percent of East German women spent 21 hours or more a week doing housework; 80 percent of men, on the other hand, spent under 20 hours a week on domestic labour. Over two-thirds of East German women regarded cooking and cleaning as their chores. When men did take on household chores they were more likely to do repairs and tasks outside the house than cooking and cleaning within (INFAS 1991: 32).

This one-sided pattern of women taking on paid work in addition to unpaid domestic work was replicated in the field of employment in terms of job distribution. Although women remained a minority in traditionally male areas of employment they did gain access to many professions from which they had been previously excluded. Yet whilst women had become visible to varying degrees throughout the labour market, including in areas which had historically been the sole preserve of male workers, there was no parallel movement of men into traditionally female areas of employment. Men did not broaden their range of labour roles to incorporate jobs traditionally associated with women, such as caring and secretarial work.

Provisions put in place by the socialist state enabled women to maintain a full-time and near continuous work profile throughout their time in the labour market. The level of female employment did not dip significantly during the years of childrearing as the over-whelming majority of women returned to full-time employment after the legislated maternity break. By 1989 childcare provision virtually covered demand. In addition to the provision of crèches and kindergarten for preschool age children, after-school clubs cared for younger school-age children in the hours between the end of school and the end of work for parents, and vacation clubs provided care for younger children during the school holidays. But whilst women in the GDR no longer had to make the stark choice between work and family, the type of work they were able to take up was often influenced by their family commitments. The failure of state policies to tackle the uneven division of labour between men and women on the domestic front compelled many women to develop individual coping strategies to ensure that work and family could be combined in some sort of manageable way. Women were more likely than men to take on a job below or unrelated to their qualification levels or to ease their workload by decreasing their hours of employment. Although women's employment was guaranteed during maternity and baby leave, many women employed in production did not return to their previous jobs after the birth of a baby (Röth 1988). Working mothers often opted for jobs closer to home or near childcare facilities even if the job in question was below their qualification level or unrelated to their training. The trend for women to switch to less qualified jobs after childbirth had led to an increasing number of women aged 26 to 30 working in jobs for which they were overqualified (Enders 1986: 35–36).

A research project undertaken by the Institute for Sociology and Social Policy in East Berlin in 1984 looked at the objective and subjective conditions of combining employment and motherhood (Institut für Soziologie und Sozialpolitik 1984; Röth 1988).[5] The results of the project indicated that women with children were more likely than both childless women and men with children to be employed on a part-time basis. A quarter of the mothers surveyed worked shortened hours compared to 10 percent of women without children (Institut für Soziologie und Sozialpolitik 1984: 8). Furthermore, women's desire for part-time employment far outweighed the actual numbers involved in part-time work. Three-quarters of the mothers surveyed wished to work fewer hours compared to around two-thirds of women without children. Interestingly, just under a third of men with children stated they would like to work fewer hours. However, nearly eight out of every ten fathers taking part in the survey wished that their partners would or could work part-time (Institut für Soziologie und Sozialpolitik 1984: 8–9).

Family and domestic commitments, the research showed, limited women's employment flexibility. Only 16 percent of the workers surveyed worked in shifts, although the researchers noted in this research project a greater willingness on the part of the workers to work in shifts than had been recorded amongst workers at the beginning of the 1970s (Institut für Soziologie und Sozialpolitik 1984: 3). But the inclination to undertake shiftwork again varied between the three groups singled out in the research project – mothers, fathers and women without children. Although over half of each group were prepared to undertake shiftwork (Institut für Soziologie und Sozialpolitik 1984: 4), the conditions under which the various groups would consider shifts differed. Women with children cited more family-orientated reasons whilst fathers and childless women put forward more individualistic reasons. For mothers, the most important conditions that had to be met before they would consider shiftwork were that their partners were in agreement and that the care of their children was ensured. The younger the age of the children the less likely women were to contemplate shiftwork. Fathers and women without children, on the other hand, were primarily motivated by financial incentives (Institut für Soziologie und Sozialpolitik 1984: 4).

But motherhood was not the only variable to influence women's work profile and care should be taken not merely to differentiate women according to whether they had children or not. Other factors, the research suggested, also influenced women's employment aspirations and possibilities. Educational background and qualification levels, for example, had a decisive impact on women's attitudes to their work roles. The higher the qualification levels the greater women's desire to work part-time. Over 90 percent of college graduates wanted to work less than the full-time week (Institut für Soziologie und Sozialpolitik 1984: 9). With regards to actual hours worked, more white-collar female workers, both with and without children, worked shortened hours than blue-collar workers. Virtually one-third of the female white-collar workers with children worked shorter hours compared to 18 percent of blue-collar workers. Of the women surveyed who did not have children, fewer than 8 percent of blue-collar workers (compared to 16 percent of white-collar workers) worked part-time (Institut für Soziologie und Sozialpolitik 1984: 8).

Although motherhood and family responsibilities had a decisive impact on women's employment opportunities, the research revealed certain commonalties between women with children and women without children, as well as clear divergences between men and women. Both women with children and women without children were, for example, less likely to take on management tasks than their male co-workers. Clearly women's lower representation at senior levels cannot be explained solely by the material constraints of motherhood. Prevalent notions of appropriate gender behaviour impinged on both the aspirations of the women themselves and the expectations of male workers and managers. Management and authority were still more closely associated with masculinity than femininity. A study undertaken by the Leipzig Institute for Youth Research in the 1980s concluded that women were underrepresented at management levels in part because of family duties, but also because of insufficient self-confidence and the underestimation of their performance by their male colleagues (Enders 1986: 34).

Policy initiatives in the GDR sent out mixed signals about women's position. Heinen (1990: 47) argues that:

> the tenacity of received ideas about women's role and appropriate employment is not the result of a popular failure to internalize legislated norms. Rather, it is the contradictions inherent in policy which create obstacles to any new thinking about gender relations.

On the one hand, state policy emphasised women's rights to equal opportunities with men in employment. On the other hand, policies supported and maintained a sexual division of labour within the home, particularly in relation to parenting, emphasising the particular significance of motherhood. Policies were contradictory in their assessment of women's position. The equal opportunities rhetoric, which stressed women's participation in paid employment, was based on the notion of equality through sameness; that men and women could be equal if women worked as well as men. However, the policy initiatives, which stressed women's particular roles in relation to childcare and domestic work, assumed a feminine difference.

The unequal division of labour in the home occurred *not* in spite of state measures to enable women enter the labour force but, in part, because of them. The state's emphasis on the reconciliation of work and *mother*hood rather than work and *parent*hood maintained and perpetuated gender segregation in the home and, in turn, in the workplace. Even though the majority of children were able to attend childcare facilities, it was still primarily women who took time off work to care for sick children and whose work patterns were thereby interrupted because of family commitments. Nearly 80 percent of East German women questioned in 1988 stated that they alone cared for their children when they were ill (Winkler 1990: 129).

Summary

If one were to use the term patriarchy to describe a situation in which men on an aggregate level held more power and had a greater command over social, economic and political resources, then state socialist East Germany could indeed be referred to as patriarchal. Within the labour market women made certain key gains – by 1989 they made up almost half of all workers and were visible in almost all areas of employment and at more senior positions. Yet, on a general level, women's labour market position was still comparatively worse than that of their male counterparts. The overwhelming majority of women workers remained clustered in a small number of traditionally female areas of employment, earned on average less than men and were less likely to take on additional responsibilities or extra hours. State socialism mobilised the large-scale employment of women but did not eradicate gender discrimination and divisions at work. To repeat a phrase used earlier, women's relationship to waged labour under state socialism involved both gains and persisting disadvantage.

Women were paternalistically granted certain concessions by the socialist state – greater access to full-time and higher levels of education, the widespread establishment of childcare places and provision of generous maternity benefits – but were not given equality in any sense of the word. The positive discrimination of women that had helped them improve their socioeconomic status in the short term by ensuring access to full-time employment, their own income, better levels of education and the ability to combine work with motherhood also reaffirmed and maintained divisions between men and women. As stated above, provisions were put in place to help women undertake paid work *in addition to* all their other roles, not to redistribute all labour, both paid and unpaid, more evenly. The Frauenpolitik pursued by the state served to reinforce women's ties to domestic labour; thereby constraining their options within paid employment. The division of labour within the home remained relatively unchanged despite women's near equal involvement in paid labour outside the home. Thus, women were never able to enter the labour force on equal terms with men. Both symbolically and practically women constituted a qualitatively different source of labour. The 'norm' by which all workers were measured was a male 'norm' – a worker unfettered by commitments beyond the workplace. Women with their additional commitments, whilst crucial to the East German economy, were seen as less flexible, less committed and more expensive. In practical terms the logistics of combining work and family, even with the comprehensive network of childcare in place, were daunting. Food shortages and a lack of labour-saving household appliances added to the difficulties of reconciling home and work.

Crucially, women were never active participants in the decision-making process. They were never directly involved in formulating the terms of these policies, which had such an enormous impact on their lives. Instead, the rights and entitlements formulated under state socialism were bestowed on them by the male elite at the top of the Politburo. Whilst women had made certain key gains in the sphere of employment, the structure of the political system had denied them the public space to articulate their own interests and set their own agenda. This system of paternalistic benevolence weakened women's hold on employment. The high level of female employment had not been achieved as the result of a long political struggle on the part of women but instead at the will of a political dictatorship. If the regime were to fail women's hold on employment may also falter. The high levels of female (and male) employment were the direct result of the state socialist political and economic system. Women's place within the labour market was awarded to them by a particular political system within a particular economic order. As the experiences post-1989 indicate, once the political system was undermined and the economic order overturned there was no guarantee that women's already tenuous hold on employment would endure. The following chapters explore in more detail the impact of post-communist change on women's relationship to the labour market.

Notes

1. Between 1947 and 1961 2.7 million Germans left the GDR for the FRG, half of whom were under twenty-five years of age (Jeffries, 1987: 6–7).
2. In a letter to Ludwig Kugelmann in 1868, Marx wrote that 'social progress can be measured accurately by the social position of the fairer sex (the ugly ones included)' (Penrose 1990: 61; Buckley 1989: 21). As Landes (1989: 21) points out, '[n]either Marx nor Engels fully escaped the patriarchal assumptions of their age, even as they sought to escape them' .
3. Article 243 of the *Arbeitsgesetzbuch* (Labour Code) introduced in 1977 prohibited nightwork for pregnant women and mothers nursing young babies. Women with preschool-age children were given the right to refuse nightwork or overtime.
4. The normal working week was 43.75 hours. However, multi-shift workers and working mothers with two or more children worked just 40 hours a week without a loss in wages.
5. The project undertaken by the Institute for Sociology and Social Policy, Sphere Woman/Family surveyed 715 women with children under 16 years of age (referred to as mothers), 350 women without children or with children over 16 years and 397 fathers across five industrial firms. The investigation took place between January and March 1984, see Institut für Soziologie und Sozialpolitik 1984; Röth 1988.

3

The Unification Process

The end of the 1980s saw the collapse of state socialism throughout Eastern and Central Europe and the dawning of a new
post-communist era in Europe. Throughout the region economic
and political reconstruction was activated, guided by market-led
economics and liberal democratic politics. To understand the particular nature and pace of post-communist transformation within
the former GDR, the specific metamorphosis of East Germany must
be placed within its unique political context – the unification of East
and West Germany after forty years of separation. Thus the mode of
economic and political restructuring adopted in East Germany cannot be disentangled from the enormous and daunting challenge of
unifying two highly disparate economic and political systems.

Unification was in essence more an annexation of East Germany
by West Germany, albeit with the expressed consent of the East
German voting populace, than an integration of the two regimes.
The terms of the unification treaty 'constituted a formidable blue-
print for institutional and legislative change in one major direction:
that from West to East' (Kolinsky 1991a: 277), thus signifying East
Germany's abrupt and complete departure, both economically and
politically, from its socialist past. A one-sided notion of convergence
– the rapid and complete assimilation of the East into the West – lay
at the heart of the unification project.

It is the aim of this chapter to outline in more detail the process
of unification and its crucial impact on the economic and political
reconstruction of East Germany. The chapter begins with an examination of the fall of state socialism followed by an account of the
political and economic dimensions of the unification project. The
discussion concludes with an evaluation of the internal cohesive-
ness of the new united Germany, assessing the implications of cul-

tural and social divisions between East and West for the durability of the newly enlarged Germany.

The Collapse of State Socialism and the Unification Process

Within the GDR the SED had held the reins of decision-making, controlling and directing policy formation and implementation. The 'repressive, communist-orientated, one-party dictatorship' (Horn 1992: 56) fomented an environment in which oppositional groups had minimal scope to exert influence on the decision-making process and to gain representation for their various interests. The parliamentary and electoral systems of the GDR paid only lip service to the notions of democratic representation and participation, creating merely the illusion of 'people's power'. The SED was able to maintain its internal power through the external support of the Soviet Union and the implementation of a repressive state apparatus, quashing internal dissent and opposing forces.

Oppositional political activity therefore existed on the margins until the 1980s, when the changing political climate in the Soviet Union (Glaessner 1992) and increasing internal instability (Andersen 1992; Horn 1992) enabled the nascent pro-democracy groups (plus the many unorganised yet disillusioned East German citizens) to take centre stage and effectively challenge the state socialist regime. The implementation of economic and political reform in the Soviet Union under the banners of *Glasnost* and *Perestroika* set the pace for reform elsewhere in the Soviet bloc. Gorbachev warned Honecker at the fortieth anniversary celebrations of the GDR that those who resisted reform might live to regret it. Yet Honecker continued to reject Gorbachev's example of reformed socialism, arguing that there was 'no model which held for all the socialist countries' (Glaessner 1992: 38).

But the GDR was growing weaker, both economically and politically. The political system of the GDR had always lacked overwhelming popular support and legitimacy (Horn 1992; Welsh 1994). The lack of democratic freedoms had been traded by many for a certain level of social and economic security (Welsh 1994: 22), in the hope of even greater prosperity in the future. Yet the system was beginning to unravel at the seams. Economic crisis was imminent (Andersen 1992) and the social contract between state and people was becoming increasingly fragile (Welsh 1994). The state's ability to counter growing unrest was undermined by the swelling mood for reform amongst its central eastern European neighbours. The opening of the Austro-Hungarian border by the Hungarian government in the summer of 1989 provided an escape route to the West for disillusioned East Germans. Reform in the Soviet Union meant East Germany could now no longer rely on any support from the Soviet Union if it were to mount a military offensive against the escalating number and size of street demonstrations. The SED was growing increasingly isolated. On 9 November 1989 the Berlin Wall, the key symbol of East–West division, was opened, signalling the beginning of the end for the SED and the state socialist regime. On 17 November a new government was formed. With hindsight, East Germany had clearly been ripe for change. Yet many had overrated the stability and durability of the regime (Grosser 1992: 1). Indeed, the swiftness of the GDR's collapse and the lack of resistance from the East German ruling elite took both East and West Germans by surprise (Lehmbruch 1990; von Beyme 1990).

At first East Germans had swelled the streets calling for the removal of the authoritarian state socialist regime and its replacement with a more democratic, participatory form of government. But proclamations by the East German people rejecting the authoritarian rule of the SED by asserting 'Wir sind das Volk' ('We are the people') were soon replaced by the pro-unification call 'Wir sind ein Volk' ('We are one people'). This crucial shift was quickly noted in the West. Initially Chancellor Kohl of West Germany had put forward a plan merely for increased cooperation between the two nations (Osmond 1992). But in response to the changing mood of the East German people and in a bid to out-manoeuvre political opponents in the West (the SPD was the first West German political party to call for national unity), Chancellor Kohl quickly altered his original plan of a confederated Germany and backed instead a speedy unification of the two German states.

The East German elections of March 1990 acted as a quasi-referendum on the unification issue (Roberts 1991: 376). Through their electoral support for Kohl and the CDU-led 'Alliance for Germany', East Germans showed their overwhelming support for a rapid unification process and in doing so handed near total control of the unification process to West Germany. Von Beyme (1992: 168) argues that the election results amounted to 'an almost complete surrender of East Germany in exchange for a pledge that it [West Germany] would take care of the economic and social integration of East Germany'. With the endorsement of the East German people unification was carried out at a lightening pace. The Monetary, Economic and Social Union came into effect on 1 July 1990, and the final Unification Treaty securing political union was introduced in October of the same year. In under a year from the fall of the Berlin Wall and the opening of East Germany's borders a new united Germany had been created.

Three points of Kohl's unification agenda proved instrumental in the future development of the new federal states and warrant further attention when considering the implications of unification for women's employment: firstly, the pledge to unify Germany according to article 23 of the Basic Law, the West German constitution; secondly, the introduction of a basic 1:1 currency union between East and West Germany; and thirdly, the promise to bring living standards and with them wage levels in the East up to West German levels. The following sections of this chapter consider each point in turn, commenting briefly on the particular implications of each aspect for women's employment opportunities. The specific impact of unification on female labour is taken up in more detail in the following chapters.

The Constitutional Framework

At the heart of the unification strategy was West Germany's reluctance to relinquish the constitutional form of the Second Republic – the Federal Republic of Germany, which came into being after the Second World War (Lehmbruch 1990: 463). Since its inception the Federal Republic of Germany (from here on West Germany) had enjoyed relative economic, political and social stability (Roberts 1991: 387). According to West Germany's own constitution two different routes to unification were possible. Article 146 of the Basic Law provided the option of drawing up an entirely new constitution for a new united Germany. Unification according to Article 23, on the other hand, ensured the preservation of West German institutions, allowing other parts of Germany to accede to the federal republic. The Saarland had joined the Federal Republic via this route in 1956. Although unification according to Article 146 afforded the opportunity to truly integrate the two German nations by creating new institutions, structures and practices as well as a new governing philosophy, it also meant that West Germans also had to accept considerable change within their own part of Germany. In addition, this form of unification rendered impossible the aim of a speedy unification. The negotiation of a new constitution acceptable to both East and West Germany would have been a lengthy process, requiring in addition the need to negotiate Germany's re-entry into the European Union.

The eventual decision to unify the two German states according to Article 23 allowed West Germany to maintain its own institutional and legal framework. As a result unification was very much a one-way process. East Germany was obliged to adapt its own institutional and legislative structures to those of West Germany after unification. In many instances this process involved the introduction of West German legislation into East Germany literally overnight. This abrupt and complete departure from the past presented East Germans with the daunting task of having to adapt quickly to legislation and institutions that were quite literally foreign to them.

Regine Hildebrandt, the Minister for Work, Social Affairs, Health and Women in Brandenburg, later summed up the enormity of the challenge whilst appearing on a television talkshow. She asked West Germans to imagine what it would have been like if the reverse situation had occurred and socialism had triumphed in West Germany. Imagine, she asked, that someone from the Central Committee of the SED had travelled to Bonn to announce that the federal government and the federal ministries were no longer needed and everything would now be governed from the East, that the existing institutions were no longer required, nor the workers and the officials. In the large firms managers and workers who were all familiar with the workings of a market economy were then told by members of the planning commission that their economic principles were old hat and to draw up a plan of action in line with socialist economic principles. Imagine then, Hildebrandt continued, that an official from the planning commission came back in just four weeks and asked impatiently why the task was not yet complete. What have you been doing? Hildebrandt's remarks point not only to the enormity of the restructuring process for East Germany but also to the frustration felt by many East Germans that the sheer scale of change demanded by unification and the implications for ordinary people's lives were never fully appreciated or recognised by West Germans.

For all East Germans, whether they were male or female, the unification process presented a massive learning process. For women, straddling the public-private divide in their dual roles as domestic and paid workers, the one-way nature of unification brought with it

specific demands. As chapter 4 illustrates in more depth, the introduction of West German legislation into East Germany meant the
introduction of an entirely different system of welfare provision,
based on a completely different understanding of women's social
roles, particularly the distribution of and the relative emphasis
accorded to their work within the private household and the public
sphere of work. Whereas the state socialist system of welfare in the
GDR had promoted the full-time employment of both parents,
including women with children, the West German system was more
firmly rooted in the male breadwinner/ female housewife model of
the family. Unification thus resulted in the removal of much state
support for working mothers (see chapter 4 for more details). At the
political level in the new united Germany, as in West Germany, there
was no real expectation of or support for the full employment for
women, especially for women who had young children in their care.

The Monetary, Economic and Social Union

Unification represented both an economic and a political challenge.
The terms of the Monetary, Economic and Social Union were key
factors in determining the fate of the East German economy in the
immediate post-unification period. But the steps taken towards
economic unity were, at times, determined more by political will
than by economic rationality. Due to the scale of the unification
project some problems were inevitable. However, others were com-
pounded by policy errors (Marsh 1993) arising at least in part from
the desire 'to subordinate economic forces to political dictation'
(*Financial Times* 11.12.92).

The introduction of a currency union at a basic 1:1 exchange rate
was met by enormous criticism from the economic establishment,
most notably by the then President of the Bundesbank, Karl-Otto
Pöhl. It was argued that the implementation of an exchange rate at
one West German Deutschmark for one East Mark – constituting a
revaluation of the East Mark by 300 to 400 percent – would render
East German industry uncompetitive (Marsh 1993). But, despite
advice to the contrary, Chancellor Kohl went ahead with the 1:1
currency conversion. With the benefit of hindsight the cautious
nature of the economic experts appears to have been fully justified.
As chapters 5 and 6 illustrate, East German industry experienced
grave difficulties adjusting to the new market system. As Marsh
(1993: 198) observes, 'East German factories were sucked into a
vortex of destruction' as a result of the currency conversion.

Advocates of the 'short sharp shock' approach to unification argued that such a strategy would curb migration from East to West. At the beginning of 1990 around 2,000 East Germans were going over to West Germany each day (Marsh 1993:198). With a scarcity of jobs and housing already in many parts of West Germany, the old federal states could not support a sustained influx of East Germans looking for work and accommodation. The 1:1 exchange rate, it was suggested, would stem the tide of East Germans settling in the West and thus divert a potentially explosive political and social situation. Paradoxically, by crippling the East German economy and sealing East German businesses' inability to compete both at home and abroad, the currency union itself, by generating job loss, generated a whole new set of problems, both economic and social. The cost of supporting an ailing economy and the mass reserve of unemployed persons put enormous strain on public funds, forcing the federal government to make unpopular policy decisions (see chapter 4). By the summer of 1992 signs of social instability in East Germany were already evident, manifesting most alarmingly in attacks on foreigners living in East Germany. Economic and social insecurity amongst East Germans had fuelled resentment against asylum seekers, exploding often into violent confrontation.

As is illustrated further in chapter 5, women workers were hardest hit by the economic downturn in East Germany, especially in the immediate period following unification. The weakness of the East German economy, the mass job loss and the low level of job creation had, of course, affected all groups of workers. With falling labour demand male as well as female workers experienced escalating economic insecurity. However, men, on an aggregate level, stood in a *comparatively* strong economic position vis-à-vis their female counterparts. Women, in part because of their already more vulnerable labour market position, were especially susceptible to unemployment (see chapter 5). As illustrated in chapter 2, women had made key gains under state socialism. Their full-time involvement in paid labour outside the home had become socially accepted and was enshrined and ensured in a multitude of laws, provisions and institutions. Areas of science, engineering and heavy industry that had traditionally been 'no-go areas' for women had been forced to open their doors to female recruits. Yet women remained concentrated in certain fields of employment and at certain levels. They generally worked for less money and with the unpaid labour they undertook within the home usually worked, all told, longer hours. The new federal states inherited a culture of gender division and discrimination;

a system of gender inequality that was built upon in the period of economic instability following unification.

The Equalisation of Wage Levels and Living Standards

Central to the notion of East–West convergence underpinning the unification process was the aim to bring living standards in East Germany in line with those in West Germany. Promises by Chancellor Kohl of a speedy equalisation of living standards created the climate for demands for wage increases in East Germany. The trade union movement backed the convergence of East German wages to West German levels, with individual unions forming agreements to achieve wage parity over a fixed period of time. As West Germany was a high-wage area the process of wage equalisation was set to transform East Germany from a low- to a high-wage economy. This process was beset with dangers. High wage levels and non-wage costs had already undermined West Germany's competitiveness in the international economy. In 1992 West Germany's unit labour costs were estimated to be 23 percent higher than the average for industrialised countries (*Financial Times*, 15.2.1994: 17). If labour costs were a problem for West Germany with its high levels of productivity, for East Germany with its significantly lower productivity levels the convergence of wage rates was to be devastating. The process of rapid wage equalisation, it has been argued, amounted to nothing less than 'collective suicide' (Wegner 1991: 38).

Wage levels were rising without a comparable rise in productivity levels. The Organisation for Economic Co-operation and Development (OECD) stressed the dangers lurking in this process, arguing that:

> the settlements which provide for complete catch-up with western levels (even allowing for the gap between basic and effective wages) are problematic, because they pre-empt any re-adjustment of wages in the light of economic events...
> ... by running ahead of underlying productivity potential, such wage increases are likely to slow the very process which would otherwise validate them (OECD 1992: 79–80).

The OECD in its analysis points to collusion between West German employers and employees in the bid to increase wage costs in the new federal states. By pushing for the rapid equalisation of wage levels, both West German capital and labour were aiming to avoid the new states becoming an area of low-wage competition within Germany. Both employers and workers, the OECD argued, had acted against the interests of the new federal states (OECD 1992). At the trade union level representatives of the movement argued that wage parity was necessary to promote social stability. Without equal wage levels in East and West Germany a mass exodus of workers from East Germany to the higher wage region of West Germany was predicted, thus increasing competition for jobs. In defence of their wage policy trade unions contended that their proposals for wage equalisation were not the cause of the economic crisis but were being used as a scapegoat in the unsettled economic climate.

Yet the owners and representatives of capital were not united in their support for wage increases. Many, especially those operating or seeking to operate in East Germany, pleaded for restraint in the process of wage bargaining. The President of the German Chamber of Commerce asserted that 'high labour costs were putting the German economy under pressure on international markets, and that union restraint in wage negotiations during 1992 would be the key to economic recovery' (Timmins 1992: 181).

In 1989 both productivity and wage levels had stood at around a third of West German levels. But whilst productivity declined after the collapse of the GDR, wage levels rose. By the end of 1991 East German wages had already reached an average 65 percent of West German wages (Timmins 1992: 178). Increases in unit labour costs exacerbated the inability of East German businesses to compete both at home and abroad. As the gulf between wage levels and productivity widened, East German businesses were unable to compete with the low-wage nations of East Central Europe to the east of their borders (see chapter 5).

The process of wage equalisation prevented East Germany from developing a low-wage, labour-intensive economy and favoured 'an excessively capital-intensive industrial structure' (OECD 1992). For women workers this shift from a labour- to a capital-intensive structure was crucial. As von Beyme (1992: 163–164) remarks; 'there are many groups which did not benefit from the trade union policy [of wage increases] such as women and unemployed people'. As women tended to be paid less than their male counterparts, they were more likely to 'benefit' in terms of jobs from a labour-intensive economic structure in which wage costs were decisive in ensuring competitiveness. Comparative analysis suggests that capital-intensive industries tend to employ a higher proportion of male labour. In West Germany the trends towards a greater capital intensity in both the textile and the electronics industry led to the replacement of labour by automation and with it the proportional increase of male employment in the production process (Figge and Quack: 1990; Raasch and Wahnschaffe 1992). As chapter 6 suggests, a similar process was underway in East Germany in the immediate period after the Wende.

A Common German Identity?

Smith (1992) suggests that the process of unification produced the Federal Republic 'writ large'. The notion of convergence had been a guiding principle behind the unification project and in technical terms at least the new united Germany exists as an enlarged version of West Germany. The transfer of the organisational superstructure of West Germany into East Germany, whilst a mammoth task in itself, constituted one of the more clear-cut processes of convergence, requiring the substitution of East German institutions and legislation by those already existing in the West (Kielmannsegg 1992). At all levels and in all areas change occurred – welfare, education, health, social security, the military, policing, labour relations, even the speed limits on the roads, to name just a few areas of public life – in accordance with West German laws and practices. It is illustrative of the formally one-way nature of unification that the new united Germany that came into existence in 1990 still bore the official title of its West German predecessor – the Federal Republic of Germany.

But the success of unification and the stability of the new united Germany rests on much more than the creation of common institutions, a common legal system and so forth. What about the inner unification of the German populace within the new nation? Willi Brandt, the former Chancellor of West Germany, spoke at the time of unification of growing together what belongs together. But after forty years of separation how alike were East and West Germans? Would the many years of division inhibit the emergence of a cohesive German identity? Would the difficulties transferring from a centrally-planned to a market-orientated system – exemplified by the high levels of unemployment – exacerbate this process further?

Even in the immediate post-unification period most Germans regardless of whether they were from the East or the West saw themselves as German. Indeed one of the commonly recognised failings of the state socialist system was its inability to foster a separate and distinct GDR national identity. But whilst just over 50 percent of East Germans identified themselves as German, 65 percent identified themselves additionally or solely as *East* German. In comparison only 40 percent of West Germans identified with the label *West* German. In the new united Germany, being German was synonymous with being West German. To be East German was to be 'other'. Built into the whole fabric of the unification process was the assumption that, over time, East Germans would become more like their West German brothers and sisters.

Yet, in the immediate post-Wende period the '*Ossie/Wessie*' distinction continued to divide Germans despite their common identification with the German nationality. On certain key issues East and West Germans displayed quite different responses. East Germans, for example, continued to be more supportive of socialism as an ideal, although few favoured a socialist planned economy over a market system in practice (Veen and Zelle 1995: 4). They also tended to place a greater emphasis on egalitarian values than their West German counterparts. Significantly for this study, research undertaken by the Konrad-Adenauer Foundation in 1993 indicated that only 49 percent of West Germans compared to 65 percent of East Germans saw 'gender equality' as 'very important' (Veen and Zelle 1995: 4). In East Germany a much greater premium was placed on women's ability to take part in the paid labour force, particularly on a full-time basis. Attitudes towards the care of young children also tended to differ. West Germans were much more likely to favour family-based care, particularly for young children. East Germans, on the other hand, tended to see the formal day-care of young children as beneficial to their development as well as vital to women's employment (see chapter 7).

Yet despite such divisions on many issues clear similarities could be observed between East and West Germans. The research by the Konrad-Adenauer Foundation in 1993 indicated that East and West Germans share broadly the same political priorities – jobs, social security, pensions, economic prosperity. Although East and West Germans ranked the four differently, both placed the desire to 'safeguard jobs' at the top. It is interesting to note that in 1990, when faced with the same question, West Germans had ranked 'protection of the environment' first (Veen and Zelle 1995: 14/15). Clearly changing economic circumstances, most notably the rise of unemployment in West Germany, had increased concern about jobs.

In terms of voting patterns both similarities and differences can be detected across the former divide. The political parties with their

roots in the West – CDU, SPD, FDP, and the Greens – have
retained as a group the lion's share of political support in East Germany (see tables 3.1–3.5). In the 1994 general election three-quarters of East German voters supported these all-German parties
(Rose and Page 1996: 20). At the same time, however, the PDS, the
reformed communist party, has gone from strength to strength. In

Table 3.1. *State elections in Brandenburg: percentage of votes gained by main political parties*

	SPD	CDU	GREEN	FDP	PDS
1994	54.1	18.7	2.9	2.2	18.7
1990	38.2	29.4	6.4	6.6	13.4

Table 3.2. *State elections in Mecklenburg-Vorpommern: percentage of votes gained by main political parties*

	SPD	CDU	GREEN	FDP	PDS
1998	34.3	30.2			24.4
1994	29.5	37.7	3.7	3.8	22.7
1990	27.0	38.3	4.2	5.5	15.7

Table 3.3. *State elections in Saxony: percentage of votes gained by main political parties*

	SPD	CDU	GREEN	FDP	PDS
1994	16.6	58.1	4.1	1.7	16.5
1990	19.1	53.8	5.6	5.3	10.2

Table 3.4. *State elections in Saxony-Anhalt: percentage of votes gained by main political parties*

	SPD	CDU	GREEN	FDP	PDS	DVU
1998	35.9	22.0	3.2	4.2	19.6	12.9
1994	34.0	34.4	5.1	3.6	19.9	—
1990	26.0	39.0	5.3	13.5	12.0	—

Table 3.5. *State elections in Thuringia: percentage of votes gained by main political parties*

	SPD	CDU	GREEN	FDP	PDS
1994	29.6	42.6	4.5	3.2	16.6
1990	22.8	45.4	6.5	9.3	9.7

the 1994 German general election the PDS polled over a fifth of the East German vote, doubling its 1990 vote in the region (Rose and Page 1996: 20). In the 1995 state and district elections in Berlin the PDS gained almost 40 percent of the vote in East Berlin (Lees 1996: 70). In 1998 the PDS again received about 20 percent of the East German vote in the federal elections, securing thirty-five seats in the Bundestag. In the 1998 state elections in Saxony-Anhalt and Mecklenburg-Vorpommern it polled around 20 and 25 percent of the respective votes. Its popularity has been confined, however, almost exclusively to East Germany. In the 1995 Berlin elections, for example, the PDS polled only 2 per cent of votes in West Berlin. Only time will tell whether the PDS will be able to retain its support in East Germany for the longer term or the extent to which its involvement in parliamentary politics may force the party to moderate its policies (Rose and Page 1996: 20). In the initial decade after the Wende the PDS has, however, been able to consolidate its position and build up its support in the East. Its growth and durability is indicative of the disquiet and dissatisfaction amongst certain sections of the East German population, particularly with the persistence of economic problems in the region.

An East–West divide is still apparent within the new Germany, whether one measures this divide in terms of economic markers, such as levels of unemployment, job creation and economic growth, or in terms of attitudes, aspirations and expectations. Indeed, the turn away from the CDU at the 1998 general election in Germany was much stronger in the new federal states than in the old. Declining support for the CDU – the party of unification – had been evident in East Germany for some time (see tables 3.1; 3.2; 3.4; 3.5). The retention of a discernible East 'German-ness' does not, however, signal the failure of the unification project or a prospective de-unification of Germany. The stability of the new united Germany does not hinge on the complete homogenisation of social values and political behaviour or on the disappearance of all regional or cultural differences. Within West Germany divisions are evident between northern and southern Germany, between rural and urban areas as well as between different social groups. Clearly East Germans have grown increasingly dissatisfied with the way in which the unification process has been governed, particularly the continuation of economic problems – unemployment was the key election issue in both East and West Germany in the 1998 elections. But despite dissatisfaction with Kohl and the CDU Germans in both East and West used the ballot box to voice their discontent and to engineer political change (see table 3.6).

Table 3.6. *German Bundestag elections: percentage of votes gained by main political parties*

	SPD	CDU /CSU	GREEN	FDP	PDS	B'90
1998	40.9	35.1	6.7	6.2	5.1	
1994	36.4	41.5	7.3	6.9	4.4	—
1990	33.5	43.8	3.8	11.0	2.4*	1.2
1987	37.0	44.3	8.3	9.1		
1983	38.2	48.8	5.6	6.9		
1980	42.9	44.5	1.5	10.6		
1976	42.6	48.6		7.9		
1972	45.8	45.8		8.4		
1969	42.7	42.7		5.8		

* In 1990 elections parties which gained 5 percent in East Germany able to enter Bundestag

Change has thus occurred within the existing political (and economic) framework. Many East Germans may be disillusioned by the economic consequences of the regime change but few actually favour abandoning the present system. Instead increasingly more looked in the 1998 elections to parties on the left to revive Germany's economic prospects.

4

Changing States: Redefining Women, Work and Welfare

> To recognize that they [the socialist states] failed to emancipate women even in terms of generally held feminist criteria, should not obscure the degree to which they implemented quite radical policies which had significant effects on women's legal, social, political and economic status.
>
> (Molyneux 1991: 51)

In the GDR the state had been instrumental in reforming women's socioeconomic position. Participation in paid labour was seen as not only the right but also the duty of each citizen, both male and female. Public policy initiatives raised and maintained the female employment quota to an internationally high level and improved women's education and training standards, thus broadening to some degree the scope of their employment opportunities. The state also provided a wide range of measures to help women reconcile both employment and motherhood, thereby maintaining women's high levels of employment even through the years of childbearing and childrearing. However, as detailed in chapter 2, equality between men and women was not achieved, not even in the sphere of employment. The labour market remained heavily gendered with higher status, better-paid jobs more frequently held by male workers. The positive discrimination of working mothers in welfare provision, whilst enabling women to work full-time relatively uninterrupted throughout their working lives, had in fact maintained a binary gender hierarchy and perpetuated unequal power relations between the sexes. Women continued to shoulder the majority of domestic labour in addition to their involvement in paid employment. Indeed, to conform to the state socialist ideal of womanhood was to be both mother and worker. For men, however, fatherhood did not carry the same significance, neither symbolically nor in practical terms.

The collapse of state socialism, the transfer from a planned to a market economy and the unification of East with West Germany put into jeopardy many of the 'gains' bestowed on women by the state during the socialist era, not least in the field of welfare provision. The West German system of welfare introduced into the new federal states (East Germany) after unification in 1990 was based on a quite different understanding of women's appropriate social and labour roles. Welfare provision in West Germany was based on the principle of subsidiarity: the family was regarded as the primary provider of welfare and the state intervened only in the last instance (Cannan 1992; Esping-Andersen 1990; Lane 1993; Langan and Ostner 1991). Whilst state policy in the GDR had enabled women to simultaneously reconcile (full-time) work and motherhood, the West German model of welfare advocated consecutive work and motherhood or the reconciliation of work and family via women's part-time employment. After unification the political will to maintain the high level of women's employment that had been achieved in the GDR was absent from the agenda of the federal government. The high female employment quota was regarded as an aberration of state socialism and unrealistic, indeed unwelcome, in the new economic and political climate.

In terms of public policy reform this chapter is concerned primarily with the ways in which state discourses constructed women's social and labour roles after unification; how these differed from socialist rhetoric and policy; and the ramifications of policy changes for women's involvement in paid labour. The discussion embraces three broad areas of policy: policies pertaining to the regulation of work and motherhood; those concerned specifically with the regulation of the post-unification labour market; as well as policy measures which indirectly impacted upon women's reproductive rights. In this case the analysis focuses on the formulation of a common abortion policy in the new united Germany. The discussion of post-Wende developments at the federal level focuses on the period of CDU-led government and is concerned primarily with the general shifts in policy direction instigated by unification. The chapter concludes with an evaluation of policy at the state level in Brandenburg, assessing the extent to which this tier of government offered an alternative approach to the issue of women's employment to that offered by the federal government.

Women, Work and Welfare in West Germany

As the unification treaty prescribed the near complete adaptation of East Germany to West German standards, systems and practices, the recognition and analysis of women's socioeconomic status in *West* Germany is of vital importance to any study of East German women's changing relationship to the labour market in the post-unification period. On creation of the new unified Germany West German legislation was introduced into the five new federal states, rendering obsolete the laws and directives from the state socialist period. In many instances legislation changed overnight, in other instances a short phasing-in period was allowed. In the case of abortion policy, to be discussed in more detail below, in the absence of any political consensus it was agreed that an all-German abortion policy would be formulated by the summer of 1992. Such was the discord around this sensitive issue that at one stage the lack of an agreed policy looked likely to derail the entire unification process (Einhorn 1993a: 96).

When the two German states were established after the end of World War Two West Germany like its socialist counterpart, included recognition of men and women's equal rights in its constitution. But contrary to the East German experience West Germany's constitutional advocacy of sexual equality was slow to permeate general legislation (Kolinsky 1993: 46). Despite amendments to the Civil Code in 1958, legislation still upheld the principle of the 'housewife marriage', that men should go out to work and women should stay in the home to take care of children and domestic tasks (Derleder 1990). A woman was 'entitled to take on paid employment, as far as this can be combined with her duties in marriage and the family' (Kolinsky 1993: 49).

It was not until the 1970s that West Germany began to seriously overhaul its legislation to accommodate the principle of sex equality. Although some initiative for legislative reform came from the SPD-led federal government (Kolinsky 1993: 50) that came to power in 1969, the main impetus for change, particularly in the realm of labour legislation, came from the European Community. Although the Treaty of Rome upheld the principle of sex equality and equal pay for men and women, it was not until the 1970s that the EC became active in ensuring compliance throughout the member states. This reawakened interest in the promotion of sex equality throughout the Community led to the formulation of three EC directives relating to women's equality at work. Member states were instructed to modify their national legislation to guarantee to men and to women equal pay, equal access to employment and parallel treatment in the workplace, and equal social security and pension rights. But, despite the EC's directives, West Germany still dragged its feet. Only in response to rulings by the European Court of Justice and criticism from the European Commission did it update its labour laws (Kolinsky 1993: 64).

In line with trends elsewhere in Western Europe the most significant upsurge in women's employment in West Germany came from the 1970s onwards. Between 1970 and 1992 the number of women employed grew by 2.7 million, increasing women's share of total employment from 36 to 41 percent (Bundesanstalt für Arbeit 1994a). Yet the level of women's employment in West Germany remained relatively low, not only in comparison to the GDR but also to many other Western European and OECD countries (Lane 1993: 281).

Two key factors limited the expansion of women's employment in West Germany: firstly, the structure of its economy (Erler 1988) and, secondly, the system of its welfare provision (Esping Andersen 1990; Lane 1993; Langan and Ostner 1991). West Germany has, in advanced capitalist, postindustrial terms, an 'atypical economic structure' (Erler 1988: 233). Throughout the advanced capitalist world the expansion of women's employment in the latter quarter of the twentieth century has been linked to economic restructuring, in particular the spectacular growth of service sector employment. In West Germany, however, the expansion of service-based employment has been much more reserved. In his comparative study of (West) Germany, Sweden and the United States, *The Three Worlds of Welfare Capitalism*, Esping-Andersen (1990) diagnosed a future of low employment for West Germany. Whilst in Sweden the expansion of the welfare state, and in the U.S. the market-led explosion of producer and personal services, had been valuable sources of employment for women, in West Germany neither the state nor the market had generated a comparable enlargement of service sector employment. The West German economy had remained orientated towards manufacturing employment with no significant upsurge in service-produced employment. Although female employment rates had increased in the postwar period, the comparatively modest expansion of the service sector had limited the growth of women's waged labour. In 1987 just over 55 percent of the West German workforce compared to over 60 percent of the U.K. and French workforces were employed in the tertiary sector (Lane 1993: 281). Esping-Andersen (1990: 214) predicted that on its present track

'Germany will remain predominantly an industrial economy, but with diminishing numbers of people in production, and an ever-increasing population of housewives, the young, and the elderly excluded from employment and dependent on the welfare state'.

In addition, the 'conservative' nature of the welfare system had a decisive impact on women's working opportunities. In all matters apart from health the family acted as the first point of welfare. State welfare provision was to be called on as a last resort. Thus, unlike the Swedish welfare system that was based on state provision of welfare services for and by women, the West German state neither generated a significant number of jobs for women in welfare services nor a growth in services facilitating women's entry to the labour market (Esping-Andersen 1990). The CDU-led coalition government advocated family-based childcare, with 'family-supplementing' (*familienergänzende*) childcare institutions (Bundesministerium für Jugend, Familie, Frauen und Gesundheit 1989: 56). Child day-care was designed to complement the care of children within the home, not to replace it. Crèche places were scarce. In 1989 places were available for just 2 per cent of children under 3 years of age. By stark contrast, kindergarten places were available for nearly 80 per cent of children between 3 and 6 years of age (Jasper 1991). West German childcare for this age group far exceeded the level of provision in Britain where working parents were still heavily reliant on informal childcare arrangements, particularly the use of the immediate and extended family. In the early 1990s only 8 percent of British children under school age attended a day nursery and 6 percent were cared for by a registered childminder (*Guardian* 6.8.94: 9).

But, despite the wider availability of formal childcare in West Germany, women with children had a much lower rate of labour force participation rate in West Germany than in Britain. Forty percent of women in West Germany with children aged between 3 and 5 years were employed, compared to 55 percent in Britain and 67 per cent in France (Lane 1993: 282). Unlike in the GDR, child day-care in West Germany was not geared towards helping women reconcile work and motherhood. Kindergarten places were usually available on a part-time basis only. Furthermore, half-day schooling and a lack of after-school care centres made women's full-time employment difficult even with school-age children (Lane 1993: 279–280). Amongst both West German men and women was an overriding consensus that the most appropriate place for the care of young children was the family unit.

In West Germany both marriage and motherhood were more likely to constrain women's involvement in paid employment outside the home than in the GDR, in France or in Britain (Lane 1993: 281). Looking at the pre-unification period only 58 percent of married women in West Germany were employed in 1988 compared to 72 percent in Britain (Lane 1993: 282). Just 16 percent of West German women with children had not interrupted their careers at all to care for children (Kolinsky 1993: 154). Of the 10.7 million women employed in West Germany in 1987 just over a quarter had children under 18 years of age and only one in nine had children under 6 years of age (Bundesministerium für Jugend, Familie, Frauen und Gesundheit 1989: 43). Whilst in France it was no longer the norm for women to take career breaks because of motherhood, in Britain short breaks from employment were still frequently taken. However, British women tended to suspend their employment for shorter periods than West German women. Although the length of employment breaks had fallen, women in West Germany still averaged an eight-year period of absence (Kolinsky 1993: 155).

To fully understand the divergent pattern of welfare in Europe, a closer examination of the ideology that underpins the formation of policy is vital. As Wilson (1977) points out, the welfare state 'is not just a set of services: it is also a set of ideas, about the family, and – not least – about women, who have a centrally important role within the family'. West German social policy was geared towards women who stayed at home (Erler 1988: 231) and defined by a 'gender ideology with a strong emphasis on women's duties as housewives and mothers' (Lane 1993: 279). The tax and benefits system was constructed around a model of the family in which one member (the man) worked full-time and continuously throughout the adult life supporting other members of the family unit (Klammer 1997: 1). The subordination of women's interests to that of the family led researchers in West Germany to conclude that '[t]he state's interest in the family does not function in the interests of women' (*die tageszeitung* 25.1.92: 13).

The victory of the CDU coalition in the 1982 elections had earmarked, supposedly, the start of a new, more 'woman-friendly', phase in welfare legislation. Under the slogans 'partnership' and 'freedom of choice' the federal government's expressed aim was to upgrade the value of family tasks (*die tageszeitung* 25.1.92: 13). Pension rights were extended to housewives and employment leave after childbirth was awarded to both men and women. The introduction of extended baby leave (*Erziehungsurlaub*) in 1986, whilst allowing parents to take career breaks, also encouraged the private care of children in their early years. Initially parents were entitled to 12 months' leave from employment after childbirth. Later the length of absence was increased to 15 months, then 18 months, and after unification to 3 years. Although there was no guarantee that parents would be able to return to their previous jobs, firms had to ensure that they were able to return to jobs on an equivalent level.

The emancipatory effects of the CDU's social policy have been hotly disputed. Kolinsky (1993: 69) argues that, by upgrading domestic work and giving both parents the option of baby leave, the measures introduced by the CDU-led coalition actually went further in reducing gender divisions than the legislation previously introduced by the SPD-led federal government. The CDU's social legislation, she suggests, broke 'new ground in the recognition of child-rearing as a contribution society should reward'.

But the welfare initiatives implemented by the CDU-led government were inconsistent in their approach to women and their relationships to the family and to work. On the one hand, certain measures stressed parental responsibility; on the other hand, provisions emphasised women's primary role in the care of children. To a large extent the CDU had merely repackaged its traditional gender ideology in a new, more 'woman-friendly' and egalitarian wrapping (*die tageszeitung* 25.1.92: 13). The swelling number of women in employment, higher education and political life, together with the concurrent growth of the new social movements, in particular the women's movements and the Green Party, meant that even parties on the right of the political spectrum could not ignore equal opportunity issues (Lane 1993: 293). How to define equality, however, remained more open-ended. The CDU adopted the line of 'equal but different' – women could be equal with men but still occupy different spaces and roles, hence the endeavours to upgrade the status of the housewife role.

Despite the federal government's attempt to upgrade the status of housework and motherhood, the rewards offered to full-time mothers and carers did not 'compensate adequately for the loss of income/opportunities/options or for the lack of childcare facilities and other services for mothers' (Langan and Ostner 1991: 138). Full-time carers still provided their services without any direct remuneration. Housewives and mothers tended to be dependent upon family or state structures for their upkeep. Not only did full-time domestic labour limit women's scope for financial autonomy but, in contrast to other workers, housewives and mothers also had no guarantee of work conditions, hours of work and so on. How many housewives have guaranteed holiday leave?

Despite the legislative commitments to parental responsibility in childcare the traditional division of labour within the home remained intact. Less than two out of every one hundred parents taking the extended baby leave were men (*die tageszeitung* 25.1.92: 14). Of course, in any instance change at the legislative level alone cannot overturn deeply embedded ideas on men and women's appropriate gender roles. But in financial terms the legislation still discriminated against women, limiting their scope for choice. As the provision for extended baby leave did not compensate fully for the loss of earnings, women were still more likely than their male partners to take advantage of the measure because of their generally lower earning power.

Reform to labour legislation occurred at the same time as welfare provisions were amended (Vogelheim 1988). Again the legislation was inconsistent in its effects on women's employment opportunities. The German Labour Law of 1985 allowed the use of temporary employment contracts that did not afford workers the same protection as permanent contracts. By allowing more precarious employment via fixed-term contracts, the law offered employers a means of avoiding additional costs. For example, pregnant women recruited on a temporary basis had no protection from dismissal (Vogelheim 1988: 116).

Yet whilst affording greater flexibility to employers by making the terms of temporary contracts more insecure, the government at the same time extended greater labour protection to part-time work. In contrast to Britain and the U.S. the West German government was far more hesitant about the virtues of labour market deregulation. In 1985 the majority of part-time workers were guaranteed the same rights and protection as full-time workers (Kolinsky 1993: 59–60; Lane 1993: 298–299; Vogelheim 1988: 115). As most part-time workers were women the increased protection for part-time workers was an important break-through for female wage labour. Whereas in Britain, at this point, employers could save massively on National Insurance contributions by creating part-time positions, in West Germany employers did not have the same incentive to hire part-time workers. Thus, whilst the West German system of welfare, with its emphasis on the family as the primary provider of care, tended to frustrate women's entry to paid labour, those women who were employed, even on a part-time basis, tended to enjoy better labour protection than many of their Western European counterparts. Para-doxically, as Lanc (1993: 280) points out in relation to women's employment, the 'overall effect of employment and family policies [in Germany] is to curtail labour force participation more strongly than in Britain and France ... [but] once women have entered the labour force they are much less disadvantaged'.

Post-Unification Policy

In the first all-German federal elections held in December 1990 the CDU/CSU/FDP coalition was victorious. Thus, the federal coali-tion government that had governed the Federal Republic since 1982 continued to hold the reins of political power in the immedi-ate post-unification period. Another victory in 1994 kept the CDU-led coalition in government at the federal level until their defeat in 1998 (see table 3.6 in chapter 3 for federal election details).

The following discussion will focus primarily on the immediate period after unification, emphasising the shifts in policy that occurred via the collapse of state socialism and the unification process. The discussion of post-unification Germany is thus con-fined to the early years after unification. The chapter begins by giv-ing a broad overview of the direction of federal welfare and labour policy under the CDU-led administration. The chapter concludes by examining the focus of policy at the state level in Brandenburg, indicating disparities in tone and content between the state and federal levels of government.

Post-Unification Policy: The Federal Welfare Agenda

After unification the tone of the federal government's welfare pol-icy was consistent with its pre-unification past. With the retention of the CDU's political dominance the conservative welfare tradition remained intact, going to even greater lengths to emphasise women's freedom to choose full-time motherhood. Whilst not overtly opposing women's right to work nor equal opportunities in the workforce, the federal government stressed East German women's newly acquired ability to choose *between* work and family. Women, it was frequently pointed out, now had the option to be workers *or* mothers and not just workers *and* mothers. Under state socialism women had been compelled both politically and economically to take up paid labour outside the home. In federal government discourse East German women's newly found ability to choose their families over employment was presented as a potential source of liberation. 'Women in the new German states', so the federal government argued, 'want more time for their children than was wished and possible in the socialist system' (Bundesministerium für Frauen und Jugend 1991a).

In line with the principles of 'partnership' and 'freedom of choice' advocated by the CDU marriage and motherhood were presented to East German women as viable career options. The government continued to emphasise the equal status of housework and motherhood to paid work outside the home. A booklet published by the Federal Press and Information Office declared that:

> The tasks of housewife and mother are actually recognised in many laws and decrees, but still it is not generally known that family work is worth exactly as much as employment outside the home. If one were to include unpaid household and family work in national economic accounts the gross national product would increase by DM 600 thousand million each year. Housewife and motherhood is a career which should not be rated less than that of a sales assistant, a teacher or a judge – for a while at least it is perhaps even the nicest job of all. (Presse- und Informationsamt der Bundesregierung 1.12.1991: 79).

As indicated above, the CDU's representation of motherhood and housework overlooked a crucial financial point. Women's domestic labour may in fact be worth millions of Deutschmarks but women performing domestic labour within their own household unit are not undertaking contractual employment with all the associated benefits nor do they usually receive direct financial compensation for their labour. Although the federal government is quite right to acknowledge that housework and childcare is work, the differences in the regulation and payment of this unpaid form of domestic work from paid labour that is subject to extensive legal controls, make it impossible to equate the two spheres of work.

In some respects the post-unification welfare agenda displayed some continuity, at an ideological level, with the welfare programme pursued under state socialism. In both the GDR and West Germany welfare policy was based on the notion that childcare was 'women's work'. However, the emphasis placed on women's private roles varied between the two systems. Whereas public policy in the GDR associated domestic labour primarily with women, it did not prioritise women's domestic roles over their wage labour roles. The

CDU-led federal government, on the other hand, accentuated women's primary association with the family. The idea of the full-time housewife had disappeared under state socialism only to be rejuvenated after unification.

Although the core of the West German welfare system remained unaltered in the new united Germany, certain salient amendments were made in the legislative realm in this immediate post-unification period – changes which had both indirect and direct implications for women's employment. Two issues in particular warrant further attention: the all-German abortion policy and the regulation of childcare.

Unification acted as an impetus to re-open the abortion debate. Throughout Eastern Europe the collapse of state socialism was accompanied by attacks on women's reproductive rights, usually with the expressed aim of criminalising or restricting women's access to abortion. With the one notable exception of Romania, abortion had been legal throughout the region during the state socialist period (Einhorn 1993a: 84; Einhorn 1993b: 64; Githens 1996: 65–66). Although relatively tardy in the liberalisation of its abortion laws, East German women were given the legal right in 1972 to terminate pregnancies within the first 12 weeks in 1972. The unification of East and West Germany thus brought together two dissimilar sets of abortion legislation. Whilst the principle of women's self-determination in the first 3 months of pregnancy was enshrined in East German legislation, West German law obstructed women's access to abortion. Paragraph 218 of the West German Penal Code only allowed abortion under certain conditions and under medical approval. A woman was entitled to an abortion up until week 12 of pregnancy if she had been raped, up to 22 weeks if the child was known to have genetic or health damage and up to any time if it would physically endanger the life of the mother. A clause stated that women were also allowed to terminate their pregnancies if there was deemed to be psychological or social need. The decision lay ultimately with the doctor. Proof of the necessity of abortion in this instance was both problematic and precarious. Not only were abortions less likely to be approved in Catholic areas; but also many doctors were unwilling to approve abortion on these grounds as inadequate proof of psychological and social need could result in the prosecution of both the doctors and women involved.[1]

Historically, Paragraph 218 of the Penal Code had been highly controversial. In the 1970s West Germany had been on the verge of liberalising its abortion laws, but amendments introduced by the federal government to make women's access to abortion easier were overruled by the Federal Constitutional Court. The Court, which acts as a constitutional watch-dog and has the power to block any legislation which it deems unconstitutional, declared that the new law contravened the constitution's pledge to uphold the rights of the unborn child.

After unification a compromise solution to create a common abortion policy in the new Germany was at first hard to find. The six legislative proposals presented varied from stiffening access to abortion to abolishing Paragraph 218 altogether. The Catholic Church made it clear that an opposition to abortion was, in its opinion, central to Christian Democratic principles, commanding the CDU (Christian Democratic Union) and the CSU (Christian Social Union) to remove 'Christian' from their titles if they were to support a more liberal line on abortion. Eventually a cross-party solution was found. A group motion put forward by the SPD and FDP, with the support of some CDU politicians, mainly from the new federal states, was able to find the two-thirds majority needed. It was agreed that abortion should be available up to the 12th week of pregnancy as long as counselling took place three days prior to the operation. On this issue East/West divisions were superimposed on party divisions, with a tendency for East German CDU politicians to adopt a more liberal approach than their West German counterparts. Interestingly, Angela Merkel, the Minister for Women and an East German, did not vote against the compromise solution but instead abstained (*Der Spiegel* 27/1992: 20).

Although the two federal chambers passed the group motion, the Constitutional Court once again challenged the legislation on constitutional grounds. In May 1993 the Court declared that abortion would be allowed within the first 12 weeks of abortion as long as the woman took part in counselling which aimed to discourage her from a termination. In addition, women would have to pay for their abortions unless the termination was proved necessary on medical grounds, making the distinction still between lawful and unlawful abortions (Clements 1994). For West German women the re-opening of the abortion debate at the parliamentary level after unification had resulted in a more liberal abortion law being introduced. But in East Germany, by contrast, unification had served to stiffen access to abortion, despite East Germany's general support for a liberal line on abortion (Einhorn 1993a: 97).[2]

To make the conditions surrounding parenthood more attractive (and also to discourage the social need for abortion), a package of social measures was introduced alongside the abortion legislation. Included within this package was a pledge by the federal government to make kindergarten places available to all children over 3 years of age by 1996. In West Germany kindergarten places were already available to around 80 percent of all children over 3 years of age. In East Germany the provision was even more extensive, with the state providing near complete childcare cover for this age-group.

However, the aim of improving the availability of kindergarten places did not represent a significant shift away from the principle of family-supplementing childcare that underpinned West German welfare policy. In West Germany, in stark contrast to East Germany, the majority of children attending kindergartens did so on a part-time basis. The new legislation, whilst aiming to provide all over-3s with day-care places, made no provision for length of opening or cost of childcare; nor did it include a similar guarantee for the provision of nursery places for the under-threes or after-school centres for school-age children. In line with the emphasis on the family as the primary providers of welfare, the federal government at the same time extended parental leave after childbirth to a maximum of 3 years. Whilst on the surface the federal government appeared to be taking on board the issue of public childcare, in fact its legislation did nothing to confront the question of how working parents should combine employment with their family responsibilities. In actuality, by not taking up the issue of opening hours, cost of childcare or provision for children outside the 3- to 6-year-old age-group, the legislation still represented a potential cutback in childcare provision for East German women.

The federal government saw part-time work for women as the most useful way of combining work and family (*Die Welt* 12.2.92: 16). In comparison with some other EU member states, West Germany has had a low part-time employment quota. In the Netherlands 34 percent of the workforce were employed part-time at the beginning of the 1990s, double the number in Germany (*Financial Times* 10.2.94). In a bid to encourage the growth of part-time employment possibilities, the federal government announced in 1994 that future vacancies in government ministries and federal agencies had to be offered on a part-time as well as a full-time basis. Of course, this represented just one section of the German workforce. In the new federal states, in particular, part-time employment was not a 'realistic possibility' for most workers, mothers or otherwise. The unstable economic climate in the immediate post-Wende period curbed the creation of part-time posts in the private sector (see chapter 5). Thus, for most East German women the option of combining parenthood with part-time employment simply did not exist.

In addition, the federal government called upon the private sector to take more responsibility in the provision of day-care for children, appealing directly to the private sector to introduce more flexible work methods and to participate more directly in the running and financing of childcare facilities. In-firm childcare in conjunction with the growth of flexible labour forms (part-time working, job sharing and partial homeworking) would, it was hoped, relieve the public sector of some of the costs of childcare provision (*Die Welt* 12.2.92: 16). However, with the East German economy in tatters, the ability and the willingness of businesses to find additional resources for childcare provision were restricted. Looking back to the pre-unification period in West Germany, the support of the private sector for working mothers had tended to ebb and flow with the demand for their labour. During the years of economic prosperity and full employment business organisations increasingly debated the problems surrounding women's employment, advocating measures to increase and maintain women's labour force participation. In a paper appearing in 1970, the Federal Institute of Industry showed a sympathetic attitude to women's difficulties in the labour market and recognised the debilitating social and economic effects of women's non-employment. It argued that employment was beneficial to both women and children and recommended the establishment of adequate childcare, identifying the need to alter work conditions to suit the requirements of women with children and to extend part-time work to facilitate women's participation in paid labour (Vogelheim 1988: 108–14).

The attitude taken by the Federal Institute of Industry was indicative of a general mood amongst employers during the period of relative economic prosperity in West Germany (Vogelheim 1988: 111–12). However, when economic crisis and growing unemployment replaced economic good fortune the interpretation of women's appropriate social and labour roles by employers and management shifted once again. As Vogelheim (1988: 113) notes; 'The terms of the discussion had clearly changed. From "unrealized potential" women had become a "problem group", but the problems were now of their own making. Women's increased motivation for work ... was what was causing the unemployment rate to rise'.

Whilst previously, in a more stable economic environment, women's employment had been seen as beneficial, in the more precarious economic climate women's employment was interpreted as a danger not only to family stability but to the whole fabric of society. Echoes of this latter position could be found in post-unification Germany. A Berlin representative of Herlitz, the paper manufacturer, when tackled about the issue of work-based childcare facilities, argued that it was more in the interests of the child for childcare to take place in the vicinity of the home than in the workplace (*Berliner Zeitung* 3.2.92: 9). In the context of high unemployment, mass job loss and economic uncertainty the economic viability of in-firm childcare was a key concern. With a mass surplus of labour in the new federal states, the economic imperative to facilitate women's entry into paid employment by assisting in the provision of childcare was missing for most firms.

In all, the moves made by the government to tackle the issue of combining work and family commitments did little to support those women wishing to combine full-time work with the care of young children. At the crux of the post-unification welfare agenda at the federal level was the (generally unarticulated) notion that the full-time employment of women with young children was undesirable. Yet despite the lack of commitment on the part of the federal government and the private sector to the provision of full-time, affordable care for preschool-age children (of all ages), childcare provision in the new federal states remained higher than in West Germany in the initial post-Wende period. In 1995 70 percent of East Germans with preschool-age children sent their children to a childcare facility compared to 58 percent of West Germans (Bundesministerium für Familie, Senioren, Frauen und Jugend: Abteilung Frauenpolitik 1996: 18–19). The higher level of provision in East Germany after unification was a direct legacy of the state socialist period rather than the effect of federal welfare policy. Not only did more childcare places already exist but also parents in East Germany were more readily disposed to the notion of childcare outside the home than West German parents. Complacency around the level of childcare in East Germany would, however, be dangerous. Public childcare, despite the comparatively high provision in East Germany, is still, as indicated above, vulnerable to cutbacks and closure.

Post-Unification Policy: Labour Legislation

The privatisation of the state-run economy was central to the transition from a state socialist command economy to a capitalist market economy. In the GDR the state was not only the legislator and upholder of the law but also the main employer. After the collapse of state socialism the interim government established the Treuhan-danstalt (THA) to take charge of the privatisation process. In total the THA became responsible for 40 percent of the surface area and 50 percent of the workforce in East Germany (Jeffries 1992: 165). Over 9,000 businesses and 4 million workers were placed under the control of the Treuhandanstalt (Flockton and Esser 1992: 290).

In the immediate post-Wende period firm closures and rationali-sation programmes led to a mass of redundancies and a sharp increase in unemployment. As chapter 5 details in more depth, within three years 40 percent of jobs had been lost, with unemployment par-ticularly high amongst women workers (Bäcker et al. 1994: 12). The Treuhandanstalt's privatisation strategy came under enormous criti-cism. Above all, the agency was accused of taking a too short-term view of the East German economy, of displaying too great a readiness to close down enterprises and too great a reluctance to rehabilitate the East German economy (Interview, Frau Smykalla, Textile and Cloth-ing Trade Union Cottbus, 17.9.92). Defending its policy, the Treu-handanstalt maintained that it was able to ascertain within a short period of time whether a firm had the chance of long-term survival. To finance *ad infinitum* an enterprise that had no chance of indepen-dent survival in the market was, it argued, a waste of resources (Inter-view, Tobia-M Engelhardt, Treuhandanstalt, 18.9.92). The cost of the privatisation process to the Treuhandanstalt was massive. In 1991 alone it suffered net losses of DM 21 billion (Flockton and Esser 1992: 291). In response to criticism the THA was forced to modify its privatisation strategy. In March 1991 it announced plans of greater cooperation with unions and state (*Land*) representatives. The emphasis of its policy would shift from closure to restructuring (Flockton and Esser 1992: 290). But, despite the shift in policy, pri-vatisation was still restrained. Confusion over property rights, the slow growth of private investment, rising wage costs and competition from exports all inhibited the recovery of East German business.

At the federal level Chancellor Kohl and the CDU-led government had miscalculated the extent to which the socioeconomic transforma-tion of the former GDR could be left to market forces, and thus grossly underestimated the amount of financial aid required to fund the tran-sitional process. As a consequence the federal government adopted 'a reactive stance, as the true scale of the restructuring needed, and the employment challenge, unfolded' (Flockton and Esser 1992: 296). In response to the near collapse of the East German economy the federal government was forced into crisis management. Originally the gov-ernment had aimed to finance the transitional process in the new fed-

eral states without tax increases in West Germany. The German Unity
Fund set aside DM 115 billion to aid restructuring in the new states
between 1990 and 1994. By August 1991 it was decided that an additional DM 6 billion would be required annually, amounting to DM 24
billion in total (Timmins 1992: 176).

By the beginning of 1993 the predicted economic upturn had still
not transpired. Unemployment remained high and the free market
was providing few compensatory jobs, by comparison with the quantity lost. It had become clear that financing unification was impossible without increasing taxes. As part of the bid to increase public
revenue, VAT was increased from 14 to 15 percent throughout the
Federal Republic in January 1993 (*Financial Times* 4.1.93). Chancellor Kohl's pledge to West Germans that they would not have to pay
for unification out of their own pockets had proved unworkable.

Such was the scale of restructuring the transition from a planned
to a market economy, the labour market necessitated a considerable
amount of state intervention to avoid complete collapse. The bulk
of labour market measures introduced by the state sought to relieve
the labour market in three key ways: by reducing the size of the
potential workforce; through job creation schemes; and by retraining the workforce to the changing needs of the economy. In the initial post-unification period early retirement schemes were the single
largest mode of labour market relief. In 1992 over 130,000 people
left the Brandenburg labour market because of early retirement,
double the number that took up places in training schemes and
double the number that found temporary employment in work creation schemes in the same period (Schuldt 1993: 9).

Initially the introduction of state-subsidised *Kurzarbeit* (short-
time working) was used as a stopgap measure to prevent the massive
and sudden swelling of unemployment in the immediate period after
unification. In the old Federal Republic Kurzarbeit had been used to
support firms through short-term difficulties. Firms, in certain
instances, were subsidised by the state to keep on their workers,
even though there was no or little work immediately available.
Through the unification of East with West Germany the system of
Kurzarbeit was extended to the new federal states. But unlike the
use of Kurzarbeit in West Germany, the introduction of short-time
working in East Germany acted merely as a means of delaying mass
redundancies. Short-time working or *Kurzarbeit Null* (where workers were still employed but were working no hours whatsoever)
served as a preliminary to unemployment for most workers. The
introduction of Kurzarbeit was a short-term solution to the prospect

of sudden, large-scale job loss; it was not a long-term cure. In 1991 a monthly average of around 250,000 workers in Brandenburg found themselves in Kurzarbeit (in some months over 300,000 workers were working shortened hours). In many ways Kurzarbeit just delayed the inevitable. It was not a viable means of labour market relief over the longer term and workers could only be involved in Kurzarbeit for a limited period of time. Over 80,000 workers in Brandenburg ended short-time working at the end of 1991 (see figure 4.1), which accounted for the sharp increase in unemployment in January 1992. As the years have gone on the number of workers involved in Kurzarbeit has steadily decreased. In January 1993 there were only 33,000 workers employed short-time, compared to over 300,000 two years earlier. By 1997 only 8,000 workers were involved in Kurzarbeit in Brandenburg (see figures 4.2 and 4.3).

Whilst early retirement schemes sought to reduce the overall number of people actively seeking or engaged in work by removing a substantial number of the preretirement-age group from the potential working population and Kurzarbeit acted as a short-term, stopgap measure, other policy initiatives were geared more towards keeping, rehabilitating and/or reintroducing workers into the labour market. Central to the state's longer-term plans to alleviate and boost the labour market has been the establishment of work-creation schemes and retraining programmes. Both have had a signif-

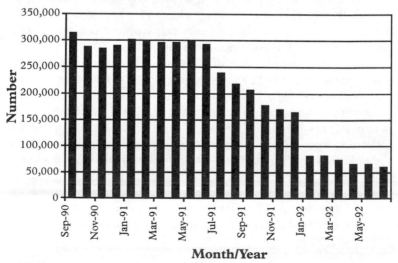

Figure 4.1. *Short-time working in Brandenburg, September 1990–June 1992.*

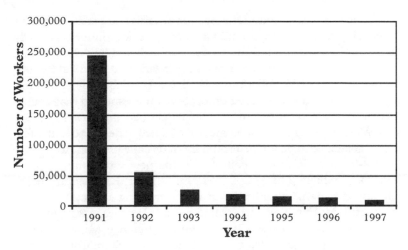

Figure 4.2. *Short-time workers. Average yearly figures for Brandenburg, 1991–1997.*

icant impact in terms of reducing the number of people registered as unemployed and have enabled workers finding themselves without a job to find the means to maintain an active involvement in the labour market and, particularly in the case of training courses, to build on existing skills or to develop expertise in new areas.

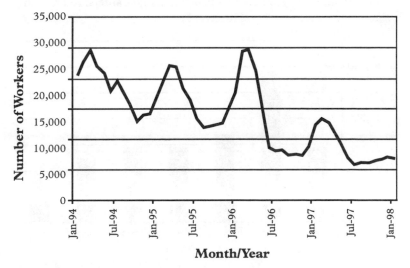

Figure 4.3. *Short-time working in Brandenburg, January 1994–January 1998.*

Yet, in spite of the continuing economic crisis and persistently high unemployment, public spending cuts were announced as early as 1993. The costs of unification had been high and had resulted in a large public sector debt. In the first thirty years of the Federal Republic of Germany the public sector had accrued a debt of DM 500 billion. In the first five years after unification it was expected that double that sum would be added to the public debt (*Financial Times* 1.3.93: 20). With such high unemployment in the new federal states the territory generated an inadequate amount of revenue itself. In April 1993 unemployment insurance collected in the new states amounted to DM 270 million (*Der Spiegel* 22/1993: 20). Yet the costs of unemployment benefit, work creation and retraining schemes totalled between DM 45 billion and DM 46 billion (*Der Spiegel* 22/1993: 20; *Financial Times* 28.1.94: 17). In total the Finance Minister, Theo Waigel, aimed to cut at least DM 20 thousand million from the federal expenditure. The year 1994, he stated, would be labelled the 'Year of Saving' (*Das Jahr des Sparens*). The Federal Labour Office alone was directed to save DM 15 thousand million (*Der Spiegel* 22/1993: 18; *Der Spiegel* 25/1993: 82). To achieve this objective the Labour Office was forced to retrench unemployment and labour market spending, leading to a cutback in the number of places available (see figures 4.4, 4.5 and 4.6). Retraining was earmarked as a 'Kann' (can) rather than a 'Muß' (must) entitlement (*Der Spiegel* 22/1993: 21). As a result, an unemployed person was no longer guaranteed full funding

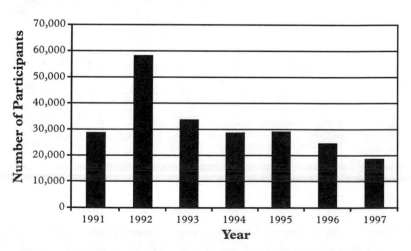

Figure 4.4. *Work-creation schemes (ABM) in Brandenburg. Yearly averages 1991–1997.*

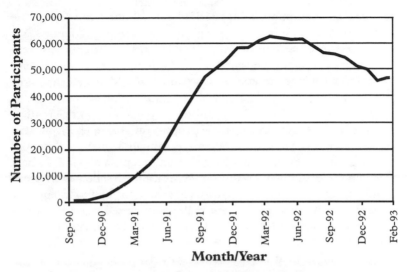

Figure 4.5. *Work-creation schemes (ABM) in Brandenburg, September 1990–February 1993.*

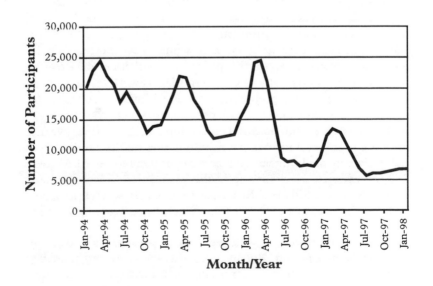

Figure 4.6. *Work-creation schemes (ABM) in Brandenburg, January 1994–January 1998.*

for retraining. Support from the Federal Labour Office would be linked to future employment prospects. For example, retraining as a pharmaceutical assistant would receive 100 percent support whereas re-training in office- or business-related schemes would only receive 70 percent backing (Interview, Director, EWA Management Berufliche Aus- und Weiterbildung GmbH, Cottbus, 7.4.94).

Interestingly, whilst the number of places in work-creation schemes has steadily dropped, the proportion of women involved in work-creation schemes has increased. Initially women's participation rates in work-creation schemes were exceptionally low. In part this can be explained by the concentration of schemes in areas requiring manual labour such as construction, environmental or industrial redevelopment where male labour predominated (Bundesanstalt für Arbeit 1994a: 91). In part it could be attributed to the more general tendency to steer women towards retraining programmes rather than work-creation schemes.

As a general principle, however, the state held that the composition of state-subsidised measures – whether they were employment schemes or training programmes – should mirror the gender profile of unemployment. Clearly, a situation where women made up just over a third of workers in ABM (37 percent of ABM workers in East Germany in 1991 were female) but two-thirds of the unemployed was wholly unsatisfactory. Initiatives on the part of both federal and individual state governments to create a more equitable distribution of places between men and women have borne fruit. By 1995 women made up over 65 percent of workers in job-creation schemes in East Germany (Tischer and Doering 1998). However, the rise in the relative proportion of women involved in work-creation schemes has coincided with overall cutbacks in the number of places available and has therefore done little to improve the absolute number of women participating in schemes. Although in 1992 women made up just 44 percent of workers in ABM, over 160,000 women were working in this area. In 1996 women made up almost two-thirds of ABM workers but their overall numbers had decreased to just over 125,000 (Tischer and Doering 1998).

In the retraining programmes women fared better in terms of representation, making up well over half of participants throughout the post-Wende period. But in the main women were channelled into programmes offering retraining in business- and computer-related skills and men into more technical and craft-based programmes, learning to be plumbers, electricians and so on. Despite the more numerically equitable participation of women in retraining programmes their employment rate after course completion fell short of their male counterparts, partly because of the type of skills they were learning and partly because of the general preference for male labour within the economy overall. The supply of workers with office skills from retraining programmes far outstripped the demand for their labour in the job market. As a result, funding for this area of training was particularly vulnerable to cutbacks (see chapter 5 for more details).

The Land Level: the Case of Brandenburg

At the state level Brandenburg was the only East German Land to elect an SPD-led coalition government in the state elections of October 1990. The other four new federal states – Saxony, Saxony-Anhalt, Thuringia and Mecklenburg-Vorpommern – elected either CDU-majority or CDU-led coalition governments (see tables 3.1 – 3.5 in chapter 3). Ideologically, the Brandenburg government adopted a quite different approach to the issue of women's employment from the CDU-led federal government. In its rhetoric, institutional structure and policy making the Brandenburg government not only recognised the additional and particular problems faced by women but also endeavoured to put into place effective measures to combat inequalities based on gender. Brandenburg was, for example, the only new state in 1990 to create a department specifically to deal with women's issues. In addition, the state appointed 120 Equality Officers throughout the state to represent women's interests at more local levels. Whilst applauding the government's initiatives in this area and the attempts it has made to loosen the male stranglehold on power within formal politics, women have still remained a minority in the Brandenburg legislature. In the first term women constituted under a quarter of all representatives in the Brandenburg Land parliament (*Landtag*). Whilst the PDS/Left List parliamentary grouping had the most favourable representation of women (six women and seven men) the sexes were less equitably represented in other parties. One-third of FDP members was female (two women and four men), 19 percent of SPD members (six women and twenty-five men) and just 15 percent of CDU politicians (four women and twenty-five men) (*betr:Frauen* Number 2/3: 14). At the ministerial level men filled the majority of posts; of the ten ministries women headed just two. The government's upper administrative posts were also male-dominated. Over 90 percent of state secretaries and department leaders, over 80 percent of bureau leaders (*ReferatsleiterInnen*) and two-thirds of bureau workers (*ReferentInnen*) were male (*betr:Frauen* Number 2/3: 11).

Ideologically, the Brandenburg government advocated greater state intervention in welfare provision and labour regulation than was generally endorsed by the federal government. Article 12 (3) of the Brandenburg constitution declares, for example that; 'Women and men have equal rights. The state [*Land*] is duty-bound *through effective measures* to ensure the equality of woman and man in work, public life, education and training, in the family as well as in the sphere of social protection' (emphasis my own – RA). In all, the Brandenburg government, whilst committed to the transition from a planned to a market economy, appeared far less willing than the federal government to write off everything associated with state socialism, believing that there were, in the words of an East German sociologist, 'assets worth saving' (Glaessner 1992: 113); most notably elements of the state socialist welfare programme. From the outset the Brandenburg government had pledged its commitment to retain the high level of women's employment characteristic of the GDR, arguing that the female employment quota in the old federal states was 'not a yardstick for Brandenburg' (*betr:Frauen* Number 2/3: 3).

One of the cornerstones of the Brandenburg government's social agenda was its childcare policy. Full-day childcare facilities were regarded by the government as 'a basic prerequisite of parental employment' (*betr:Frauen* Number 2/3: 4). But whereas the state socialist regime had seen state-subsidised childcare as an essential precondition of maternal employment, the Brandenburg government recognised paternal as well as maternal responsibility for childcare. It thereby sought to avoid the specific targeting of women in its policies dealing with the reconciliation of work and family, a stance that had proved to be such a double-edged sword for East German women in the state socialist regime.

To ensure the practical application of the government's ideological commitment to provide full-day childcare, the Brandenburg government introduced the *Kitagesetz* (Childcare law) in June 1992, outlining the terms and conditions of childcare within the state. By guaranteeing not only the quantity of places in kindergartens, crèches and after-school centres but also the length of opening hours and the cost to the parents, the state legislation went far beyond the federal government's commitment to make kindergarten places available to the over-3s.

The Brandenburg Kitagesetz aimed to meet the needs of both child and parents. Facilities were directed to stay open according to the demands of the parent, up to a maximum of 10 hours a day for each child. Parental contributions to the cost of childcare were to be regulated according to parental income, the age and the number of children attending a nursery facility. With regard to the quantity of childcare places, the Brandenburg government aimed to 'meet demand' (*bedarfgerecht*). In order to achieve this objective the state legislated to provide crèche places for 40 percent of children under 3, kindergarten places for 90 percent of children over 3 and after-school places for 40 percent of primary school children. At the beginning of 1992, prior to the introduction of the legislation, the Brandenburg government still provided a childcare service that exceeded the demands of the Kitagesetz. Ninety percent of preschool-age children over 3 attended a kindergarten and between 60 and 70 percent of children under 3 had a crèche place (Interview Frau Rabe, MASGF, 7.2.92). But closures had already taken place, mainly as the result of childcare mergers and the decreasing demand for childcare places arising from a falling birth rate.

State (*Länder*) budgets were severely constrained in the immediate transitional period. Soon after unification Kurt Biedenkopf, Prime Minister of Saxony, announced that his state – along with the other new federal states – stood on the edge of bankruptcy (Timmins 1992: 175). The five new states had started off after unification with no debts at all. In 1993 it was expected that they would borrow DM 28 billion. By the end of 1994 it was predicted that their debts would total DM 76 billion (*Financial Times* 1.3.93: 20). In Brandenburg, the available financial resources limited the state's childcare policy. Manfred Stolpe, outlining the strain of childcare provision on the state and local government's budget, confessed that; 'We in Brandenburg have been able to ward off the threatening cutbacks in childcare facilities, but with a show of strength that has pushed many of the local communities to the limits of their financial capacity' (*betr:Frauen* Number 2/3: 3).

Although as a result of budgetary constraints the Brandenburg government could not aim to rival the level of state subsidisation that had existed in the GDR, it already contributed as much or more out of its own coffers to childcare than many of the other new states. In February 1992 Brandenburg had provided 42 percent of the overall costs of childcare out of state funds. Whilst the state of Saxony-Anhalt matched Brandenburg's level of financing, Thuringia contributed just 29 percent of crèche costs and 38 percent of kindergarten costs (Interview, Frau Rabe, MASGF, 7.2.92). In Berlin, due to financial constraints, the Senate was planning to shorten the opening hours of childcare facilities and thereby curb spending (*Berliner Zeitung* 3.2.92: 9). In Saxony after-school centres had been closed down altogether because of a lack of state funds (Kolinsky 1993: 285).

Budgetary constraints restricted the extent to which the state could provide other social measures, for example, its planned provision of free contraceptives. From the inception of the government's term in office it pledged to continue the cost-free supply of medically prescribed contraceptives that had existed in the GDR. However, the state was only able to extend this provision to persons under 21 years of age (in line with the federal legislation) and for women below a certain income (*betr:Frauen* Number 4: 4). Although the original resolution to provide a free service for all, regardless of age or income, could not be met, the Brandenburg legislation again went beyond the terms of federal law. The regulation passed was still subject to criticism from within the *Landtag*. As resources were scarce, the allocation of public funds was highly controversial. Alfred Pracht, speaker on women's issues for the FDP in the Brandenburg parliament, argued that the provision diverted too much money away from other areas of social policy, suggesting that the money could be better spent on the care of the elderly (Interview, Alfred Pracht, Potsdam, 23.9.92). In 1992 the state of Brandenburg had put aside DM 35 million for the reimbursement of contraceptive costs (*betr:Frauen* Number 4: 4).

The Brandenburg government actively supported women's right to employment. However, as the Federal Labour Office was the main instrument of labour market support, the Brandenburg government was limited in the financial assistance it could provide to the region's labour market in general, and specifically to women in the labour market. As was pointed out, 'The policy of the state of Brandenburg can no way compensate the savings of the Bund with its financial resources. However, the state policy can – to a modest extent – flank, supplement and set its own tone to federal policy' (MASGF Brandenburg 1993c). The state initiated and funded programmes to help older women get back to work; to encourage small and medium-sized firms to take on female apprentices; to assist women's employment projects; and to help the long-term unemployed, many of whom were women, to find jobs (MASGF Brandenburg 1994).

Despite the Brandenburg government's support for such initiatives unemployment in the region still grew apace with other states. Likewise, levels of female unemployment in Brandenburg were comparable to those elsewhere in East Germany (see chapter 5). At the state level the scope to intervene to effect change was of course limited. As the Brandenburg government noted in its 1996 labour market report; 'It is clear that the state government cannot determine key factors affecting the employment situation. It can, however, adapt and optimise its own instruments in order to achieve the desired objectives' (MASGF Brandenburg 1997a: 39). Moreover, the sheer scale and speed of economic dismantling and job loss put both the state and federal governments in a reactive position, fighting, particularly at the state level, an uphill battle against job loss. The government's overall strategy to stimulate job creation was thus inextricably linked to the general rehabilitation of the regional economy. Without creating the general conditions for economic stability and growth, it argued, jobs would not follow (MASGF Brandenburg 1997a: 39). Furthermore, the policies directed specifically at improving women's access to employment were operating in a context of already existing and deeply entrenched gender stereotypes. This is not to discount or devalue the endeavours and achievements of the Brandenburg Land government. At the very least the Brandenburg was able to keep the debate around women and employment alive in the public arena, and in so doing provide a source of opposition to the more conservative rhetoric of the CDU-led federal government. The state government in its support for women's full-time employment had fostered a climate in which women had been encouraged to maintain their claim to employment. Indeed, perhaps the biggest achievement of state policy was to curb the growth of a 'silent reserve' of economically inactive women by encouraging long-term unemployed women to continue registering as unemployed even when they were (no longer) eligible for benefits (Interview, Sabine Hübner, MASGF, 15.4.94).

Postscript: 1998 Federal Elections

In September 1998 the CDU's 16-year hold on power at the federal level was halted. Germany voted overwhelmingly in the 1998 general elections for a change of government. The polls were marked by a clear swing to the left. The SPD gained 298 seats in the Bundestag, the CDU and CSU combined just 245. With the Green Party the SPD was able to form a coalition government; the first centre-left federal government in West Germany since the end of the SPD/FDP coalition government in 1982 and the first ever since unification. But what will the change of government mean for women in Germany, particularly for women living in the new federal states?

The SPD manifesto stated that 'If our society is going to meet the challenges of the future then the intellectual potential, creativity and initiative of women must be able to blossom'. It pledged to begin a 'Women and Work' action programme, aiming for the equal participation of women in working life; increased support for women starting businesses; the more just division of waged and domestic work between men and women through more flexible working times and improved conditions for part-time work; and the provision of more childcare facilities by increasing the financial strength of states and local authorities. Overall the SPD pledged in its manifesto to ensure that neither women nor men are forced to choose between career and family.

How the election promises translate into actual policy measures remains to be seen. Likewise only time will reveal the effectiveness of the red-green coalition at the helm of the federal government. The SPD-led coalition government begins its term of office against the backdrop of mounting economic anxiety worldwide – illustrated by the financial crisis in South-East Asia and the near economic collapse of Russia. Unemployment was the key issue at the 1998 elections. The German populace regarded the SPD as best equipped to deal with the internal economic problems facing Germany. However, the extent to which the SPD coalition government will be able to overturn Germany's domestic economic problems, most notably the mounting unemployment, will be contingent upon developments in the global markets.

Notes

1. In May 1989 a gynaecologist in Memmingen was convicted of carrying out illegal abortions. He had terminated pregnancies within the first 12 weeks of pregnancy, sanctioning the abortions according to the provision in German law that allowed terminations for women in social need. He was sentenced to two and a half years in prison. Over a hundred women were also convicted of having illegal abortions; fifteen men were fined for assisting the women obtain abortions.
2 . The author's own interviews with thirty-two women revealed that all bar one of the women taking part were in favour of maintaining women's right to decide on abortion.

5

The 'Defeminisation' of
Waged Labour

After the collapse of state socialism East Germany entered a
period of economic instability. Many firms were unable to withstand the transition to market economic conditions and the exposure
of the East Germany economy to the rigour of competition in the
global capitalist economy (see chapter 6) and were forced to either
downsize or to close completely. Post-communist economic transformation was entwined with the unification process. As illustrated in
chapter 3, the conditions of unification, most notably the introduction of a 1:1 currency conversion and the policy to equalise wage
rates, all added to the vulnerability of the East Germany economy.

A key offshoot of the economic crisis was the rapid and extensive
displacement of workers from the labour market. In the immediate
period following the Wende high levels of unemployment replaced the
full employment that had existed in the GDR. By the end of 1993
around 40 percent of jobs had been lost in the former GDR, with job
casualties particularly high in agriculture and the industrial sector
(Bäcker et al. 1994: 12). Some estimates put job losses as high as 70
percent in farming and forestry in the first three years after unification
(*Brandaktuell* Number 3: 2/3). In industry over 2 million persons were
still employed in 1991, but within two years the number had
decreased to three-quarters of a million, a fall of around 65 percent
(Bäcker et al. 1994: 12). The process of deindustrialisation had taken
hold so rapidly and completely that already in 1992 politicians and
members of the Treuhandanstalt were debating ways of salvaging the
'industrial nucleus' of East Germany (Hofman and Rink 1993: 29).

This chapter examines employment and unemployment trends in
the initial post-Wende period, focusing on the gendered nature of

labour market change. A key objective of this chapter is to further our understanding of why women have been comparatively more vulnerable to unemployment since the fall of state socialism. The chapter begins by exploring the extent to which women's disproportional exclusion from the labour market has been assisted by the gendered segregation of labour. Have women been more vulnerable to unemployment because areas in which women have predominated have been more susceptible to rationalisation? Are new jobs emerging in areas traditionally associated with male labour? How flexible is sex segregation in the workplace? The chapter goes on to take a closer look at the changing range, level and form of women's employment in the post-unification labour market of East Germany. For those women fortunate enough to retain or find employment, what is working in the new market economy like? The chapter concludes by examining the diversity of women's work experiences, looking at the extent to which women's relationship to the labour market is moulded by factors other than their gender. On the whole, the data used refer either generally to East Germany or specifically to Land Brandenburg, the new federal state profiled in this study. Unless otherwise indicated the statistical data is compiled by the author from the monthly labour statistics produced by either the State Labour Office in Berlin/Brandenburg or the Federal Labour Office in Nuremberg.

Unemployment: Gender Difference

Unemployment rates in the former GDR rose rapidly in the immediate post-Wende period. By January 1992 the official unemployment quota had tripled its pre-unification level, despite high levels of migration and attempts by the state to reduce unemployment through early retirement schemes and other state-sponsored labour market measures (see chapter 4). In September 1989 1.3 million persons had been employed in Land Brandenburg (excluding those persons working in the armed forces and state security). By the end of November 1990 this figure had already fallen to 1.19 million (MASGF Brandenburg 1993a: 28). It was estimated that in Brandenburg over 130,000 persons were removed from the labour market by early retirement schemes in 1992 and an additional 110,000 persons commuted outside Brandenburg to their place of employment (Schuldt 1993: 9). Between November 1989 and March 1991 880,000 persons had migrated from Brandenburg (MASGF Brandenburg 1993a: 28). Despite these forms of labour market relief unemployment still grew rapidly. In September 1990, on the eve of unification, unemployment in Brandenburg stood at just over 5 percent. By 1992 it was already at 14 percent. Unemployment in the new federal states soon outstripped that in the old federal states. By June 1993 unemployment in East Germany as a whole stood at 15.1 percent, almost double that in West Germany.

Through 1994 and 1995 the employment situation began to show some signs of stabilisation; the unemployment rate in Brandenburg, for example, fell from an annual average of 15.3 percent in 1994 to 14.2 percent the following year. However, the period of remission was short-lived and by the end of 1995 signs of further deterioration were already evident. The year 1996 saw a rise in the yearly unemployment average for the first time since 1992. A further rise in unemployment occurred in the following year, increasing the yearly average of unemployment from 16.2 percent in 1996 to 18.9 percent in 1997 (see figure 5.1). Across the whole of East Germany the average yearly number of unemployed persons increased by almost 122,000 between 1995 and 1996 (Tischer and Doering, 1998: Abb. 13.2). A decade on from the fall of the Berlin Wall the employment situation in East Germany remained bleak. The hopes of a rapid recovery had proved misguided.

Despite the high levels of female employment achieved under state socialism, it is women who have been hardest hit by unemployment since the fall of the Berlin Wall. In the immediate period

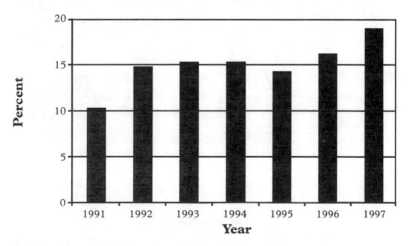

Figure 5.1. *Unemployment in Brandenburg. Yearly averages 1991–1997.*

of restructuring the gap between male and female levels of unemployment quickly widened. In September 1990 there was just one
point separating male and female unemployment quotas in Brandenburg. By July 1993, the female unemployment rate was over
double that of the male rate, standing at over 21 percent for women
and just over 10 percent for men (see figure 5.2). In the same
month women constituted on average two-thirds of unemployed
persons in Brandenburg; in some localities women's share of the
unemployed reached over 70 percent of the total. In July 1993 70.1
percent of unemployed persons in the district of Forst and 73.1
percent of unemployed persons in the district of Calau (both in the
Cottbus region of Brandenburg) were female. Although women
made up slightly more than half of all workers entering unemployment in the immediate post-unification phase, their susceptibility to
redundancy in itself did not account for the large disparity between
male and female unemployment rates. It was women's much lower
chance of finding re-employment or places in state-subsidised
employment schemes once out of work that was the main determinant of their high unemployment. In Brandenburg from December
1991 to July 1993 women constituted on average 52 percent of
workers joining the unemployed. In July 1993 women constituted
fewer than 40 percent of persons finding re-employment.

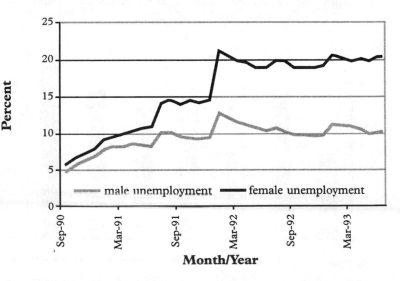

Figure 5.2. *Male and female unemployment in Brandenburg,
September 1990–June 1993.*

A slight shift in the gender-balance of unemployment has been evident since the end of 1995 at the point when unemployment began to rise again. In this period, in contrast to the initial five years after unification, the downturn in the labour market has been borne most heavily by male workers (see figure 5.3). Between 1995 and 1996 just 5,000 women but 93,000 men lost their jobs across East Germany (Tischer and Doering 1998: 13). In Brandenburg male unemployment increased by 3.1 percent during this period. In contrast female unemployment grew by just 0.9 percent. As a result, women's share of unemployment overall has started to fall. In 1997 women made up just 57 percent of the unemployed in Brandenburg compared to 65.1 percent four years earlier. Across the new federal states women constituted 58 percent of the unemployed in September 1997, almost 2 percent less than a year previously.

But in spite of the proportionally higher increase of male unemployment between 1995 and 1997, women's employment chances are still less favourable than those of men. Firstly, women's unemployment rates remain significantly higher than male unemployment rates. In 1997 the average yearly unemployment for women in East Germany was 22.5 percent, still considerably higher than the 16.6 percent recorded for men. Secondly, unemployed women continue to have a significantly lower rate of finding re-employment in the 'free market' than unemployed men. In 1996 fewer than four in every ten workers finding work in the nonsubsidised sector were

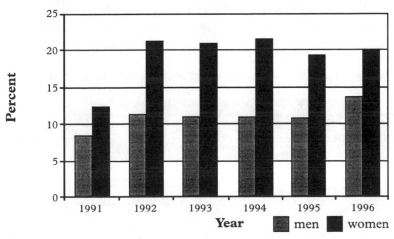

Figure 5.3. *Average yearly unemployment quotas in East Germany, 1991–1996.*

female. Finally, as a result of their persisting difficulties re-entering the workforce once unemployed, women are much more susceptible to periods of long-term unemployment than their male counterparts. One in three women unemployed in 1996 had been out of work for more than 12 months compared to just a quarter of unemployed men. Age is also a determining factor. Over half of the long-term unemployed are over 45 years of age (Landesarbeitsamt Berlin-Brandenburg 1997: 11). Older women, due to the combination of age and gender, are especially vulnerable to prolonged periods out of work (Bundesanstalt für Arbeit 1994a: 57). Long term unemployment acts as a vicious circle. The longer anyone is out of work the more difficult it is to re-enter the workforce. Lengthy involuntary absences from the labour force can not only lead to a loss of self-confidence (*Berliner Zeitung* 10.9.92: 23) and increased poverty, but also to a reduction in the marketability of skills. As Michael Böhm from the Berlin-Brandenburg branch of IG-Metall aptly remarked, a 'skilled worker who is unemployed for more than a year is no longer a skilled worker' (*Berliner Zeitung* 16.9.92).

But how do we adequately explain women's greater susceptibility to unemployment? Chapter 3 examined the nature of the transformation process, indicating the impact of reconstruction on the economic sphere, productivity and job availability. But this analysis in itself did not adequately explain why it is *women* who have disproportionately borne the fallout from economic restructuring. Chapter 4 charted the discursive, legal and the institutional changes at the level of state, examining the impact of such change on women's relationship to the labour market. Yet this examination alone, by concentrating on policy reform, did not illustrate fully the processes by which women have been marginalised in the workforce. The following section starts to take this analysis further by looking at the ways in which sex segregation at work have affected men's and women's employment opportunities in the post-Wende labour market. The analysis suggests that whilst the occupational segregation of men and women is a crucial factor in explaining gendered employment trends, it is not a solely sufficient rationale.

Occupational Segregation

As indicated in chapter 2, despite the high level of female employment achieved under state socialism sex segregation in the workplace persisted. Women had made certain inroads into traditionally male areas but still the majority of women had worked in predominantly female areas. In the immediate post-Wende period not only were female-dominated job categories slightly more vulnerable to redundancy, but also, most significantly, re-employment occurred predominantly in traditionally male fields of employment. In Brandenburg, four of the five job categories with the highest levels of unemployment – office and administration work, retail employment, the food processing industry and cleaning jobs – were occupations that had employed primarily female workers. At the end of June 1993 nearly 15 percent of all unemployment in Brandenburg, and nearly one in five of all women out of work, stemmed from office-based occupations. By West German standards there had been a considerable amount of 'excess employment' in the GDR. The East German economy was much more labour-intensive, with labour productivity rates in the former GDR just 40 percent of those in West Germany. Inefficient production systems, low levels of technology and large, unwieldy bureaucratic structures had all increased the demand for labour. About 10 percent of the workforce in light industry existed, it has been argued, because of the shortcomings of the planned economic system, and a further 5 percent of the workforce in order to perform social and political tasks within the workplace (Breitenacher 1991: 26). Enormous amounts of red tape in a system which remained largely uncomputerised had created a huge demand for secretaries and administration workers, the majority of whom were women. After the collapse of state socialism and the opening up of the East German economy to world trading conditions, the necessity to close the technology gap has led to substantial labour rationalisation in this area, thereby inducing sizeable job losses for women workers.

Yet difficulties were not confined solely to 'female' occupations, such as cleaning and office, or female-dominated sectors such as textile and clothing (see chapter 6). Male strongholds of employment – car manufacturing, heavy industry and coal mining – also suffered significant job losses in the immediate post-Wende period. In the early months after unification it was predicted that by June 1991 the size of the mechanical engineering workforce would be just a third of its September 1989 size, and that the tractor and car industry labour force would be just a quarter of its former magnitude (IAB-Kurzbericht 13.5.91).

But in the initial restructuring period male workers benefited considerably from the buoyancy of the construction sector. One-fifth of re-employment in 1992 occurred in building and construction-related employment, over 90 percent of which was filled by male labour. Improvements to East Germany's infrastructure were crucial to the transformation of its economy and improved efficiency. Roads, buildings, communication networks, gas and water supplies required modernisation in order to bring the region in line with West German and European standards, to increase productivity and, ultimately, to attract much needed investment into the region. Ironically, even the collapse of the economy created jobs. The widespread closure of factories and enterprises generated work, usually for male labour. Often a certain number of employees were retained to clear and strip former work sites after production had ceased.

For women the fortitude of the construction sector created few job opportunities. In the first six months of 1993 women constituted fewer than 10 percent of persons finding re-employment in building-related occupations in Brandenburg. In the early years after unification such was the demand for employment in construction that in some regions of the state a shortage of suitably qualified and regionally mobile workers was recorded in building-related occupations. Yet, labour shortages aside, women made little progress within the building sector. However, the domination of the building-related employment by male workers meant that when the construction began to make cutbacks it was male employment that was hardest struck. Indeed, the downturn in male employment opportunities between the end of 1995 and 1997, marked by men's rising share of unemployment overall, can be attributed, at least in part, to the deterioration of the construction industry and the impact of its decline on related occupations.

In advanced capitalist countries the growth of female employment in the postwar period had resulted largely from the expansion of the service sector. In Britain, whilst women were more susceptible to redundancy during the recession of the 1970s, particularly in the manufacturing sector, the rise of female unemployment was, in part, offset by the growth of jobs for women in the tertiary sector (Bruegel 1979). The service sector in the GDR (as elsewhere in the Eastern bloc) was underdeveloped by general Western standards. At the end of 1990 only 47 percent of the East German workforce had been employed in this area compared to 57 percent in West Germany, a figure resembling West German levels in the mid-1970s (Wegner 1991; *Berliner Zeitung* 7.2.92). It was thus reasonable to expect, firstly, a significant rise in the number of service sector jobs within the East German economy and, secondly, for women in particular to benefit from this increase.

But despite the growth of service sector jobs after the collapse of state socialism, the expansion and emergence of new jobs in this area has not transpired at a rate to counteract the loss of jobs both within the sector and elsewhere. Between 1992 and 1993 10,000 jobs were created in the Brandenburg service sector. However, in the same time-period 76,500 jobs were lost in industry and a further 42,600 were shed from the agricultural sector (Landesamt für Datenverarbeitung und Statistik Brandenburg 1993a; Landesamt für Datenverarbeitung und Statistik Brandenburg 1993b). Entirely new jobs have emerged in banking, insurance, consultancy and training. Employment in credit institutes and insurance companies in Brandenburg increased by 30 percent between April 1991 and January 1992 (MWMT Brandenburg 1994: 48). But in other areas of the tertiary sector substantial job losses had been incurred. Tailors, cobblers, public sector workers, kitchen and cleaning staff were all particularly susceptible to unemployment (*Berliner Zeitung* 7.2.92). In addition, the general poor health of the East German economy, high unemployment, low levels of income and restricted consumer spending have impeded the potential expansion of the service sector.

As a consequence the service sector has not fulfilled its anticipated role as a panacea to women's employment problems. Expectations that the service sector could adequately absorb displaced female labour in East Germany were based not only the presumption that service expansion would be greater in the initial post-Wende period than it actually was, but also on the assumption that demand for employment amongst women would drop to levels more in line with Western nations, such as West Germany. Instead the demand for employment amongst East German women has remained high after unification, and in comparison with West Germany the demand for full-time employment is significantly greater. In addition, as the following section explores further, it cannot be assumed a priori that expansion of employment in all service sector areas will benefit female above male workers. As will be argued below, whilst women continue to dominate service sector employment, a slight shift towards male recruitment has been noted.

Redrawing the Boundaries of Male and Female Employment

As the analysis above indicates, women's greater susceptibility to unemployment resulted, in part, from the gendered division of jobs within the labour market. Because of the sex segregation at work, firm closures, redundancies and recruitment have had an uneven impact on male and female labour, contributing to the overrepresentation of women in unemployment, their weaker position in the recruitment process and the general 'defeminisation' of waged labour after unification. However, the scale of women's unemployment, this chapter suggests, cannot be explained solely by the reference to the occupational segregation of men and women. In specific areas of the labour market the boundaries of male and female employment have been shown to be quite flexible and a resegregation of male and female labour, overwhelmingly in favour of male labour, has occurred. During the period of economic dismantling and reconstruction, male workers, I would argue, were able to bolster their representation in traditionally male as well as some mixed-sex and some customarily female areas of employment.

Under state socialism many traditionally male areas of employment recruited a substantial number of women workers, not only to fill the expanding number of white-collar bureaucratic jobs but also to perform the manual, blue-collar labour customarily undertaken by men (see chapter 2). During the period of downsizing after the Wende there has been a tendency for these traditionally males areas to 're-masculinise'. The mining and energy sector, for example, has incurred particularly high personnel losses. Yet job losses have not been borne equally by both male and female workers. Despite the inroads women had made into both white-collar and blue-collar sections of the mining workforce, they were still hardest hit by the wave of redundancies that swept through the sector following the collapse of state socialism (IGBE 1991).

Women working in the mining sector have been more vulnerable to job losses not only because of the loss of typically female jobs, but also as a direct result of discrimination in favour of men. Increased competition for jobs within the sector meant that traditionally female jobs, such as signal box work, were attracting male workers and the qualified technical areas of employment were becoming 'women-free' zones. Both management and male workers have been implicated in the marginalisation of women within the sector and their removal from it. Where women were directly confronted with large waves of redundancies, either in the firm as a whole or within a specific department, women have reported a rise in discriminatory comments and behaviour on the part of male workers. A representative of the Trade Union for Energy and Mining (IGBE) in Cottbus recounted a '*schreckliche Wende*' (awful turning point) in the attitudes of male to female workers and an increase in the (reported) harassment of women by male workers (Interview, representative of IGBE, Cottbus, 17.9.92). As Jasper (1991: 13) comments in reference to East German men:

> Either the 'old Adam' hardly changed or he is developing anew at a lightning speed. The general opinion is that everyone should have work as long as possible, but when unemployment is unavoidable, then the opinion is: it affects women less. (According to the motto: men become unemployed; women become housewives).

The transfer of West German systems, personnel and styles of management practice to East Germany as a result of unification has also assisted the mounting exclusion of women from areas of employment traditionally associated with male labour. In West Germany a far smaller percentage of workers in the mining sector is female and the small number of women working in the sector are employed almost exclusively in white-collar functions, usually as office and administrative workers (IGBE 1991). After the Wende, labour and personnel structures in East German industry, in an attempt to adapt to the new economic conditions, have begun to assimilate Western standards and practices, a process galvanised by the strong presence of West German managers and advisers within the economy. As a result, the parameters of what is considered to be suitable 'women's work' is being newly redefined, resulting in blue-collar areas of heavy industry, such as mining, once again becoming associated primarily with male labour. However, the disassociation of women with heavy, manual labour has been made more by male management and workers than by the women themselves. Research indicates that the majority of women workers in the mining industry still identified positively with their jobs and the sector after unification and, given the choice, would have continued working in the sector. But many women have simply not had the option to stay on. As one woman remarked, 'For years we were good enough and now all of a sudden we have to go' (Schütte and Minx 1993: 5). Clearly, women's inclusion in traditionally and/or predominantly male areas of employment was not enough to make their jobs as secure as the jobs of their male co-workers. The vulnerability of their position has, however, only been fully exposed once the economic and political conditions surrounding employment changed and competition for employment emerged.

The relative strengthening of men's position within the labour market vis-à-vis women has not been confined to areas historically and traditionally associated with male employment. In some mixed-sex and traditionally female areas a similar process has been observable. The service sector, as indicated above, has been hailed by some commentators as the panacea to women's ailing employment position, if not in the short-term at least in the medium- to long-term. Not only has a significant upsurge in jobs in the tertiary sector still yet to fully materialise but also this sector, which is traditionally viewed as a predominantly female domain, has become an increasingly attractive source of employment for male workers. Increased competition from men for traditionally 'female' jobs has been especially prevalent in areas of service sector employment, which have become more prestigious and better remunerated. In banking, insurance and trade, for example, there was in the immediate post-Wende period a proportionately higher employment rate of men compared to women (Engelbrech 1991).

Thus, the sex typing of jobs has not shown itself to be irrevocably fixed but at times fluid and redefinable, enabling the boundaries of male and female labour to be redrawn during the period of economic reconstruction. Yet this remapping of male and female employment has overwhelmingly benefited male workers. The movement of men into some traditionally female areas of employment has not been accompanied by the parallel motion of women into male-dominated areas. An IAB study summed up this process by stating that, 'All economic spheres whether they are contracting, stagnating or prospering, whether they previously showed a high or a low level of female employment, have recorded a relative increase in the employment of men and a decrease of women' (Engelbrech 1993).

This preference for male labour has been evident throughout the recruitment process. Employers in the nonsubsidised labour market as well as recruitment officers in the allocation of apprenticeship and training places, it has been argued, have often discriminated against women applicants. The Ministry for Work, Social Affairs, Health and Women (MASGF) in Brandenburg noted that the rights of women were not always recognised during the interview procedure. During job interviews women had been asked about their desire for children, marriage plans, and even for proof of sterilisation: all practices prohibited in Germany. Men tend to be seen by many employers as a more flexible and thus more desirable source of labour. Employers, careers advisers and teaching staff have cited women's family ties and their *perceived* lower productivity, technical abilities and analytical competence as reasons for the bias against women in the distribution of training places (*betr:Frauen* Number 7/8: 8–12).[1]

A Reserve Army of Labour?

It is perhaps tempting to associate women's changing fortunes solely or predominantly with the changing demand for labour within the economy and to explain women's vacillating position within the labour market by reference to the 'reserve army of labour' model. In other words, women's fluctuating employment levels exist in response to the altering demand for workers; that women are brought into waged labour when needed and discarded when demand falls, never really securing a firm foothold in employment. Clearly, the mass mobilisation of women into the East German workforce under state socialism coincided with a dire shortage of workers. Likewise, the increasing marginalisation of women in the workforce and their disproportional expulsion from it after the collapse of state socialism coincided with a slump in the demand for labour. But such an explanation elides the composite and complex nature of the situation and ignores in particular the areas where women do retain a firm footing within the labour market.

Even during this period of high unemployment and economic crisis in East Germany's history certain areas of the workforce have remained predominantly feminine. A wholesale re-masculinisation of labour has not occurred despite the mass surplus of labour within the economy. This may appear quite an obvious statement, but it is vital to note that the movement of male workers into female areas of employment has tended to transpire only under certain conditions. The tendency has been for men to strengthen their position in historically male areas of employment and certain mixed-sex and traditionally female areas of employment when those areas have gained status, better pay or have become more technologically intensive. In East Germany women were able to retain their dominance within certain sections of the workforce, admittedly where the tasks involved were usually low-paid, low status or associated with supposedly 'natural' female attributes. As illustrated in chapter 6, the employment of women remained crucial to the remaining sections of the garment-making industry because of the relatively low level of their wages and what was perceived to be their greater natural aptitude to such tasks. Similar reasons were used to vindicate the employment of women in caring professions. The boundaries between male and female employment may be flexible, but in the East German context this flexibility occurs within certain limits. Thus, whilst male labour appeared on an aggregate level to fare

97

better in the post-unification economy of East Germany, in certain specific areas women were able to safeguard their position.

What remains significant, however, is that during the process of economic reconstruction in East Germany women's employment prospects have deteriorated not just in terms of the quantity of jobs available to women but also in terms of the quality of employment on offer to women. The following section takes a closer look at changes within employment, to give a broader account of the gendered nature of labour market developments.

Female Employment

The level of female employment has dropped significantly since unification. Under state socialism over 90 per cent of women were classified as 'employed', if one counted women who were in education or training as well as in employment. If one took into account solely those women who were engaged in paid work and excluded those in education, about 80 percent of East German women could be counted as employed. By the middle of the 1990s slightly fewer than three-quarters of East German women were economically active, in that they were either in work or registered as looking for work, i.e. officially classified as unemployed. Because of the high rates of unemployment in East Germany a substantial number of those women counted as economically active (employed either in the free market or a state-subsidised work scheme) were actually out of work and registered as unemployed. Just 56 percent of East German women in 1996 were actively employed. Significantly, by 1996 the level of women's employment, if taken as the number of women in work, was only 1 percent higher in East Germany than in West Germany. The participation of women in paid work had been so depleted after unification that if one were to exclude the number of women in work-creation schemes from the figures and look just at employment in the free economy, the level of women's employment in East Germany was in fact lower than in West Germany by 1996 (MASGF Brandenburg1997b: 16). Although demand for employment amongst East German women remained considerably higher than in West Germany, the process of economic reconstruction had already brought the actual level of female employment down to West German levels within seven years of unification.

However alarming the rapid and extensive exclusion of women from the labour market, any analysis of women's changing relationship to the labour market after unification needs also to take account of shifting patterns within the labour market. Running parallel to the disproportional displacement of women *from* the labour market during the period of restructuring has been the reconfiguration of the level, range and form of women's employment *within* the labour market. Falling levels of employment overall have, as already indicated above, been accompanied by a restructuring of the employment profile for men and particularly women.

Women's relative share of employment in industry has decreased rapidly since the Wende. Between 1991 and 1995 six out of every ten jobs in manufacturing that had been filled by a woman were dismantled, compared to one out of every two jobs taken by men. At an aggregate level industry was re-masculinising. Whilst male industrial employment in Brandenburg fell by under 10 percent between 1991 and 1992, female industrial employment decreased by a staggering 30 percent. Despite the drop in the absolute number of men working in industry, the proportion of male employment engaged in industrial activity remained constant over the period studied. In both 1991 and 1992 employment in industry accounted for half of all male employment. This constancy did not apply to female workers. Whereas a quarter of employed women had worked in industry in 1991, employment in this area accounted for just a fifth of women's employment by 1992. Similar trends were evident in agriculture and the sphere of trade, transport and communications. In these areas the absolute number of both male and female workers declined rapidly in the immediate post-unification period. Yet in all instances female employment fell more sharply than male employment, thus reducing their relative share of employment in these fields (Landesamt für Datenverarbeitung und Statistik Brandenburg 1993a; Landesamt für Datenverarbeitung und Statistik Brandenburg 1993b). Although the service sector remained a key source of employment for many women, women's share of employment in this area has also been vulnerable to erosion. In 1992 half of women working in Brandenburg were employed in the service sector compared to just a quarter of men (Landesamt für Datenverarbeitung und Statistik Brandenburg 1993a; Landesamt für Datenverarbeitung und Statistik Brandenburg 1993b). However, men's share of new service employment has been steadily growing. Between 1991 and 1992, for example, male service sector employment rose by 2.9 percent in Brandenburg. In comparison, female service sector employment increased by just 2 percent (Landesamt für Datenverarbeitung und Statistik Brandenburg 1993a; Landesamt für Datenverarbeitung und Statistik Brandenburg 1993b). Figures for the whole of East Germany indicate that in the period 1991 to 1995 employment loss for women in service occupations has been double that for men. In stark contrast to trends in West Germany, men have profited from job creation in many areas of the service sector, most notably, although not exclusively in the sphere of service retail (Tischer and Doering 1998: 16).

Alongside shifts in the distribution of male and female labour have been changes to the qualitative aspects of employment. The remainder of this section probes further into the calibre and content of women's employment in East Germany, assessing, for example, how women's work hours, income and access to senior positions have altered as the result of the shift from a command to market economy and German unification. In addition, the discussion looks at factors influencing women's access to jobs, such as training and individual mobility. The section concludes by looking at the incidence of black-market labour within East Germany and women's role within this sphere of work.

Work Hours

In the GDR there had been little latitude for flexible working arrangements. Although part-time work was a virtually all-female enclave, the vast majority of women worked full-time regardless of their family commitments. However, as indicated in chapter 2, the desire for part-time labour amongst women in the GDR exceeded the amount available. In West Germany the part-time labour quota was much higher amongst women than in the GDR. Although the level of part-time labour in West Germany was comparatively lower than in certain other West European countries, the expansion of female wage labour in West Germany from the 1970s onwards had still been based largely on the expansion of part-time work opportunities (Bundesanstalt für Arbeit 1994a: 3). As a result of the transformation of the East Germany economy, did the volume begin to approximate West German levels? Under the changed economic conditions did women's desire for part-time labour persist, lessen or increase?

Part-time labour for women in West Germany increased from 24 per cent of women's employment in 1970 to 35 percent in 1992 (Bundesanstalt für Arbeit 1994a: 3). By 1995 part-time employment accounted for around 40 per cent of all women's jobs and 58 percent of married women's employment (Tischer and Doering

1998: 12). Part-time work was usually available in a narrower career spectrum than full-time employment, mostly in traditionally female job categories and in unskilled or semiskilled occupations where the prospects of promotion were low. Some part-time work was available in better-qualified jobs, most notably in the public sphere (see chapter 4), but, looking at the economy as a whole, part-time opportunities at the higher end of the career spectrum were few and far between (Bäcker et al. 1994: 35). As chapter 4 illustrated, the demand for part-time jobs was high in West Germany. Societal attitudes towards the reconciliation of work and family which stressed mothers' direct involvement in the care of young children, together with a scarcity of full-time childcare places and half-day schooling, meant that for many women part-time work was either preferable or their only possibility. But part-time work was not confined to women with young children attempting to combine family responsibilities and work. In comparison with Britain a much higher proportion of women without young children worked part-time hours in West Germany. In the early 1990s half of all female part-timers in West Germany did not have children under 16 years of age (Lane 1993: 285).

In the GDR the structure of part-time employment differed from that in West Germany. Although under state socialism women with children expressed a greater desire for part-time labour than women without children, part-time workers had mostly been older women (Bundesanstalt für Arbeit 1994a: 27). The majority of women with young children, once they had returned from baby leave, worked on a full-time basis. Furthermore, part-time workers in East Germany tended to work more hours than in West Germany, most over 20 hours a week (Winkler 1990: 83/84). This trend continued after the Wende. Whereas more than one in five women employees in the old states were working less than 20 hours a week in 1991, just 3.5 percent of women were doing so in the new states (Bundesanstalt für Arbeit 1994a: 26).

In the immediate post-Wende period the volume of part-time employment did not increase. In fact, the German micro-census of 1991 indicated a fall in women's part-time employment in the new federal states. This decline was primarily the result of the mass exodus of older women from the labour market. The erosion of employment for women over 55 years of age was staggering. In 1992 only 27.1 percent of women aged between 55 and 60 years of age and just 2.7 percent of 60- to 65-year-olds were still employed (Bäcker et al. 1994: 39).

By 1995 the part-time labour quota for women in East Germany stood at around 22 per cent for women overall (3.3 percent for men) (Tischer and Doering 1998: 13). The poor state of the East German economy had inhibited the growth of part-time labour. In the precarious economic climate after the Wende the option to work part-time was in many instances simply not available. The shortage of part-time posts in the new states corresponded to trends already recognised in West Germany (Bäcker et al. 1994: 39). There, the expansion of part-time jobs had also been slow in phases of higher unemployment and declining employment. Firms were often reluctant to adopt part-time work strategies and take on more workers, as they feared that this step would increase personnel costs (Interview, Frau Kummer, Landesarbeitsamt Berlin-Brandenburg, Berlin, 12.4.94).

Despite the oft-cited difficulties of combining work and family the vast majority of East German women wished to continue working full-time after the Wende. According to research undertaken by the IAB in the early 1990s, just a quarter of all employed women were interested in part-time work; a third of all married working women with children under 16 years of age and 40 per cent of married women with children under 6 years of age (Engelbrech 1993). Indeed, one in two women working part-time wanted full-time employment. Women sought full-time work for a number of reasons. Clearly, full-time employment offered the opportunity to earn more money. It was also considered more secure than part-time employment. Furthermore, career pathways were still very much designed according to male time-structures and to the principle of a full-time working week. For women seeking to establish a career full-time employment was often the only means to secure their full integration into firms and to place themselves on the rungs of the career ladder. In addition, the higher level of childcare provision in East Germany made the reconciliation of full-time work and motherhood a realistic possibility for many women. In 1995 just a quarter of married women in East Germany compared to over half of married women in West Germany, worked part-time (Tischer and Doering 1998: 13).

Income

Under state socialism women continued to earn, on average, less than men; gendered pay differentials were nonetheless slightly narrower than in West Germany. After the Wende this relationship was not overturned. Women continued to earn on average less than men but fared slightly more favourably in terms of relative pay than their West German counterparts. In 1996 the average weekly income of female blue-collar workers in industry was 23 percent less than that of their male colleagues. For white-collar workers in the same area women's wages were around 75 percent of men's. In trade, credit and insurance institutions the difference was less pronounced, even though women earned still just 85 percent of male wages. Pay differentials between East and West Germany persist, with average male pay in East Germany still resembling more closely full-time female pay levels than male pay levels in West Germany. Even as late as 1996 average male earnings in East Germany were only 75 percent of male earnings in West Germany (Tischer and Doering 1998: 24).

Women's subordinate earning potential was defined not just by the lower levels of pay accorded to 'women's' jobs but also by their lower access to more senior and, therefore, better remunerated levels of employment. In the post-Wende period, the vertical segregation of men and women was intensified. Although East German women still fared better than their West German counterparts in terms of representation at management levels, the proportion of East German women in senior positions had decreased during the transformation process. Well-qualified women workers, particularly those in management positions, were more adversely affected by personnel reductions than their male colleagues (MASGF 1993a; betr:Frauen Number 4: 3). A third of women workers had been employed at management levels in the GDR (Winkler 1990: 95). By 1991 just one in five women were employed at this level (Bundesanstalt für Arbeit 1994a: 49).

With the high levels of unemployment in East Germany, particularly amongst women workers, wages were not the only indicators of income levels. The mass surplus of labour resulting from the transformation of the economy caused many former workers to be dependent upon state support for their survival. According to German social security laws persons eligible for unemployment benefit received a percentage of their last net wage. As women in the GDR had on average a lower income than male workers, unemployed women tended to have a lower income than unemployed male workers. In June 1991 women received an average unemployment or social security benefit (*Arbeitslosengeld* or *Arbeitslosenhilfe*) of DM 562 per month compared to DM 725 for men (Jasper 1992).

Women of retirement age were particularly vulnerable to low income. In West Germany female pensioners are especially vulnerable to poverty because of their intermittent work patterns, relatively low rates of pay and higher levels of part-time working, all influencing the amount of money contributed towards a pension and thus the final sum received. In June 1992 only a quarter of women pensioners in West Germany received a pension of DM 1,000 or more compared to three-quarters of male pensioners (Klammer 1997: 4). In East Germany a gendered gap in pension levels also existed despite the higher rate of continuous, full-time female employment and the slightly narrower differentials between male and female pay. In July 1995, whilst almost 97 percent of retired men who had previously worked in blue-collar employment received a pension of over DM 1,000 only 58 percent of retired female blue-collar workers were in receipt of such a sum. White-collar pensions displayed a similarly gendered pattern. Almost 95 per cent of male pensioners who had previously been employed in white-collar work received over DM 1,000 (30 percent over DM 2,000). Only 42 percent of women in this category had secured a pension of DM 1,000 or more. Just 1.2 percent obtained over DM 2,000 a month in pension (Klammer 1997: 4).

Accessing Employment: Mobility

With jobs scarce, workers had to be increasingly mobile in their search for employment. With Berlin located in the heart of Brandenburg the capital city provided an important source of jobs for the residents of Brandenburg. After early retirement working beyond the borders of Brandenburg was the second most significant means of labour market relief within the state in the initial post-Wende period. In the summer of 1992 72,000 Brandenburg residents commuted to employment outside Brandenburg (Schuldt 1991: 9). In contrast, just 23,000 persons resident outside Brandenburg were employed within the state (Schuldt 1991: 12). By 1996 almost 60,000 people working in West Berlin lived in Brandenburg. Overall, 104,000 people travelled from Brandenburg into Berlin to work, 56,000 more than commuted in the opposite direction (MASGF Brandenburg 1997a: 26).

Mobility is gendered. Analysis of mobility patterns in Brandenburg indicated that women are less likely than men to commute outside Brandenburg to work (at the beginning of the 1990s women were a quarter of all commuters), and those that do tend to commute closer to home. Indeed the shorter the distance the higher the proportion of women workers amongst commuters (Schuldt

1991: 18). The archetypal working woman commuting to her place of employment is young, childless and lives alone. In the early 1990s half of all female commuters in Brandenburg lived alone, compared to ùnder 20 percent of male commuters. The evidence indicates that family responsibilities, particularly childcare, restrict women's mobility to a greater extent than they do men's (Schuldt 1991: 26). Not only are women with children less likely to work outside Brandenburg than men with children but within their own neighbourhoods women tend to face greater obstacles to their mobility. Car ownership in East Germany was less widespread than in the west. In households with one car the male partner often had priority over use of the vehicle during work hours. In the GDR the transport network had been geared towards moving people to and from work and fares were subsidised by the state to make them affordable. The city of Cottbus in Brandenburg boasted the cheapest trams in the world in GDR-times. After unification, endeavours to cut public spending reduced services and increased fares (*Berliner Zeitung* 12/13.9.93: 16). Poor transport services severely restrict women's mobility, particularly for women in rural areas. To combat this problem some East German women have developed their own strategies. In Luckenwalde in Brandenburg women established a private minibus service for women to increase their mobility and thereby assist their employment opportunities (*Berliner Zeitung* 4.3.92: 15). But unfortunately such initiatives are few and far between and many women are left reliant on deteriorating public services to move to and from employment.

Accessing Employment: Training of School-Leavers

For younger East Germans leaving school and endeavouring to forge out careers the transformation of the economy and the adaptation of education and training institutions to the West German system has brought many difficulties. In the GDR school-leavers had been guaranteed training places or employment after finishing their education. Likewise, apprentices had been assured of jobs after the completion of training. In the post-Wende period neither the availability of apprenticeships nor the prospect of employment after training were assured. On a general level, the mass closure of firms and the rationalisation of industries and administrations have reduced the possibilities for in-firm training and apprenticeships. In the new states 38 percent of trainees undertook their training within a firm compared to 42 percent in West Germany in 1991 (Bundesanstalt für Arbeit 1994a: 39). But, whilst both male and female school-leavers face additional difficulties, it has been women who have had the most problems finding either apprenticeship places or jobs after training (Bundesanstalt für Arbeit 1994a: 43).

To a certain extent the problems encountered by young women are attributable to severe reductions in the personnel and training capacities of traditionally female areas of employment, such as administrative and social institutions and trade and retail outlets (Bundesanstalt für Arbeit 1994a: 38). Compounding young women's problems, however, has been a tendency for employers to take on male rather than female trainees, thus mirroring trends already identified within recruitment in general. In certain firms, about half of all training places, it has been argued, have been unofficially reserved for male apprentices, a practice which has occurred even in the typically female areas of trade, banking and education (*betr:Frauen* Number 5/6: 15). Whilst women are sometimes reluctant to enter 'male' training areas, employers also tend to regard male workers as a more flexible and therefore more productive source of labour. In Brandenburg just one out of every two girls applying for a training place for the year 1993/1994 was successful compared to two-thirds of male applicants (*betr:Frauen* Number 7/8: 11). Young women looking for training places had to make more concessions in their search for a place than men in a similar situation (Bundesanstalt für Arbeit 1994a: 38). As a result of more restricted choice in the training market, women have been more likely to take on an apprenticeship or training that was not in their desired profession, to undertake out-of-firm training that offered less secure job chances than in-firm training or to delay their entry to the training market by staying on at school (*betr:Frauen* Number 7/8: 10).

Even when young women have managed to secure a training place their chances of finding secure employment after finishing are still much lower than their male counterparts'. A survey conducted by the Federal Institute for Vocational Training between November 1995 and January 1996 indicated that only half of women in the new federal states completing their training between 1994 and 1995 had been successful in finding a job compared to three-quarters of male 'graduates'. Over 40 percent of the young women were unemployed after training compared to 20 percent of men. Women who found themselves unemployed after training were out of work for an average of 7 months; men in this position averaged about 4 months without a job. In addition, women finding work were more likely than their male counterparts to end up in precarious employment and thus more vulnerable to future periods of unemployment (Tischer and Doering 1998: 7).

Accessing Employment: Retraining

For many workers the updating of old skills or the acquisition of new skills has been necessary in the changing economic climate. Retraining courses provide a vital link between the previous employment structure and the demands for labour in the new economic system. With the economic structure undergoing such a dramatic process of change, the pattern of employment and therefore demand for skills has been refashioned. In addition, the validity and applicability of East German qualifications were reassessed on the unification of the two German states. The resulting devaluation of many East German qualifications has been a particular problem for women workers. In many instances qualifications gained from the special study courses for women (*Frauensonderstudien*), which the socialist state had introduced to improve women's qualification levels, are no longer recognised in the new unified Germany (Jasper 1991:13).

Numerically, women have been well represented in vocational training programmes, principally because of the high number of retraining programmes in office and business skills. But, as illustrated in chapter 4, the number of places available for retraining was soon reduced. By 1993 both new entries to training courses and the number of participants overall had begun to decrease, despite the continued high level of unemployment. In the Cottbus region of Brandenburg, only one-third as many people started courses in the first six months of 1993 as in the same time period a year earlier. Whereas in 1991 a yearly average of virtually 125,000 people had entered retraining programmes in Brandenburg, the yearly figure had dropped by almost 100,000 six years later (see figure 5.4).

Despite women's better quantitative representation in vocational training, the ability of many training courses to adapt labour to the changing demands of the East German economy remains questionable. On a general level, criticism has been levelled against measures for being too short and of low quality. Indeed, between October 1991 and April 1992 almost two-thirds of places in vocational training in the Cottbus region were for courses which lasted six months or less. Fewer than one in five courses started in this time-period lasted for more than a year. Further education and vocational training soon became big business in East Germany,

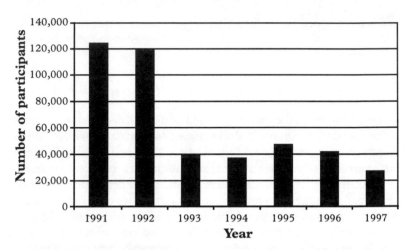

Figure 5.4. *Average yearly entry into vocational further training in Brandenburg, 1991–1997.*

constituting two of the few growth industries in an otherwise struggling service sector. Labour Office and government officials have often expressed concern about the haphazard nature of many courses and the lack of forethought and organisation. Too many women, it was argued, were taking courses that did not produce a qualification at the end or had no relation to their previous occupation (*Wochenpost* 5.3.92*)*. The quality of courses varies considerably. Whilst some institutions have good links with local businesses and can secure a relatively good employment rate, others are unable to offer participants similar opportunities (Interview, Sabine Hübner, MASGF, Potsdam, 15.4.97).

Furthermore, the allocation of training places has remained gender-specific. In the past women have usually been guided towards office-based training programmes whilst male labour has been retrained in construction-related and technical skills. As the interviews with the women in retraining programmes detailed in chapter 7 indicate, the choice of retraining programmes available to women was often severely restricted. A strengthening of gender stereotyping in the retraining process is evident. Courses run by the Chamber for Industry and Commerce reveal clear gender divisions in the distribution of training places. In 1990 women made up 43 percent of all participants in the new states, but were overwhelmingly concentrated in traditionally female domains, most notably office-orientated courses. Women constituted 99.9 percent of participants in secretarial courses and 96 percent in typing courses. Of the near 9,000 students taking metal and electro-industrial examinations only 44 were women (*Lausitzer Wirtschaft* May 1992: 54).

Despite women's slightly higher success rate in course completion, women finishing training have had a much higher tendency to become unemployed than male graduates did. In 1995 only 35 percent of women completing a vocational training programme found employment compared to just over half of men (Tischer and Doering 1998: 28). Women with all levels of qualifications have tended to be channelled into the same courses – usually in office and administrative skills – regardless of their previous qualifications. For some, then, the retraining process has actually served as a form of downgrading or deskilling. Demand for workers holding qualifications in office skills has been well below supply. As a consequence the labour market has become saturated with women holding office and business-related qualifications and thus their re-employment chances have been diluted.

Black-Market Labour

The above analysis has highlighted the greater difficulties women have experienced in securing employment in both the subsidised and nonsubsidised labour markets. But what of unofficial employment? To provide an accurate exposition of change within the East German labour market it is necessary to monitor employment in the black market as well as in the free and state-subsidised labour markets. However, by its very nature it is extremely difficult to observe and quantify illegal employment.

Illegal or unofficial employment is an umbrella term that covers a broad range of activities. For example, the employment of foreigners without valid work visas, illegal work practices that contravene Health and Safety Codes and undeclared, cash-in-hand work are all facets of illegal employment. It is the latter form of work, most commonly labelled black-market employment, which the following discussion considers further (Marschall 1983: 72). Quantifying the exact extent of illegal employment in the new federal states is difficult. Nonetheless, it is anticipated that illegal, undeclared employment does exist to a significant degree. In the GDR work 'on-the-side' in the after-work hours, during holiday periods and after retirement was welcomed by the state, even praised as a form of leisure activity as it provided a means of covering the general lack of goods and services. In the initial post-unification period federal government agencies were therefore concerned that many people in East Germany would be unaware of the illegality of such undeclared work under federal law.

In the immediate post-Wende period it is impossible to calculate the exact scope of black-market activity in the new federal states, let alone the gendered division of labour within illegal employment. However, in terms of officially recognised social security fraud, in 1993 95 percent of cases in the new states involved the misuse of wage replacement moneys and child allowances. Furthermore, experience of the nature of black-market employment in West Germany provides some clues as to the possible sectors in which illegal employment would predominate in the new states. It is likely that construction work, taxi driving, hotel work and private and office cleaning are particular havens of undeclared, cash-in-hand employment. It is also probable that the majority of illegal employment would be in less qualified, 'unskilled' tasks. Given the sexual division of labour noted in the subsidised and free labour markets, it is plausible to assume that women have a greater tendency to find work on the black-market in hotel and cleaning rather than in the building trade (Interview, Frank Brandes, Landesarbeitsamt Berlin-Brandenburg, Berlin 12.4.94).

Interviews with former textile and clothing workers (as detailed in chapter 7) provide some oral evidence of black-market work amongst the women participating. Although none of the women stated that they were currently working illegally, the interviews revealed that 4 of the thirty-two women had been working on the side while they were in Kurzarbeit. Three of the women had been working from home selling either cosmetics or household products; one had worked, cash-in-hand, as a cleaner:

> It was not well paid but it helped me out. I cleaned in a hospital, four hours a day. It was better than sitting at home. I earned DM4.95 an hour. It wasn't a lot. I was the only German. I worked with about 10, no, 14 Russian women. It was badly paid but I was in *Kurzarbeit* and did it on the side. So in effect I earned in a month what I normally earned at TKC.

Clearly, whilst the cleaning work was poorly paid it still provided an important source of income. In the climate of high unemployment and job insecurity women have had to develop individual coping strategies to maintain an acceptable standard of living. When chances for employment have not materialised in the formal sphere of employment women have demonstrated their resourcefulness by seeking employment in the informal sector.

It is interesting to note that many of the women working along-side the woman interviewee were Russian women. With jobs so scarce foreign and migrant women have faced additional problems finding work in the formal labour market. Cash-in-hand work in the informal arena, albeit without any job security and for low levels of pay, often constitutes a vital means of earning money for migrant or foreign women.

Commonality and Diversity of Women's Experiences

The analysis above has focused primarily on women's employment position in direct relation either to that of their male counterparts in East Germany, in comparison to female employment in West Germany, or in relation to their own pre-Wende labour roles. Women have been treated overwhelmingly as a unitary category, with potential differences between women's experiences of employment being pushed to the background. But how diverse are women's experiences of employment and unemployment? To what extent, and in what ways, are women's relationships to the labour market constituted by other cultural, social and material factors as well as by gender? If one were to take age, family position, qualification level or regional economic structure as the key unit of analysis instead of gender, would distinct gender differences still exist?

Perhaps the most influential factor to differentiate women's opportunities in the labour market has been qualification level (Tischer and Doering 1998: 9). Despite the limited success of retraining courses to reintroduce women workers to the labour market, women without training and qualifications have found it hardest to secure employment. In East Germany women with no training qualifications, women who have been trained in areas that are no longer in demand and women holding internal company (as opposed to externally-validated) qualifications have all been disproportionately vulnerable to unemployment (Tischer and Doering 1998: 1). In general, the risk of unemployment has been lower for white-collar rather than blue-collar workers (Bundesanstalt für Arbeit 1994a: 55) and lower the higher the level of qualification (Bundesanstalt für Arbeit 1994a: 56). Yet whilst being better qualified may improve chances of finding or retaining a job, as the above discussion in relation to retraining for women has indicated, it was, all the same, no guarantee of employment.

111

As a result of regional economic differences the process of structural adaptation has had varying implications for regional and local labour markets (Völkel 1991). Although no area of East Germany has been unaffected by firm closure and job loss, geographical location does play a part in determining employment opportunities. Comparing rates of unemployment at the state level reveals some slight differences. In June 1998 unemployment was highest in Saxony-Anhalt (20.6 percent overall, 23.3 percent for women) and lowest in Thuringia (17 percent overall, 19.8 percent for women). More pronounced differences exist, however, at the regional and local levels. Looking within the state of Brandenburg, clear regional differences are observable. Unemployment levels in the Potsdam region are considerably lower than in other regions of Brandenburg, most notably in comparison with Cottbus, Eberswalde and Neuruppin. Potsdam's roles as capital of Brandenburg and the seat of government and administration have all provided additional sources of employment. Also its proximity to the Berlin labour market (particularly West Berlin) has been pivotal in keeping unemployment down. A higher percentage of workers from Potsdam commute outside Brandenburg to work than in any other region of Brandenburg (Schuldt 1991: 18; MASGF Brandenburg 1997a: 26). In June 1998 unemployment levels in Potsdam stood at just 14.1 percent compared to 20.4 percent in Cottbus and Eberswalde and 18.7 percent in Neuruppin. The region with the nearest level of unemployment was Frankfurt/Oder. But even here unemployment was 2.4 percent higher than in Potsdam. Similar variations at the regional level were observable in other East German states. In Saxony, for example, 20 percent of the working population of the Bautzen region were unemployed in June 1998. Yet in nearby Pirna unemployment was almost 5 percent lower.

Levels of female unemployment, in line with overall unemployment figures, thus differ according to geographical location. A woman's chances of being out of work are at least in part dependent upon the economic profile of the region in which she resides. In the Potsdam area of Brandenburg women's unemployment was actually lower than male unemployment in Cottbus, Eberswalde and Neuruppin (15.6 percent compared to 17.8 percent, 17.9 percent and 16.3 percent respectively) in June 1998. Again the employment stemming from Potsdam's political and administrative functions and its nearness to West Berlin have all assisted in boosting women's employment levels in this area.

Across East Germany age has been a central factor in determining women's employment opportunities in the post-Wende period.

Under state socialism women's involvement in waged labour had been relatively secure until retirement. In 1989 over 80 percent of women aged between 50 and 55 and nearly three-quarters of women aged 55–60 were still in employment (Winkler 1990: 64). But it has been precisely these groups of women, most especially the over-55 age-group, that have been struck hardest in the process of job loss and labour restructuring. Already by 1992 just a quarter of East German women aged between 55 and 60 remained in employment (Bäcker et al. 1994: 39). Although many had left the labour market via early retirement schemes, unemployment was still rife in the 50 to 55 age-groups, making up one in five of all unemployed women – a higher proportion than for men of the same age group (Bundesanstalt für Arbeit 1994a: 55). For unemployed women over 55 years of age the chances of working again once unemployed were remote (MASGF 1993a: 45). With a large pool of workers to choose from employers opted in the main to recruit younger workers.

Labour market difficulties have not been confined to the older age group of women. Younger women, most particularly women with dependent children, also face specific problems in the new market economy. The high employment rate of women with children had been one of the most striking features of women's employment in the GDR. As detailed in chapter 2, the vast array of provisions put in place by the state enabled women to combine the dual roles of mother and worker. The introduction of West German welfare regulations into East Germany through unification resulted in leave to care for sick children and the financial support for maternity leave being reduced. In addition access to childcare has been made more difficult for many women, not only through the closure of some childcare facilities (after-school centres have been particularly vulnerable to axing) but also in terms of hours of opening being restricted and the price of childcare rising. Nonetheless the system of childcare remains more comprehensive and better developed than in West Germany, indeed in comparison to many other parts of the European Union. In 1995 84 percent of women working with young children took their children to a crèche or a kindergarten (Bundesministerium für Familie, Senioren, Frauen und Jugend 1996: 19).

Still, my own study of the clothing industry suggests that younger women with caring commitments have found it particularly hard to hold on their jobs during the process of labour rationalisation (see chapters 6 and 7). Moreover, the interviews with East German women documented in chapter 7 indicate a predominant feeling amongst the interviewees that women with young children do face additional difficulties finding employment. Dominant discourses increasingly define women with young children as a problem group who hold less of a claim to employment than other social groups, particularly men. The notion that women have an equal right to full-time employment even when they have young children, an idea prevalent under state socialism, has been perceptibly eroded. The women interviewed argued, for example, that not only were firms less likely to recruit women with small children, but the Federal Labour Office was less likely to put them forward for job vacancies. Of course, the Federal Labour Office has been quick to distance itself from rumours of collusion in sexual discrimination. A Labour Office circular stated that:

> Primarily in the NFL [new federal states] complaints are increasingly being lodged against gender-specific discrimination in the filling of jobs. Discriminatory behaviour is to be actively opposed. Employers and women looking for work must not be given the impression that the Labour Offices tolerate such a stance (*betr:Frauen* Number 7/8: 14).

However, regardless of the extent of actual discrimination the overall *perception* amongst women was that women, particularly women with young children, had greater difficulties maintaining or securing employment. This observation, grounded or not, has had important knock-on effects, influencing the individual strategies employed by women to improve their job possibilities. Many women are, for example, reluctant even to take advantage of the leave available to them to care for ill children for fear of identifying themselves as less committed to their jobs or less productive than their colleagues. Women have also been more disinclined to have children. After the Wende the birth rate dropped dramatically. In part the decline was the result of the migration of many young people to West Germany. However, the fall in the number of babies born was also an expression of economic insecurity. Children were quite simply a luxury that many could no longer afford. In the first two years after the Wende the birth rate fell by half. The number of sterilisations in the new states also sharply increased in the immediate post-Wende period. Reports indicated that in some areas sterilisation had become the most popular form of contraception. In some clinics where previously only two or three sterilisations were performed per year there were now three or four operations per day taking place (*Berliner Zeitung* 7.2.92: 5; *Neues Deutschland* 7.2.92: 1). In the GDR, sterilisation was quite uncommon. Hence, in part, the rise in the number of sterilisations was the result of a backlog of women wishing to be sterilised. But, perhaps most alarmingly, there were reports of women, even younger women, seeking sterilisation specifically to improve their chances of employment (Einhorn 1994: 28).

In the GDR one in five households had been headed by a single parent – the majority of single parents being women. In the GDR employment had been secure and the vast array of special provisions in place to enable women to combine work and family had included special provisions for single mothers. In the new federal states, given the restructuring of the welfare system and the greater competition for jobs, were single mothers particularly hard hit? When examining the relationship of single mothers to employment in Germany one of the first things to notice is the clear difference between East and West Germany. According to a survey of single parenthood conducted between October 1995 and January 1996, 35 percent of single mothers were working full-time in West Germany compared to just 13 percent of mothers living with their partners (Harder 1996). In contrast the full-time employment rate of single and married/cohabiting women in East Germany was not significantly different – around half of each group were engaged in full-time labour. However, unemployment rates were significantly higher for single mothers as opposed to mothers in dual-partner households in both parts of Germany. In West Germany 14 percent of single mothers surveyed were registered unemployed, almost treble the rate of unemployment for women in dual-partner households. In East Germany registered unemployment for single mothers was a staggering 30 percent compared to just over 20 percent for mothers in dual-partner families (Harder 1996: 80–81). Single parenthood has had a decisive impact on women's vulnerability to unemployment or at least their likelihood to be registered as unemployed once out of work. Although a much smaller sample of single fathers was included in the survey single parenthood appeared equally detrimental to men's employment chances. Only 60 percent of single fathers were in full-time employment compared to almost 90 percent of fathers in dual-partner households. Twenty-eight percent of single fathers taking part in the survey were out of work, almost four times as many as married or cohabiting fathers (Harder 1996: 81).

Clearly women's experiences of employment in the post-Wende period have been diverse, varying, amongst other things, according to their age, qualification levels, domestic role and the development of the local economy in which they live. Yet whilst women's employment patterns indicate a certain amount of disparity, a considerable degree of uniformity is also evident in women's relationship to the labour market. In spite of varying levels of unemployment throughout Brandenburg women have consistently constituted the majority of the unemployed in all regions of the state, regardless of the local economic structure. Moreover, in no region of Brandenburg have women's rates of re-employment corresponded to their levels of unemployment. Whilst the analysis of the Brandenburg labour market indicates that women's unemployment rates vary according to their age, qualification, locality and so on, in most instances, women fare worse than men in a similar social or geographical position. For example, women between 50 and 55 years of age have been particularly vulnerable to unemployment. However, women in this age group have, at the same time, been more susceptible to unemployment than men of the same age. Likewise, whilst female unemployment rate has been lower in Potsdam than elsewhere in Brandenburg it has still far exceeded the male unemployment rate in the area. Interestingly, unemployment was disproportionately high amongst single fathers as well as single mothers. However, as over 90 per cent of single parents are women the number of single fathers, let alone the number of unemployed single fathers, constitutes a significantly smaller section of the society than single mothers and single mothers out of work. This study therefore suggests that whilst 'in-gender' divisions are apparent, and women's experiences of the labour market are shaped by factors in addition to their gender, there is also a sufficient degree of commonality between different groups of women, particularly their disproportional rates of unemployment vis-à-vis men, to justify the use of gender as an analytical category within the context of the East German labour market. In many instances women have lost out in the labour market because of their gender.

Note

1. *betr:Frauen* is a magazine produced by the Ministry for Work, Social Affairs, Health and Women (MASGF) in Brandenburg.

6

Linking the Local and the Global: Women in the Textile and Clothing Industry

It is the aim of this chapter to explore the process of economic transformation in East Germany from a sectoral perspective, looking specifically at the restructuring of the textile and clothing industry and its implications for female waged labour. The textile and clothing sector is a useful starting point in the analysis of gender and sectoral change, for a number of reasons. Firstly, the deindustrialisation of the East German economy has been one of the key consequences of economic reconstruction of the new federal states in the initial period of restructuring (see chapter 5). Under state socialism industrial production formed the backbone of the East German economy. Amongst the socialist bloc of nations in Europe the GDR was regarded as having the most developed and successful industrial economy (Andersen 1992: 109). Although statistics provided by the socialist state had depicted the ailing economy in rather healthy and thus deceptive terms (Andersen 1992: 115), the rapid decimation of the industrial sector following the collapse of state socialism still sent shock waves throughout Europe. The transformation from socialist to capitalist relations of production throughout Eastern Europe was a mammoth and unprecedented task. Although the end goal – capitalism – was known the means of achieving the goal were untested. The rapid decline of industrial activity in East Germany was thus greeted with a sense of foreboding. If the industrial sector of East Germany, the most industrialised nation in Eastern Europe, could collapse, surely anything was possible? Analysis of a particular branch within the industrial sector thus affords the opportunity to explore in more depth the processes by which deindustrialisation occurred.

As the focus of this study is on women's employment, the second motive for selecting the textile and clothing industry is related to the gender composition of its workforce. Overall 40 percent of the entire industrial workforce was female, making up around a third of women's total employment (Winkler 1990: 66). But whilst female labour was present throughout the industrial sector (see chapter 2) women workers, particularly those engaged in blue-collar work, remained clustered in certain key industries. The textile and clothing industry was one of the largest industrial employers of women in the GDR; around two-thirds of the 320,000 workers in the textile and clothing sector were women. As the textile and clothing industry was concentrated in specific regions of the GDR – Saxony, Thuringia and southeast Brandenburg – in certain local economies the textile and clothing industries constituted one of the main employers of female labour.

Thirdly, an analysis of the textile and clothing industries necessitates consideration of global economic factors and their impact on the restructuring process. A new international division of labour in world capitalist trade emerged in the postwar period. From the mid-1960s onwards there was a substantial shift of manufacturing, particularly labour-intensive production, from the advanced capitalist economies to newly industrialising countries. The textile and clothing industry was 'a typical example of industrial production transfer to less costly LDCs [less developed countries]' (Raasch and Wahnschaffe 1992: 110) within global capitalism. The state socialist nations of Eastern Europe had stood on the edges of this process, continuing to perform the majority of trade with other state socialist nations. Under state socialism two-thirds of East Germany's foreign trade had been conducted with other socialist states (Andersen 1992: 109), around 40 percent solely with the Soviet Union (Andersen 1992: 109; Falke 1994:180). As a member of the Comecon trading system, East Germany's trade with nonsocialist countries, apart from West Germany, had been limited.[1] The collapse of state socialism in the USSR and Eastern Europe, together with the introduction of market reforms in many of the remaining communist states, have repositioned the so-called 'Second World' within the world trade system, triggering a reordering of the international division of labour. In East Germany, for example, the fall of the Berlin Wall not only paved the way for market reform and the democratisation of the political system but also opened up the East German economy to the full rigor of the global capitalist system.

With a few notable exceptions (Moghadam 1993; Molyneux 1991) analyses of female labour in state socialist or post-communist societies have tended to overlook or underanalyse the role of global economic factors in shaping women's relationship to the domestic labour market. This chapter hopes to take some modest steps towards filling this gap. Through analysis of the East German textile and clothing industries this chapter begins to explore the implications of East Germany's changing role within the global economy for women's employment opportunities within the domestic market. The exposition considers two key questions: is there a future for East German women in domestic industrial production? Or is their economic future tied firmly to service sector expansion?

The exploration of female labour within the textile and clothing industries takes place at both the local and the global levels. The discussion begins with a general analysis of the sector's changing position during the process of economic restructuring, looking at the extent and causes of its decline, before moving on to consider the case of a particular textile and clothing firm in Cottbus, southeast Brandenburg. The micro-level study is used specifically to chart the impact of reconstruction on the gender composition of the workforce. The case study suggests, firstly, that the transfer from labour-intensive to capital-intensive production in the textile industry was accompanied by the increased marginalisation of women within the workforce, particularly in production. Secondly, it proposes that whilst the employment of women remained central to clothing production, mass job loss from the sector was not borne equally by all women. Length of service, age and caring commitments appear to have impinged upon women's employment chances during the rationalisation process.

The Textile and Clothing Sector in the GDR

East Germany has a long history of textile and clothing production. Before the division of Germany after the Second World War a comparatively high amount of textile production was situated in the territory which later formed the GDR. Thirty-eight percent of the entire textile capacity of Germany was located in this area compared to 22 percent of the population (Breitenacher et al. 1991: 5). Garment making was much more evenly spread across eastern and western parts of Germany, although within East Germany East Berlin was already a noted centre of clothing production. After the division of Germany planners in East Germany sought to reduce the over-capacity of the textile sector in relation to the size of the GDR population and to reorientate the range of textile and clothing production to the needs of the new command economy. However, textile and clothing production, as with all light industry, was not a strategic economic priority of the GDR government. Instead heavy industry, engineering and the primary sector were prioritised in the allocation of state investment, to the detriment of the development of consumer and light industries.

Yet despite the emphasis on areas such as heavy industry, the textile and clothing sector retained a significant position in the economic profile of the GDR. Firstly, the GDR sought as far as possible to become economically self-sufficient and to keep the import of produced goods to a minimum. The retention of a domestic textile and clothing industry was thus vital in this process. Secondly, the sale of garments to the West was a critical source of foreign currency for the GDR. The export of textiles and clothing to other socialist states also acted as a counter-balance to the importation of raw materials and was important in the formation of trading agreements. Finally, given the state's ideological emphasis on the full employment of both women and men, the textile and clothing industry – a traditionally female area of employment – constituted an important source of jobs for women in some regions of the GDR. Thus, the textile and clothing industry, however underfunded by the state, was in both economic and ideological terms an essential resource.

In 1989 nearly 4 percent of all East German workers and an eighth of industrial workers were employed in the textile and clothing sector. Two-thirds of workers in the sector were engaged in textile production, the remainder in garment making. Because of the uneven regional distribution of textile and, to a lesser extent, clothing production, the textile and clothing industry was one of the key, if not the main provider of jobs in some areas of the GDR. Saxony was the leading regional centre for textile and clothing production – over 70 percent of all textile workers and around half of clothing workers in the GDR were employed in Saxony (Breitenacher et al. 1991: 24). In areas such as Chemnitz (Landkreis) and Glauchau in Saxony around a quarter of all workers in the locality were employed in textile production (Rudolph 1990b: 500–501). But even beyond Saxony important pockets of textile production existed. In the Apolda district of Thuringia, for example, the textile industry was the largest industrial branch, accounting for 25 percent of all employment in the area (Rudolph 1990b: 499).

Under state socialism the emphasis within the textile and clothing industry was on mass production for the mass market, using Fordist methods – large-scale production by assembly-line workers. During the 1970s smaller firms were joined together to form larger units – combines (*Kombinate*) – with the aim of standardising and expediting production. The organisation of firms into combines facilitated the central control of production. Decisions on the range and scale of production were made outside the firm by central planning groups and then disseminated via the combine management. In all, seven textile and three clothing combines were established. Usually textile and clothing production was kept separate; however, the textile combine in Cottbus, profiled later on, incorporated garment making as well as textile production. The size of the combines varied. ESDA Thalheim, for example, included just eight firms with a total workforce of around 15,000 in 1989. Baumwolle, Chemnitz, on the other hand, was much larger, combining twenty-nine firms and employing nearly 70,000 workers overall (Breitenacher at al. 1991: 80).

As a result of the introduction of combines textile and clothing workers, as with industrial workers generally, found themselves working in large production units. In the GDR over 80 percent of textile workers and nearly 70 percent of clothing workers were employed in enterprises with over 1,000 employees (IHK 1992: 11). Internal production and employment structures were geared towards the demands and functions of the command economic system. Consequently a higher proportion of workers was engaged in tasks that were not directly related to production than was usual under market economic conditions. Enterprises in the GDR assumed a near autarchic structure, usually with maintenance, research and development units incorporated within the firm. Often social services, such as childcare facilities and medical centres, accommodation offices and party political appointments were incorporated into the structure of the firm, thus increasing the number of nonproduction workers employed within the industrial sector. In addition, a substantial number of administration workers were employed as a result of the low level of office technology, cumbersome bureaucratic structures and the subsequent inefficiencies of the system. Taking into consideration the deployment of labour for social and political tasks and the labour absorbed by the particularities of the planned economy, it has been estimated that in 1989 there was a 'surplus' (in market economic terms) of 50,000 workers in the textile and clothing industry (Breitenacher et al. 1991: 26). This figure does not, however, take into account the potential saving on labour that could have been achieved if newer, more labour efficient technology had been introduced. One of the paradoxes of the East German economy was that an endemic shortage of labour went hand-in-hand with a labour intensity arising not only out of low levels of technology but also inefficient work practices.

In both the textile and clothing industries the production processes remained highly labour-intensive with a low level of capital intensity. Whilst both branches together employed 12 percent of industrial labour, they made up just 9 percent of total industrial production in the GDR. As indicated above, light and consumer industries were bypassed in the distribution of state funds in favour of heavier industry. Investment in the capital stock of light industries, such as textiles and clothing, was therefore low by comparison. The capital intensity (calculated as gross fixed assets per employee) of the textile industry was particularly low, standing at 30 percent below the industrial average (Breitenacher et al. 1991: 30). As a result, the machinery used in production was infrequently updated. A survey of textile industries in autumn 1990 suggested that over 70 percent of firms were using machinery that was more than 10 years old (Breitenacher et al. 1991: 44); the average 'shelf-life' of machinery in the textile industry was 28 years (Breitenacher et al. 1991: 34). For the textile industry the lack of capital investment was decisive in structuring the mode and efficiency of its production process. In the past two decades considerable advances have been made within textile technology worldwide, resulting in much greater automation. By the end of the state socialist period a technology gap between East and West Germany in terms of textile machinery had become evident. Without the funds or the political will to buy or develop more technologically-intensive machinery the textile industry in the GDR remained highly labour intensive. By contrast, textile production in advanced capitalist countries had become more automated and much less reliant on the use of labour (see below).

In comparison with West Germany the level of output in the textile and clothing sector of the GDR appears quite high. Although the GDR was just a quarter of the size of its West German neighbour output in the GDR textile industry, in terms of quantity of goods produced, was around 50 to 60 percent and clothing output about half of West German levels (Breitenacher et al. 1991: 14). Clear-cut comparisons are, however, hard to make and can lead to misleading conclusions. The textile and clothing industries in both states were operating under widely divergent economic and political systems which had varying relationships to both domestic and external markets. In the postwar period, under different economic and political pressures, the textile and clothing industries in each part of Germany had evolved in distinct and different directions. In West Germany, as will be discussed in more detail below, the industry, in trying to carve out a niche in the international market, had moved towards more small-scale, high-quality production. In contrast, both textile and clothing industries in the GDR continued to orientate themselves more towards the large-scale production of medium and lower quality goods. Looking at output figures within this context, then, it is not surprising that the volume of goods produced in the GDR, with its emphasis on mass production, was comparatively higher than in West Germany. Comparisons made solely on volume of goods produced do not, however, account for differences in the quality and type of good made.

Similar difficulties also arise when attempting to compare levels of labour productivity in planned and market systems. Labour productivity can be calculated in a number of ways – for example, goods produced per employee or number of hours worked, volume of goods produced per square metre – but again these kinds of comparisons are more reliable and useful if one is comparing like with like. If one is trying to compare productivity levels between divergent economic systems, with different modes of production, different accounting systems and nonconvertible currencies the results one produces must be viewed with some caution. In addition, estimates of labour productivity levels do not take into account the difference in the quality of goods made. As argued above, the type of goods produced in the clothing industry of the GDR was generally of a lower quality than those garments produced in West Germany. Again, the stumbling block in producing reliable and useful comparative data is that in many ways one is trying to compare chalk with cheese; in this case, high quality with lower quality goods. However, taking into account all such caveats, the message from the research undertaken (Breitenacher et al. 1991: 51) is that productivity levels in the GDR were significantly lower than those in Western European countries, particularly West Germany, a significant factor when assessing the industry's survival chances in the post-Wende market system.

Imports into the GDR and exports from the GDR were strictly controlled and monitored by state agencies. Individual combines or firms did not trade directly with external partners as in a market economy. Instead the level of exports, the type of goods exported and the destination of exports were decided by the state and laid down in export trading agreements. Likewise, decisions over what was imported were made by the state. As a result the East German market had been relatively shielded from restructuring of global (capitalist) markets that had led in particular to the decline of clothing production in advanced capitalist countries. The majority of textiles and garments produced in the GDR was destined for the domestic market. Over 80 percent of textiles and nearly two-thirds of garments were for the internal East German market. Nonetheless the textile and clothing industry was the second most important exporting industry in the GDR during the state socialist period (Breitenacher et al.1991: 90). Although the industry had been neglected in the distribution of public finances, the sector, most particularly the clothing branch, was important in the export field as a trade-off for raw materials and as a means of gaining foreign currencies. As a result two standards of goods were produced in the GDR – a higher quality for Western export markets and a lower quality for internal and other state socialist markets. About two-thirds of exports were destined for socialist markets, with the Soviet Union the single biggest importer of East German textiles and garments, receiving almost 50 percent of all exports. The overwhelming majority of export trade with the West was conducted with West Germany. Around a quarter of exports were sold to West Germany, usually to warehouse and mail order firms. Because of the dire need for foreign, convertible currencies the state subsidised clothing export trade with the West. As a result, the majority of products retailed in West Germany were sold at a loss (Breitenacher et al. 1991: 91–92). The necessity to subsidise the price of goods for external western markets points to the lack of marketability and competitiveness of East German goods when placed within the global market economy and as such did not bode well for the industry's survival after the Wende.

The West German Textile and Clothing Production: a Comparison

As indicated above, both the textile and the clothing branches in the GDR were characterised by a high deployment of labour. Despite the difference in size of the two states, 320,000 persons were working in the East German textile and clothing industry prior to the Wende, just 60,000 less than in West Germany (Breitenacher et al. 1991: 18–19). Whereas in the GDR textile and clothing sector workers accounted for 3.7 percent of the entire workforce, in West Germany just 1.9 percent of the workforce was employed in the sector prior to the Wende.

The West German textile and clothing industry had been in crisis since the mid-1960s, a trend that was evident throughout Western Europe. Between 1960 and 1977 the textile workforce in countries making up the then EEC diminished by a third (Robert 1983: 23). In West Germany 60 percent of textile and clothing workers lost their jobs from the 1960s onwards (Breitenacher et al. 1991:19). The decline of the textile and clothing industry in West Germany, as elsewhere in Western Europe, was largely attributable to the emergence of low-cost competition from newly industrialising countries (NICs) as well as to stagnating internal demand (Raasch and Wahnschaffe 1992: 112). The industrial expansion of lower-cost, less-developed countries (LDCs) threatened the survival of labour-intensive, manufacturing industries in the advanced capitalist economies. Garments could be produced much more cheaply in developing countries than in higher-wage countries, such as West Germany. As a result, the advanced capitalist countries increasingly lost their share of the world garment trade. In 1970 clothing manufacturers from developed nations accounted for 65 percent of export trade. Already by 1976 their share had already dropped to 50 percent. By contrast, LDCs had increased their stake in the world export market by 17 percent in the same time-period. In 1976 they already controlled 38 percent of world export trade in garment manufacturing (Robert 1983: 21).

To enhance their positions on the world market the textile and clothing producers in West Germany adopted differing survival strategies (Raasch and Wahnschaffe 1992: 113). Whilst the textile branch fought competition in the global economy by a process of technological rationalisation, the clothing industry increasingly relocated production to areas offering lower wages. To maximise its survival chances West German textile manufacturing developed a more capital-intensive production base, with a growing emphasis on the production of technical and artificial fibres. In 1978 the average cost of establishing a new job in the textile industry was DM 250,000, compared to an industrial average of just DM 160,000 (Raasch and Wahnschaffe 1992: 125). In 1988 the capital investment in the textile industry was almost one-fifth higher than the average for processing industries (Breitenacher et al. 1991: 30).

The clothing industry, on the other hand, adopted a quite different strategy. Despite some automation in garment making, the clothing industry in West Germany still relied heavily on the use of large amounts of labour (Raasch and Wahnschaffe 1992: 125).

Instead, in a bid to cut production costs and to increase their competitiveness, many clothing firms either relocated production to lower-wage areas of West Germany (Figge and Quack 1990: 11–12; Raasch and Wahnschaffe 1992: 114) or to lower-cost countries. Although relocating in LDCs offered West German firms substantial wage cost advantages, a certain amount of clothing manufacturing remained on West German soil. The extent to which low-wage costs were the decisive determinant of competitiveness depended upon the type of product being manufactured. For the production of high-quality, quick-changing, fashion items proximity to the market was crucial. As Raasch and Wahnschaffe (1992: 125) point out:

> Large-scale serial production that can be pre-planned can take place in market-distant, but cost-effective locations, while for quickly changing products and small-lot volumes, domestic production offers advantages due to its shorter delivery periods and its higher level of worker qualifications.

Whereas in the GDR the textile and clothing industry was still organised according to Fordist principles of production, industrial production located in West Germany had increasingly moved away from large economies of scale towards more flexible methods of production that were more responsive to changing consumer demand. To compete with the mass influx of low-cost imports the West German industry concentrated on the production of high-quality, more expensive, short-range goods. Post-Fordist production methods allowed a larger variety of products, market diversification and product 'nicheing'. The organisation of production into smaller units was crucial to the restructuring process. In 1987 60 percent of textile firms in West Germany employed between 20 and 99 workers. Two-thirds of clothing firms employed between 20 and 49 workers (Figge and Quack 1990: 8).

In addition, textile production in West Germany had moved increasingly towards the production of technical and artificial textiles and the finishing of textiles. In contrast the East German textile industry was focused more on the preparation of textile raw materials and the manufacturing of garments in the machine branch of the textile industry. Before the Wende the production of artificial fibres accounted for just 5 percent of textile production in the GDR, compared to 20 percent in West Germany (Breitenacher et al. 1991: 16). Within the sector as a whole clothing production had stronger weighting within West Germany than in the GDR. In part this was due to the faster changing fashion cycles in West Germany which increased demand and the need for production, but also in part because an element of garment production in the GDR was undertaken within the textile industry.

Whilst a certain amount of both textile and clothing production was retained in West Germany, the industry's endeavours to increase its competitiveness did not prevent the decline of West German textile and clothing production nor the mass loss of labour from the sector. In 1955 630,000 workers had been employed in the textile industry and 290,000 in the clothing industry. By 1989 the amount of labour engaged had decreased to 213,000 and 167,000 respectively (Breitenacher et al. 1991: 19). The importance of the textile and clothing industry for women's overall employment decreased. In 1976 6.3 percent of all women workers had been employed in the sector. By 1987 the textile and clothing sector accounted for just 3.8 percent of female waged labour (Figge and Quack 1990: 56).

In West Germany the textile and clothing branches' differing responses to the process of global restructuring had had varying implications for the gender composition of the industrial workforces. Despite significant workforce cutbacks – 75,000 fewer women were employed in garment manufacturing in 1987 than in 1977 – clothing production remained labour-intensive and continued to employ predominantly female workers. However, the shift to technologically- and capital-intensive modes of production in the textile branch led to the proportional increase of male workers in textile production. In the period between 1977 and 1987 the number of women textile workers decreased by 32 percent, compared to just 24 percent for men (Figge and Quack 1990: 76). Only in white-collar work within the industry were women able to retain their share of employment (Figge and Quack 1990: 79).

Transition to the Market: the Decline of Textile and Clothing Industry in East Germany

Whereas the West German and Western European textile and clothing manufacturers had been caught in a spiral of decline since the 1970s, the industry in the GDR, in stark contrast, had actually increased output in this period. Under state socialism the textile and clothing industry in the GDR was not exposed to the same domestic and international pressures in the postwar period as in the capitalist West and, as a result, was not subject to the same processes of restructuring and the same magnitude of job cutbacks. Whereas the workforce in West Germany decreased by 60 percent from the middle of the 1960s onwards, the East German textile and clothing workforce declined by just 20 percent in the same time-period (Breitenacher et al. 1991: 19).

Even taking a brief glance at the textile and clothing industries of the GDR and West Germany before the Wende suggests that in its pre-Wende form the East German industry would have had certain difficulties surviving the transition to market economic conditions. Over the previous two decades the West German industry, in line with trends elsewhere in the Western world, had had to make massive structural adjustments to retain a stake in the market. Adjustments included the mass displacement of labour from the sector within West Germany, the relocation of production sites to cheaper regions of the world, increased capital investment, particularly in the textile industry, a shift towards smaller, more flexible production units and the reorientation of the range and types of goods produced. The large inflexible production units in the GDR geared towards mass production, the relatively high proportion of nonproduction workers within the industry, the low levels of capital investment that had led to the predominance of outmoded machinery (particularly in the textile branch) and the reliance on state subsidies to compete in Western markets all signalled problems ahead for the East German textile and clothing industry after 1989.

As detailed in chapter 5, the collapse of state socialism and the later unification of Germany had a devastating effect on the East German labour market. On an aggregate level East German industry shed around 65 percent of its workforce. The textile and clothing industry fared particularly badly. Initially it was predicted that only 20 to 30 percent of the former textile and clothing industry would survive the transitional process (Interview, Tobias-M Engelhardt, Treuhandanstalt, Berlin, 18.9.92). Yet the reality of the situation exceeded even the bleakest predictions. In the Upper Lausitz region of Saxony, the textile and clothing centre of the GDR, 90 percent of jobs in the textile branch and 75 percent of those in the clothing branch were lost between 1989 and January 1992 (IHK 1992: 10). In the city of Cottbus in Land Brandenburg over 5,000 persons had been employed in the textile industry before the Wende. By 1993 only 430 textile workers remained, just 8 per cent of the original workforce (Buttler et al. 1993).

Given the structure of the East German textile and clothing industry, particularly the high level of employment in nonproduction jobs, personnel reductions were an unavoidable upshot of the restructuring process (Interview, Tobias-M Engelhardt, Treuhand-anstalt, Berlin, 18.9.92). However, two points need to be made to qualify the situation. Firstly, although a substantial amount of labour was excessive to the requirements of a market economic system, at the same time some new jobs had to be created. In the GDR production had paid very little attention to consumer demand, as was indicated by the production of an inferior standard of garments for domestic and Eastern export markets (Breitenacher et al. 1991: 89). Managers in the GDR played a very different role from managers in capitalist economies. Regulation of output and production was undertaken by central planning authorities, whilst in-firm management took responsibility for the internal running of the firm. It was not the task of management, for example, to forge or win new contracts. Likewise East German managers had no direct experience of trading on the world markets. In the GDR textile and clothing firms sold their goods abroad via state agencies (Breitenacher et al. 1991: 89) and, as a consequence, there was at most minimal but usually no contact between the site of production and the buyers. To compete in the capitalist system the establishment of new-style managerial, marketing and retailing posts was essential to optimise competitiveness. There was also much more scope for independent designers in the new market system. In West Germany clothing production had had a much stronger weighting within the sector as a whole than had been the case in the GDR. In part this was because some garments were produced under the umbrella of the textile industry in the GDR but most significantly it was attributable to the much shorter fashion cycles in the West than in the East. Central planners rather than in-house or independent designers had directed fashion styles in the GDR. To survive in the highly competitive market after the Wende massive adjustments were imperative not only in terms of marketing and distribution but also in terms of the design of goods produced.

Secondly, whilst the collapse of the textile and clothing industry in East Germany can be explained at least in part by reference to the particularities and inefficiencies of the planned economic system – lower levels of productivity, inflexible production systems geared towards mass production, lack of capital investment, old, out-dated machinery, the lack of market competitivity – its rapid decline cannot be explained *solely* by these factors. The near annihilation of the industry and the extent of job losses within the sector that occurred after the collapse of state socialism can only be fully understood if further consideration is given to the particular conditions of unification and to East Germany's renegotiated role within the global economy. This chapter thus proposes that three interrelated factors were instrumental in the decline of textile and clothing production in East Germany: firstly, the legacy of the state socialist production and employment structures; secondly, the political conditions of unification which favoured a high-tech high-wage transformation process; and, thirdly, the exposure of the sector to international competition after the opening of the East German borders. As attention has been paid above to the specific characteristics of production under state socialism, the following analysis will focus on the latter two points – the impact of unification and East Germany's changing role within the global economy. The analysis of unification will focus in particular on the implications of the currency union, the lack of state support and wage increases for the textile and clothing industry.

The Currency Union

The sector's adjustment problems were exacerbated by the conditions of the currency union in the summer of 1990. The introduction of the West German mark (Deutschmark) into East Germany at a basic conversion rate of one West mark to one East mark (re-evaluating the East mark by 300 to 400 percent) together with the abrupt ending of state-financed export subsidies, rendered many East German firms unable to compete. For the textile and clothing industry the economic union of the two German states resulted in the loss of virtually all markets, both domestic and foreign. As an official from the East German textile industry remarked shortly after the Wende, 'At the moment we are practising a market economy without a market' (*Handelsblatt* 6.8.91).

Prior to the Wende, the textile and clothing industry had been the second most important exporting industry in the GDR (Breitenacher et al. 1991: 90). After the currency union the demand for East German goods fell both at home and abroad. The end of state subsidisation meant that East German goods lost their price advantage in Western markets. Moreover, the goods were not of a high enough quality to sustain a marked increase in prices. With regard to the Eastern export markets, the introduction of the Deutschmark into East Germany made East German goods unaffordable in the former Eastern bloc countries. East Germany's Eastern neighbours were unable to pay Western prices for East German goods. Although demand for textiles and clothing expanded in the internal market in the immediate post- Wende period, East Germans with their newly acquired Deutschmarks and greater consumer power initially rejected internally produced goods in favour of West German and foreign goods, thus compounding the problems caused by the collapse of export trade. Tired of the limited product range and poor quality offered by domestic producers, East Germans chose imported goods rather than internally produced ones (Breitenacher et al. 1991: 103).

The loss of markets was doubly devastating for the textile industry. Textile enterprises were hit two ways: firstly, by the influx of textiles from abroad and, secondly, by the collapse of the East German clothing industry. As the clothing industry was the textile industry's main customer its own fate was closely intertwined with that of the clothing branch. In December 1990, just six months after the currency union, clothing production was down 57 percent on its preyear level. Textile production had, however, declined by 70 percent in the same time period (Breitenacher et al. 1991: 109).

Wage Increases

Difficulties in adjusting to the conditions of the market were heightened by the policy to close the wage gap between East and West Germany, by bringing wages in East Germany closer to West German levels. Rising wage and production costs aggravated the industry's ability to adapt to the new economic conditions by not only pricing East German textile and clothing enterprises out of the market but also by dampening outside investment interest. Lower wages with comparable productivity levels existed just beyond the borders of the former GDR in the former Czechoslovakia, in Poland and in the Baltic States. Businesses were therefore looking further eastwards for investment (*Die Welt* 12.2.92).

In general rising wage costs in East Germany favoured the growth of capital- rather than labour-intensive industries (OECD 1992). In West Germany, whilst the clothing industry had been more limited in the extent to which it could replace labour by technology, the textile industry had developed a technologically- and capital-intensive industrial production base (Raasch and Wahnschaffe 1992: 125–29). East German textile producers faced difficulties in replicating this strategy to stay in the market, as the installation of more technologically intensive equipment required a high capital outlay. As the textile industry in West Germany was still in crisis it was limited in the extent to which it could invest in East Germany. In the first four months of 1992 textile production in West Germany was down 5 percent on the previous year (*Lausitzer Rundschau* 7.4.94: 23). Declining output was accompanied by falling personnel numbers. In April 1992 350,000 workers were employed in the West German textile and clothing sector, compared to 365,000 a year previously (THA 1992). A survey of textile managers in Saxony and Thuringia revealed that 60 percent considered the structural crisis in the West German textile industry as the main hurdle to privatisation (Management Partner GmbH 1992).

Lack of State Support

Despite the rapid decline of the textile and clothing sector in the new states, the demise of the industry called forth no more than minimal state support. Willi Arens, head of the German textile and clothing trade union (GTB), was critical of the lack of state support for the sector, suggesting that its neglect was in part the result of it being a female-dominated industrial branch. Other industries in crisis, such as shipbuilding and steel, which employed predominantly male labour, he argued, received greater public attention even though they were of comparable size to the textile and clothing industry (*textil bekleidung*, 1992, Number 5: 3,10,11). Even in the federal aid programme to the new states 'Upturn East' (*Aufschwung Ost*) DM 0.53 billion of the DM 24 billion budget for 1991 and 1992 had been allocated to the shipbuilding industry (*Scala* 1991 Number 5: 14).

The Treuhandanstalt's policy of privatisation rather than redevelopment also came under enormous criticism. The Treuhandanstalt argued that it knew if a firm was going to be successful or not within a short period of time. If there was no future for the enterprise it saw no need to prolong its financial support of it and would thus close it down (Interview, Tobias-M Engelhardt, Treuhandanstalt, Berlin, 18.9.92). The GTB claimed that the agency, because of its unwillingness to invest in the East German textile and clothing industry, did not give firms a fair chance to establish themselves within the market and to adapt to market economic conditions. Whilst in some industries between DM 500,000 and DM 1 million were invested per job, investment in the textile industry often fell short of DM 10,000 per job (*textil/bekleidung*, 1992, Number 5).

Regardless of whether the lack of state attention to the crisis in the East German textile and clothing industry was motivated by gender bias, the fact still remained that the sector was neglected in the distribution of state finances in the new united Germany. Although in

West Germany the decline of the industry had also received minimal state attention (Figge and Quack 1990: 89), its demise had been much more gradual. The erosion of the West German textile and clothing industry had taken place over decades, whereas in East Germany the contraction of the industry was concentrated into a two- to three-year period. The lack of state support for the ailing industry in East Germany was thus particularly hard felt.

The Changing International Division of Labour

Under state socialism the majority of textiles and clothing on sale within East Germany were produced within East Germany. In line with the GDR's autarchic aims, textile and clothing imports had been kept to a minimum. Whereas in West Germany the domestic industry had been forced to compete with imports from low-wage countries, the GDR imported very little from lower-cost countries, with the exception of China. Imports from Yugoslavia, South Korea, Taiwan, India and Brazil in 1989 were fifty-five times higher in West Germany than in the GDR. Even though China was the biggest source of textile and clothing imports in the GDR, the People's Republic of China still exported three and a half times as much to West Germany as to the GDR (Breitenacher et al. 1991: 95).

As already indicated, clothing exports generated an important source of foreign exchange for East Germany. To make East German garments attractive in foreign markets the state often subsidised the sale price, minimising or losing any actual profit on the goods but increasing the amount of 'hard' currency available to East Germany. With East Germany particularly reliant on the import of certain raw materials from other socialist countries, the export of East German textiles and garments to other areas of the Eastern bloc was also an important aspect of trade relations within the socialist trading area. The USSR was a particularly important destination for textile and clothing goods, receiving almost 50 per cent of all East German exports in this area (Breitenacher et al. 1991: 92). The collapse of state socialism and the transition to a market economy brought an end to the subsidisation of goods to the West. Under market conditions East German goods could no longer compete; the relatively low quality of goods could not withstand a hike in prices necessitated by the cessation of subsidies. At the same time, the rising price of East German goods induced by the 1:1 currency union undermined the sale of garments and textiles to other former socialist bloc economies. East German goods were simply too expensive to sustain previous export levels with these countries.

Problems were not confined solely to the loss of trade in foreign markets. The fall of the Berlin Wall opened the floodgates for a mass influx of foreign goods into East Germany, undermining the domestic industry's hold over the internal market. As indicated above, East Germany provided a relatively untapped market for foreign traders as imports had been kept as low as possible. The net result of economic restructuring in East Germany was the decimation of external markets for East German textile and clothing producers and the near complete substitution of internal domestic production by imports (THA 1992: 5). In general terms the end of the Cold War signified a new phase in international trade. The economic liberalisation of former and existing communist countries yielded new markets and new producers. China and Vietnam replaced many of the Southeast Asian 'tiger' economies as the cheapest clothing and textile producers. But whilst the textile and clothing industries elsewhere in East Central Europe could not rival the low costs of China, they could produce textiles and clothing at a much cheaper rate than in East Germany. They also had the advantage over Asian producers of being located much closer to the European market. For the East German clothing industry the existence of low-wage competition so near to home placed a major hurdle in the way of its redevelopment. Why invest in East German clothing enterprises when just a few miles further eastwards similar levels of productivity could be achieved at a much lower cost? East Central Europe provided both the advantages of lower-cost production and the benefits of market proximity.

Thus to understand the decline of employment opportunities for women in the textile and clothing industry attention to the changing role of the East German economy within the world trade system is crucial. Entwined with the transition to a market economy was the full exposure of East Germany to the global capitalist economy. The structure of state socialist production was undoubtedly a key factor in determining the weakness of the East German textile and clothing industry on the world markets but the inheritance of, by global standards, outdated production techniques was not the only factor undermining East Germany's international competitiveness. The conditions of unification, most notably the 1:1 currency exchange and the attempt to increase wage levels in East Germany to match West German levels, all hindered East Germany's ability to retain a stake in the market.

Post-Wende Developments: a Summary

After the Wende the East German textile and clothing industry was caught in an economic 'no-man's land'. It could rival neither the high productivity levels of West Germany nor the low-production costs of East Central Europe. Not only did indigenous enterprises lack high productivity levels, market flexibility and the management know-how of West Germany, but also their cost advantages were rapidly undermined by wage increases. Although the workforce in the GDR was well trained and highly qualified, many still lacked flexibility and adequate experience of new technology (Breitenacher et al. 1991: 174). Moreover, the textile and clothing industry in the GDR had specialised in mass production with the emphasis on bulk rather than on quality. As a result East German firms lacked the ability to respond quickly to market changes.

To enhance industrial competitiveness and to increase the chances of survival and privatisation one of the first steps taken by the Treuhandanstalt, the agency designated the task of privatising East Germany's nationalised industries, was to split the large combines into smaller units. Nonproduction tasks were either closed down or, in the case of in-firm childcare facilities, transferred to the jurisdiction of local authorities.

Despite the division of the combines into smaller units the East German enterprises still faced considerable difficulties of adaptation. One major disadvantage of East German enterprises was their lack of experience of functioning in a market economic system and of dealing on the international market. As indicated above, the role of the manager in East German factories had been vastly different from that of a manager operating within a capitalist system. Under the conditions of the planned economy there was little attention paid to costs, now a central factor in the market economy. The THA argued that lack of management know-how was a major hurdle to a firm's survival. Importing a manager from West Germany to assist in, or to take over, the running of a concern was considered a major advantage (Interview, Tobias-M Engelhardt, Treuhandanstalt, Berlin, 18.9.92).

The transition from a centrally planned to a market-dominated economy, and from a state socialist to a liberal democratic form of government, had destructive consequences on production and employment levels in the textile and clothing sector. A survey of textile firms in Saxony and Thuringia in the immediate post-Wende period revealed that only 20 percent of managers had experienced an increase in production and profits since the currency union.

Almost six out of ten recorded a decline in production levels (Management Partner GmbH 1992). Falling production levels were accompanied by mass firm closures and the large-scale loss of jobs within the sector.

Throughout the 1990s the German textile industry, in the West as well as the East, has been caught in a downward spiral. Although the textile industry remains, in terms of turnover and number of employees, one of the ten largest industrial groupings in Germany, orders, employment numbers and production levels have constantly fallen during the past decade. In 1992 217,000 workers were employed in the textile industry across Germany. By 1997 the size of the workforce had decreased to 130,000. Orders for textiles in 1997 were just three-quarters of 1991 levels. Production in 1997 was 69 percent of 1991 levels. More and more (West) German companies sought to remain competitive by relocating production sites to cheaper areas of the world. Increasingly the trend was for Western Europe to house the management, research and design side of textile and clothing production and for the actual production sites to be located further afield. Despite all efforts on the part of the industry to keep its head above water Germany was still losing the import war, continuing to import more textiles than it was exporting. In 1997 the import surplus stood at DM 20,475 million (Information compiled from gesamttextil website).

For women the decline of the textile and clothing industry has had crucial implications. As illustrated above, the decline of the textile industry in West Germany had a particularly negative effect on female employment within the branch. Rationalisation and the introduction of high-tech machinery altered the ratio of male to female workers in favour of male workers. The experience of the West German textile industry (along with that of the electronics industry) suggests that automation within industry tends to replace women's labour by men's in blue-collar areas (Raasch and Wahnschaffe 1992: 134). Only in white-collar employment was the loss of female labour less than that of male labour. Even so, women working in white-collar jobs tended to be employed in administrative functions whereas the more technical posts (forepersons, technicians) and managerial positions were filled by men (Figge and Quack 1990: 79). But whilst male workers had strengthened their position in the West German textile industry, the clothing workforce, despite substantial job losses, had retained a high proportion of female workers.

The decline of the textile and clothing industry in East Germany was compressed into a relatively short time-scale and was in many ways much more devastating in its effects on local economies because of the rapidity of its degeneration. Whilst job displacement in the West German textile and clothing sector had taken place gradually over decades, job loss in the East German sector took place over a matter of years. The swift decline of the industry had, as a result, a sudden and devastating effect on local workforces. As women constituted the majority of workers in this field of employment, the collapse of textile and clothing production had particularly gendered implications. The following case study of a textile and clothing firm in East Germany examines the impact of downsizing and restructuring on the gender composition of the workforce. To what extent did the East German textile and clothing industry replicate the experiences of the West German industry?

Case Study: Textilkombinat Cottbus (TKC)

To explore further the impact of the Wende on women's employment within the textile and clothing industry, the following analysis examines the effects of the transformation process on one particular textile and clothing firm. The case study intersects both the sectoral analysis of the textile and clothing industry and the regional study of Brandenburg. The enterprise in focus is the former main site of the Textilkombinat Cottbus (TKC), situated in southeast Brandenburg. Prior to the Wende, the combine (*Kombinat*) had employed almost 20,000 workers over twenty-two different firms, spanning both textile and clothing production.[2] The Cottbus site had particular significance within TKC as it housed the combine's headquarters. Of the 4,200 workers employed on the site, 230 were involved in the management and administration of the combine. The case study was undertaken between 1992 and 1994 and thus provides only a snapshot picture of the impact of restructuring on the gender composition of the workforce. The analysis is thus concerned solely with the immediate period after the Wende, looking at how the sudden degeneration of the industry impinged on women's employment opportunities within this field. The case study does not include examination of developments after 1994.

Regional Context

Although the majority of textile and clothing production in the GDR was situated in Land Saxony, the Lower Lausitz region of Branden-

137

burg, in which Cottbus is located, had a long textile tradition. The area around Cottbus, Guben and Forst was known as the Lower Lausitz Textile Triangle. The region had become famous for its cloth production in the Middle Ages, enjoying a revival first in the nineteenth century (Buttler et al. 1993: 7) and then under state socialism.

Mining and energy production constituted the main source of industrial employment in the Cottbus area in which TKC was located, but predominantly for male workers (Interviews, Frau Smykalla GTB, Cottbus, 19.9.92; representative of Betriebsrat, TKC, Cottbus, 25.3.92). Within the Brandenburg economy the Cottbus area of southeast Brandenburg was, economically, a problem region. Not only was the local economy overindustrialised but the region was also dependent upon brown coal mining and the energy sector for a large proportion of its employment. Seventy percent of energy in the GDR had been derived from brown coal (MWMT 1991: 14); 65 percent of which came from the Cottbus area (MASGF Brandenburg 1993a: 90). In many of the districts one industry predominated. In the district of Spremberg, for example, over 60 percent of workers had been employed in energy and mining alone (Rudolph 1990b).

But after unification the virtual monopolistic use of brown coal in energy production was programmed to end. Energy policy set out plans to phase out the majority of brown coal production. Brown coal was to be largely replaced by other energy sources, and remaining production was to become more cost-effective and environmentally friendly (MWMT 1991). The scale-down of the industry would involve substantial job losses. In 1990 670,000 workers were still employed in the sector. Yet it was foreseen that by the end of the century only 10,000 workers would remained employed in the sector (Buttler et al. 1993: 10, 26). Initially redundancies were implemented incrementally. Unlike many industrial sectors the energy and mining sector did not shed a substantial proportion of workers at the end of 1991 when short-time work regulations came to an end, but instead sustained a more gradual loss of labour. As a result, until the beginning of 1993 the Cottbus region as a whole was relatively favourably placed in terms of (male) unemployment. However, from 1993, the employment situation began to quickly deteriorate. The region's overdependency upon brown coal and industrial production and significant cutbacks in this area contributed to a rise in unemployment, to bring joblessness in the area above the Brandenburg average for the first time. By 1998 the Cottbus area had the highest regional unemployment in the state of Brandenburg.

Although the mining and energy sector predominated in the locality, the textile and clothing industries were important providers of
jobs for women in the area. Prior to the Wende, over 10,000 workers
in this region were employed in the textile branch alone, the majority
of whom were women (MWMT 1992). In so far as the entire GDR
textile production was concerned the Lower Lausitz region occupied
a modest position. Whereas the Chemnitz district in Saxony produced over 50 percent of the gross industrial production of the GDR
textile industry, the textile industry in the Cottbus area produced
just 2.7 percent (IAW 1992: 94, 95). Of the five new federal states
that were established after the collapse of the GDR, Brandenburg
ranked third in terms of textile and clothing production behind Saxony and Thuringia. Seventy percent of all textile workers and almost
half of all clothing workers were located in Saxony (IAB 22.5.91).
However, within the Brandenburg regional economy the Lower
Lausitz area was the primary location of textile production and garment making. The Lower Lausitz town of Forst, situated close to the
Polish Border, was the largest textile producer in Brandenburg, both
in terms of production volume and the size of the workforce. In all it
accounted for over 17 percent of Brandenburg's textile production
and one in five textile employees in the state (IAW 1992: 95). Forst's
local economy was strongly tied to textile production. The industry
was the single, largest employer in the town, engaging over 14 percent
of all workers (Rudolph 1990b). The rapid decline of the textile and
clothing industry thus had a decisive and negative impact on
women's employment opportunities in the region.

TKC Production in the GDR

As part of the drive by the state to create larger units of production
the Textilkombinat Cottbus (TKC) had been established in the early
1970s. TKC incorporated all textile and clothing firms in the Cottbus
area and in nearby locations. At the Cottbus site three main pillars of
production existed: garment making, with a particular emphasis on
women's outer clothing; carpet yarn; and artificial fibres.

The site at Cottbus resembled the autarchic structures familiar
throughout East German industry. The plant was not only the site of
production but also of research and technology, maintenance, welfare
and political functions. Employees of TKC performed all maintenance and repairs on site. A technology department and a rationalisation centre were established to develop new ideas. Structures were
also in place to deal with the workers' welfare. Hot meals were pro-

vided in in-firm canteens. A medical centre was situated on site to care for the health of the workers. Three childcare units – a crèche with places for 65 children, a kindergarten with 160 places and a week-long childcare facility for the children of shift workers – were located at the Cottbus plant. Provisions were even made for the workers' leisure time. An arts centre (*Kulturhaus*) was established to provide a venue for dancing, theatrical and work team (*Brigade*) activities, a sports' field was installed and a restaurant/bar (*Gaststätte*) opened for the workers' use. The Party (the SED) had a high profile within the firm structure. Party political meetings took place at the work site and trade union workers within the firm dealt with the allocation of accommodation for workers. Even the workers' holidays could be organised by and within the structure of the firm. Employees at the Cottbus plant had access to holiday homes by the Baltic Sea and in the Harz Mountains (Interview, Betriebsrat, TKC, 25.3.92).

The Workforce at the Cottbus Site of TKC

In line with general trends in the GDR a substantial proportion of the TKC workforce was not engaged in the actual production process. Of the 4,200 employees working at the Cottbus site in 1989, only 55 percent were working directly in production. The remainder worked in management, research and design, maintenance, and in the numerous services located on site. Of the 4,000–strong workforce 500 were foreign workers from Vietnam. Because of labour scarcity the GDR government did use foreign labour agreed by intergovernmental contracts between the GDR and other socialist/communist nations. In a bid to distance themselves from accusations of exploitation or imperialism, official rhetoric stressed that foreign workers were employed in the GDR as part of training programmes to improve their skills, the idea being that once the required skills were gained the workers would return to their home countries. At TKC, however, the Vietnamese workers were employed either in unskilled or in low-skilled tasks, suggesting that their employment there was more to cover labour needs than to provide specialist training.

Three-quarters of the workforce in TKC (*Stammbetrieb*) were women (Interview, Frau Liebger, Personnel TKC, 25.3.92). Although female workers worked in all areas of the firm, occupational segregation according to sex did exist, both vertically and horizontally. Women were near excluded from top level management, although a woman had filled the post of personnel manager. They were better represented in middle and lower level management although even at this level the number of women managers did not correspond to women's share of employment overall. Women made up three-quarters of all workers at TKC, but just half of all shift leaders. In addition, transport and storage work, technical and research tasks were carried out, for the most part, by men. In the technology department 70 percent of workers were male. In blue-collar production men were concentrated in certain key areas, usually the heavier tasks – pressing, cutting and finishing. Occupational segregation also provided the scope for gender-based wage differentials. In line with a general trend in the East German economy, male workers at TKC earned on average more than their female counterparts.

Yet the lines of male and female segregation were blurred. Although men were clustered in certain areas women were represented across the board, even in traditionally male jobs – as mechanics, transport workers and storepersons. But female enclaves of employment still existed. East German men did not work at the sewing machines, in a secretarial capacity or looking after children in the on-site childcare facilities.

Analysis of the age structure of the TKC workforce suggests that a substantial proportion of the women working were probably working mothers, although exact data on the subject was not available. Sixty percent of women working were under 35 years old; 45 percent were under 30 years of age. In the GDR the average age for a woman to have her first child was 22.9 years of age in 1989. The majority of births were to women between 20 and 25 years of age (Winkler 1990: 27). If one also takes into account that over 90 percent of East German women became mothers then the age structure of the TKC workforce points to a high proportion of women employees with children.

Post-Wende Developments

As with all state-owned industry TKC came under the control of the Treuhandanstalt (THA) in the post-Wende period. One of the first key tasks undertaken by the THA was to split the combine into smaller, individual units, with a view to making the separate components more competitive and easier to privatise. As the main aim of the THA was to privatise as much as possible, streamlining took place at every level to ensure maximum efficiency and competitiveness. Hence, the nonproductive units of the firm were closed down, sold off or transferred to the local authorities. In January 1992 the last of the eating-halls was closed down. The three childcare facilities were passed over to local authority control. The polyclinic set up as an independent medical practice. The *Kulturhaus* was sold to a West German company and maintenance units set up independently.

The Managing Director, a former accountant at TKC, pointed to the currency union in July 1990 as the watershed mark in TKC's history (Interviews, Managing Director of TKC, 4.5.92; 16.6.92; 13.4.94). As the majority of the clothing production had been produced for export, the introduction of the 1:1 currency conversion and the cessation of export subsidies severely undermined the enterprise's ability to compete and resulted in the loss of many of their former markets. Prior to the Wende half of the garment production at the TKC main site had been exported to the Soviet Union and a further 30 percent to West Germany. Only 20 percent of the garments made were destined for the domestic market. Although in comparison the textile units at TKC did very little export trade (30 percent of total trade), they had supplied primarily East German garment manufacturers. As a result, the collapse of the export contracts for the clothing industry had negative consequences for textile production at TKC, leading quickly to the closure of the entire textile plant. The production of artificial fibres ceased in June 1991 and of carpet yarn in January 1992.

Although the clothing production at TKC was running at a loss, the THA resolved to retain and financially support some clothing production with the view to later privatisation. Initially under the trademark '*Lady Chic*' and later the label '*Cottbuser Moden*' (*CoMo*) the manufacturing of women's outer clothing continued at the Cottbus site. Privatisation did occur. By April 1994 only the clothing production at the Cottbus and Forst sites remained in THA hands. The Cottbus site had been transformed into a business park. A wide range of business activities was situated on the former TKC site, reflecting the changing nature of the East German economy. Spar had set up a large supermarket and garden centre at the front of the site. The former site and combine administrative building housed a local authority department and a solicitors' office. In the other buildings, cafeterias, management and environmental consultancy firms, engineering offices and small workshops were situated. Both textile and clothing production continued at the site. Garment manufacturing continued at the THA-owned firm Cottbuser Moden (formerly Lady Chic) and by the West German group, Steilmann. Two textile firms had located production plants at the Cottbus site – Rhône-Poulenc Rhotex GmbH and EMBO

Textilproduktionsgesellschaft mbH & Co. KG. Prior to the Wende around 4,000 workers had been employed at the Cottbus plant. In 1994 about 2,000 persons were still working at the site, although the majority was engaged in work unrelated to the textile and clothing sector (Interview, Managing Director of TKC, 13.4.94).

Post-Wende Textile Production

The following analysis considers the level and structure of employment at one of the textile plants opened at the TKC site after the Wende – Rhotex. The information on the employee and production profile of the firm was gained from an interview with the manager of the site. Production at Rhotex, in comparison with production at the Cottbus plant before the Wende, was technologically intensive. The purchasing of new machinery for the plant required a capital investment of DM 900,000. Although it was widely reported that the privatisation contract with the THA had secured the retention of 140 jobs, in April 1994 just 56 were employed at the plant. The Managing Director of Rhotex foresaw the possibility of a future expansion to 65 workers at most. Prior to the closing down of the artificial fibre production at TKC the plant had produced 6,000 tonnes per year with 650 workers. Under the Rhotex management the plant produced 3,000 tonnes per year with less than 60 workers, representing an average increase in annual productivity from 9 to 50 tonnes per worker.

As a subsidiary of a much larger multinational organisation, the plant at Rhotex was a site of production. Decision making existed outside the firm's structure. Rhône-Poulenc had wanted a production unit in the new federal states and had chosen to locate at the Cottbus site. Unlike the clothing industry in Cottbus, locating in the new federal states did not provide the West German textile industry with any major wage-cost advantages over West Germany. In 1994 wages in the East German textile industry were already 83–84 percent of those in West Germany. However, the Cottbus site, the manager argued, did provide locational advantages. Despite the generally poor state of the German textile industry, the expansion of and investment in the clothing industry in East Central Europe, he suggested, was potentially of benefit to the textile industry in East Germany. Since the beginning of 1994 when the factory was taken over by the joint venture the proportion of material supplied to European markets had increased. Up to the end of 1993 2,400 tonnes of nylon were produced. Half was sold outside Europe, a quarter was destined for the German market and a quarter for markets elsewhere in

Europe. From January 1994 the production capacity had increased to 3,000 tonnes; 35 percent was for the domestic market whilst the rest was heading for other European countries.

At the Rhotex textile factory 32 of the 56-strong workforce (57 percent) were women clearly indicating a proportional increase of male workers in textile production when compared to pre-Wende days at TKC. The management of the firm was male-dominated. Although the production manager was a woman, the general manager of Rhotex, along with three of the four shift managers, were men. All of the workers in the internal transport department and in the firm's workshop were men, whilst all of the workers employed in quality control and in packing were women. Whilst the distribution of tasks outside the production process was clearly gendered, there was a more even division of male and female workers within production; 12 of the 25 workers in this section were women. The employment profile of Rhotex does, however, indicate a shift from the female-dominated production workforce of the pre-Wende period to a mixed-sex production workforce, thus echoing developments already seen during restructuring in West Germany during the transfer from labour-intensive to capital-intensive production techniques (Figge and Quack 1990; Raasch and Wahnschaffe 1992).

When asked about sex segregation in the workforce, the manager was at first very reluctant to acknowledge any distinct lines of occupational segregation. However, he later added that women were concentrated in certain areas because of their greater suitability to more intricate and routine work as a result of their more nimble fingers and their greater patience. The manager was an East German who had worked at TKC prior to the Wende. His recourse to very traditional ideas on women's supposedly 'natural' traits indicates the potential for gender discrimination in the recruitment process. Even though women had made up nearly 50 percent of the workforce in the GDR, had succeeded in penetrating male areas of employment and were well qualified, his attitude clearly illustrated that, in some quarters at least, traditional gender attitudes had been retained. Women's socioeconomic status may have improved under socialism but they were still looked upon by many as a qualitatively different set of workers.

Some of the women taking part in the author's own interviews, detailed in chapter 7, had worked in textile production at TKC and had applied unsuccessfully for jobs at Rhotex. Many felt they had been disadvantaged in the recruitment process because they were women. One such worker who had worked at TKC for seven years before being made redundant said:

They told me that I was too thin and too small. They mainly employ men now who are stronger. They say that women cannot manage it any-more. They have got new machines now and it's heavier.

Another former TKC worker with a 3-year-old child believed she was turned down for the job because of her childcare commitments.

I'm sure that was the main reason why I did not get the job. They did not say so, but it was on my mind. My child was just a year old then. At that age they are more susceptible to illness. I really do think that that was the main reason.

A former shift leader at TKC had wanted to apply for a job at Rhotex but had heard they were only taking on men. She had been employed as a shift leader for six years during her fourteen years of working at TKC.

I could have applied for a job at the new firm, but not as a shift leader, because there aren't any more female shift leaders. That went right at the beginning. They told me straightaway that there were just going to be male shift leaders. It would have been possible to be a foreperson. They took women on in exceptional cases. In the west men usually fill this position. The foreperson would have had the same duties as the shift leader but would have worked at the machines as well. I didn't want that. That's why I have done the further training and everything. I did not want to work on the machines. I can't because of health reasons.

In fact, one of the three shift workers employed at the production site was female. But whilst the realm of shift leadership had not become exclusively male it is significant that this former worker perceived this sphere of employment as being out of bounds for women. The information gained about the employee profile of Rho-tex does suggest that the changing nature of textile production – the move from labour to capital-intensive techniques – had been accompanied by the greater involvement of male workers within the production process. It bears testament to the assertion made in the previous chapter that, under certain circumstances, for example, when an occupation previously filled by female labour becomes more prestigious, better paid or more technologically-intensive, there is a greater tendency for women to become marginalised. With the boundaries of male and female employment within the textile industry shifting, women were having to learn that certain occupations were becoming less accessible to them, not necessarily because of their qualifications, experience or aptitude to learn but because of their gender.

Treuhand-Owned Production: Garment Making

In 1994 clothing production was still taking place in the THA-administered concern.[3] The garment-making unit at the Cottbus plant had been given by the THA until the end of 1993 to become financially viable. It was a sign of the enterprise's success that, despite still being under THA ownership in April 1994 and still awaiting privatisation, clothing production continued at the Cottbus plant, albeit in a much reduced form. Before the Wende 1,400 employees had worked in the clothing plant at TKC, producing 1.5 million pieces of clothing annually. In April 1994 130 workers were employed in the THA-owned Cottbuser Moden with an output of 140,000 garments per year. The Managing Director anticipated that further cutbacks in the size of the workforce would take place in future, reducing the capacity to between 80 and 90 workers.

To court investment from the West German Steilmann group the enterprise had been given first pick of the workers from the clothing unit at TKC. Although Lady Chic/Cottbuser Moden had to recruit its workers from the remaining workforce, by 1994 the THA-owned unit, the managing director reported, had matched the productivity levels of the Steilmann workers. After the loss of the majority of its markets in the post-Wende period the THA-owned clothing unit faced additional problems carving out a new niche in the market as goods for export in the GDR had been sold via a state agency. To improve its chances of surviving in the new economic climate a West German who had previously worked in the clothing industry was brought into the firm in an advisory capacity.

Also under the control of the THA and the management at the Cottbus plant was a garment-manufacturing plant in the nearby town of Forst (Interview, Production Manager, Forst, 15.9.92). Production there differed from that at the Cottbus site in that the Forst plant did not produce goods under its own label but instead subcontracted work from other firms. In September 1993 the plant had a contract to produce women's coats for a West German concern. Productivity levels had been improved by the installation of new, more efficient machinery, financed by the THA. In April 1994 a potential buyer had been found for the Forst plant, and privatisation was in the last stages of negotiation. Around a hundred workers were still employed at the plant and the prospective buyer was looking to keep on 80 workers after privatisation. Various concerns had been interested in purchasing Lady Chic/CoMo but as of April 1994 the terms of privatisation had not yet met THA requirements. Either the firms expressing an interest had been unwilling to meet the THA's demands on the sale price or had been unwilling to keep on enough workers after privatisation.

In the clothing production at the Cottbus site (including the Steilmann project) and at the Forst plant, although the size of the workforce was radically reduced during the restructuring process, women's share of total employment actually increased in the immediate post-Wende period. Before the Wende women had constituted 75 percent of all workers at the Cottbus site. By June 1992, although the absolute number of clothing workers had reduced dramatically, women made up around 86 percent of the entire THA workforce. Included within this number were workers employed in the deconstruction and renovation of the site, trainees finishing their apprenticeships, as well as the employees involved in the clothing production at Lady Chic, the Steilmann plant and at the Forst site. If one looked solely at the workforces of Lady Chic, the Steilmann project and the Forst plant, the concentration of female workers was even higher than for TKC as a whole – women constituted 95 percent of the Lady Chic, Steilmann and Forst workforces.[4]

Although many traditionally female jobs in social and welfare functions as well as in administration had been lost at TKC, many positions which had been filled by male labour had also been displaced in the restructuring process, thus accounting for the proportional increase in women working at TKC. For example, the technological and rationalisation centres, the maintenance and repair units, as well as the stores and transport sections of the firm had all been removed, thus eliminating from the TKC workforce a substantial core of male employment. The majority of men retained by the Treuhandanstalt were engaged in the manual and administrative dismantling of the firm. Men constituted 60 percent of the labour employed in these areas.

The reorganisation of clothing production at TKC resulted not only in a higher proportion of women workers, but also a higher proportion of workers in the 30–50 age-group. In October 1989 40 percent of the entire workforce (excluding apprentices) and 45 percent of the women workers at TKC had been under 30 years of age. In June 1992 less than a quarter of the employees working at Lady Chic/CoMo, at the Forst plant or in the Steilmann project were below 30 years old. At Forst only one in five workers fell into this category. Although the workforces were on average much older after reorganisation – in the Steilmann project nearly three-quarters of the workers were between 30 and 49 years of age – the proportion of workers over 55 years of age had fallen. At TKC nearly 8 percent of the entire workforce had been above 55 prior to the Wende. However, less than 2.5 percent of workers employed at Lady Chic, at the Forst plant or in the Steilmann project were aged 55 and above in 1992.

Both management and workers' representatives at the THA enterprise at TKC argued that although social factors were taken into account when deciding on redundancies (for example, single parenthood, partner's employment status, number of children and so on) the main factor involved in the selection procedure was work performance. The more productive and efficient (*leistungsfähig*) workers were retained. But what factors constituted greater efficiency and productivity? Why did younger workers appear more vulnerable to redundancy? Older workers in the 30–50 age-group may have been preferred in the selection procedure because of their greater length of work experience. But older workers, it could be argued, also offered greater reliability. They tended to be more free of childcare commitments and therefore less likely to take time off work because of pregnancy, baby leave or to care for sick children.

A former department leader in the garment manufacturing at TKC suggested that there was a hidden policy not to recruit women with young children to work in the Steilmann project.

> To attract Steilmann the management decided to get the best machinery, the best workers together and put them into one hall... This obviously pleased Mr. Steilmann... I was left with the worst machinery, the worst people and so on... I wanted to have extra training for the people left but I was not successful. There just wasn't the time... No one was prepared to stay on after work to learn. Many had small children, or had family members to care for. These were handicaps... The other two groups hadn't taken on these people. They knew it was a risk. A woman with two small children cannot do overtime... The only women with small children who were taken on had a grandmother or an aunt who could look after the children.

At the Forst plant there had also been a greater propensity to keep on older workers, predominantly between 30 and 49 years of age. At the Forst site 230 workers, including eighty Vietnamese workers, had been employed prior to the Wende. By September 1992 the workforce had decreased by 55 percent to 102 workers.

The contracts of all the Vietnamese workers had been terminated and a further forty-eight workers had been made redundant. Of the remaining workforce, nine persons were employed in white-collar jobs (including the forepersons), two were mechanics, one was a cleaner, one a transport worker and eighty-nine worked in production. Just three members of the entire workforce were men: the manager, the transport worker and one of the mechanics.

Most workers were either married or cohabiting and were parents. More than eight out of every ten workers had children, although the majority had grown-up children – just a third had school-age children (6–16 years of age) and fewer than 15 percent had preschool-age children (5 years and under). All of the workers' children who were under school age attended a childcare facility whilst their mothers were at work (none of the men taking part in the survey had preschool-age children). However, in three cases day-care was supplemented by care from relatives or partner of the mother.

Half of the workers surveyed had been employed at the Forst plant for 20 years or more; 22 percent of the employees had worked at the Forst site for over 30 years. In the GDR mobility tended to take place on an intra-firm rather than an inter-firm level. The majority of the workers at the Forst plant had been employed there since their teens, many presumably since leaving school. Only three of the workers were not working at the firm in October 1989 when the borders were opened. But, whilst the majority of workers had a long history at the factory, nearly a quarter of the workers (23 percent) had been employed in different jobs during their period of employment at the Forst plant, indicating a certain amount of internal mobility.

If one compares the social structure of the Forst plant in 1992 with that of the TKC workforce before the Wende, there appears to be a trend towards the employment of older (30–49 years), well-qualified women. In line with trends evident in clothing production at the Cottbus plant, older workers with more work experience and, at the same time, fewer family commitments, appear to have been retained during the rationalisation process.

Gender and Employment in the Textile and Clothing Industry: Summary

With the emergence of a surplus of labour in the East German economy, management had a large pool of workers from which to select their workforces. In the textile and clothing branch two gender-related trends were evident in the selection process. Firstly, in certain instances, there existed a preference for male over female labour. Secondly, certain groups of women workers were favoured over others. Although we cannot assume that the case study is representative of the entire textile and clothing sector, the information obtained from the analysis of changing employment structures at the former TKC plant suggests that whilst the textile industry had been transformed from a predominantly female to a mixed-sex branch, the clothing industry remained a female enclave of employment. However, the women remaining in the clothing industry after the Wende were on average older than the TKC workforce in the GDR. Women below 30 years of age, and therefore often women with young children, were less likely to maintain their employment posts.

In West Germany the automation of industrial branches (including the textile industry) had led to the proportional decrease of female labour in blue-collar production work. Looking at the particular example of the electronics company Phillips/Valvo in Hamburg, Raasch and Wahnschaffe (1992: 134) state that 'many original female manual labourers were replaced by a highly trained technician for whose work women are still seldom qualified'. Figge and Quack (1990: 76, 79), in their analysis of the West German textile and clothing industry, indicate that the growing demand for higher qualified workers in the production process of the textile industry also favoured the employment of male workers. The study of the former TKC plant suggests that similar processes were in operation in East Germany in the post-Wende period, despite the relatively high levels of training and education women had achieved under state socialism.

Overall, the analysis of Rhotex suggests that textiles had shifted from a predominantly female to a mixed-sex industry, although within the enterprise certain tasks were performed overwhelmingly by one sex. The employee profile of workers on the 'shopfloor', i.e. directly employed in the production of the artificial fibres, was mixed-sex in that there was a fairly even split between men and women. On the one hand, this signifies a deconstruction of gender segregation. However, when placed within the general context of female employment in the GDR characterised by women's disproportionately high levels of unemployment and low job take-up rate, this shift appears less favourable in that it signifies the increasing marginalisation of women in a once female stronghold. The remarks made by the manager alluding to women's 'natural' capabilities suggest that women and men were seen as different types of labour, with innately different strengths and weaknesses. At another textile enterprise in the area the hiring practices were much more directly skewed in favour of employing male workers on the shopfloor. The Managing Director of the *Spremberger Textilwerk*, another textile enterprise in the Lower Lausitz region, stated that she was more likely to hire male workers because she saw them as more efficient and adaptable workers. The factory that she managed had just installed more modern machinery. She argued that women would not be correctly trained for the job and, in addition, the machines now produced larger spools of cloth that were too heavy for women workers to move around (Interview, Managing Director, Spremberger Textilwerk, 3.4.92). In the end, neither male nor female workers benefited from the introduction of a new, more technologically-intensive production process as the firm closed down at the end of 1992 (Interview, representative of GTB Cottbus, 17.9.92).

Whilst the textile workforce shifted from a female-dominated to a mixed-sex branch, employment in the clothing branch remained filled predominantly by female workers. But, as the analysis of clothing production at TKC suggests, younger women and therefore women with younger children were more disposable in the redundancy process. Of course, we can only speculate that the tendency to retain older women was linked at least in part to their lesser likelihood to have young children. Their experience in the field was undoubtedly a crucial factor in the selection process. However, one must bear in mind that in the clothing industry wage costs were a key determinant of competitiveness in the post-Wende period. Indeed, as a result garment manufacturing had remained relatively free from the infiltration of male (and more expensive) labour. Older workers may have been preferred over younger workers because of their greater work experience. However, women with younger children are also perceived to be less flexible and, as a result, a more expensive form of labour. Through absenteeism to care for sick children and maternity leave, employers incur additional employment costs, thus decreasing the cheapness of female labour derived from low wage levels.

Taking a long-term view, although a core of the textile and clothing industry has remained in the Lower Lausitz region, it is highly improbable that the industry will undergo any substantial expansion in the foreseeable future, thus the industry will generate neither white-collar nor blue-collar jobs for women. As a consequence thousands of former textile and clothing workers left the industry holding obsolete skills. The following chapter will look further at the specific case of a group of former TKC employees trying to adapt to the new economic climate. But on a general level what did the future hold for the many women who had been made redundant from employment in the textile and clothing industry? Is service-based employment the way forward?

The Way Forward: Services?

Analysis of the general trends in the textile and clothing industry and of the particular fate of TKC shows clearly that at both macro- and micro-levels production and employment structures were unable to continue in their pre-Wende forms under the new economic system. By international (capitalist) standards the East German government had subsidised and maintained an inefficient industrial structure lacking competitive edge. Once laid open to global capitalist relations the weaknesses and deficiencies of the East German textile and clothing sector were fully uncovered. Employment cutbacks were an inescapable repercussion of the restructuring process. Yet the scale of job loss and the intensity of adjustmental difficulties were heightened by the political (mis)management of economic restructuring. Labour costs were decisive determinants of the sector's competitiveness, especially that of the clothing branch. Hence, the 1:1 currency union, government calls for a rapid convergence of living standards and trade union support for wage parity pushed up labour and therefore production costs in the new federal states.

This chapter illustrates the key role the nature of the transformation strategy plays in shaping the economic structures of post-communist states. The high-wage, high-tech transformation strategy adopted in East Germany reduced its competitiveness on the world markets in the immediate post-Wende period. As neither high-quality nor low-cost producers East German industries had enormous difficulties carving out their own niche in the global economy. Whilst East Germany was set on a preprogrammed course of wage equali-'sation with the West German high-wage economy, lower-cost production continued to the east of Germany's borders. Germany's Eastern European neighbours could offer not only cheaper goods but were also close enough to ensure relative speed of delivery.

The rapid approximation to West German wage levels and the emergence of low-cost producers in East Central Europe precluded the growth of a labour-intensive industrial structure in East Germany. The shift from labour-intensive to high-tech industries in the new federal states not only reduced the number of industrial workers needed, it also resulted in the proportional decrease of female labour employed in the production process. The comparative cheapness of female waged labour generally makes them an attractive source of workers in labour-intensive industries; for example, the clothing industry, itself labour-intensive, employs predominantly female labour. But, as this chapter has shown, rising wage costs in East Germany undermined the competitiveness of East German clothing manufacturers, leading to job loss and firm closures. The shift to a capital-intensive employment structure marginalises women in the production proces. Although the example of the Rhotex factory in Cottbus alone cannot be regarded as representative of the East German textile industry (let alone industry in general), the results of the case study are significant in that they indicate that the growing capital-intensity in the branch was accompanied by a proportional decrease in female blue-collar employment. Within the textile industry women were becoming increasingly concentrated in more routine white-collar work, or in areas such as packing or quality control.

If one accepts that the future of German industry, in both West and East Germany, is based in high-tech, capital-intensive industries, the expansion of the service sector, it could be argued, remains the most promising way to stimulate job creation, particularly for women. Although, as indicated in chapter 5, the growth of the service sector in East Germany in the immediate post-Wende has not produced enough employment to compensate for the vast loss of jobs, including the loss of women's jobs, the IAB predicts the long-term growth of the tertiary employment in both East and West Germany (Bundesanstalt für Arbeit 1994a: 67, 69). As the head of a European management consultancy firm remarked, in relation to Germany:

> It is not that we shall stop producing things. The question is what we produce. There are too many businessmen still trying to pay yesterday's game... They cannot see further than manufacturing the best-quality product, and are driven by ever higher costs into ever narrower niches... One should no longer think of Germany as a production centre, but of companies such as Volkswagen or Bayer as production centres. Each will be present in many different countries [...] our services are on average 25 per cent less productive than those in America or France. Remedying this will be the major challenge of the Nineties (*Independent on Sunday* 25.4.93: 25).

However, the extent to which any further expansion of the service sector would provide employment opportunities for women depends very much upon the type of service industries that develop. Traditionally women have been better represented in primary service activities as sales assistants, retail and office workers, cleaners and so on, and have been less well represented in secondary services such as management, research and development and consultancy work. It is predicted that in the period up to the year 2010, production-orientated services (manufacturing, repairs) in Germany will undergo substantial job losses, employment in the primary service sector will decline more gradually and secondary services will expand (Bundesanstalt für Arbeit 1994a: 67, 69). Thus, whilst service sector growth may well provide job opportunities for women, the expansion of the tertiary sector does not unreservedly benefit women workers. As has been observed already in relation to the East German labour market, even those areas of service activity traditionally associated with women, such as service retail and banking, have become increasingly attractive to male workers.

Notes

1. The one key exception was West Germany. Intra-German trade was handled as domestic rather than foreign trade and as a result was not subject to the usual tariffs, quotas and other barriers placed on trade with foreign/non-EC states. West Germany's support of open trade with East Germany was politically motivated, based on its refusal to recognise the division of Germany as a permanent situation and thus to recognise its East German neighbour as a foreign country. West Germany's political position was to East Germany's economic benefit. 'Technically, with a few exceptions, the GDR had free access to the largest market in the Community and was frequently called the thirteenth member state' (Falke 1994: 166).
2. In 1989 there were ten combines in the textile and clothing industry, incorporating 264 firms and over 300,000 workers (Breitenacher et al. 1991: 80).
3. Information on THA-production, unless indicated otherwise, obtained from interviews with Herr Hoffman, Managing Director, 4.5.92, 16.6.92 and 13.4.94; Herr Hoffmann, representative from the *Betriebsrat* 25.3.92; Frau Leibger, Personnel Department, TKC, 25.3.92.
4. Compiled from company records: personnel figures as of 1 June 1992.

7

Hearing Voices: Women's Responses to Change

East German society was structured with the workplace at its centre. The larger workplaces were much more than mere sites of employment, they also housed a whole host of welfare agencies – medical centres, childcare facilities, and accommodation offices – as well as cultural and sporting facilities. Work played a pivotal role in the structuring of social life. The network of public transport was constructed with workers' daily movements to and from work in mind. Childcare facilities were open to accommodate the time structures of workers. Such was the degree of interaction between work and childcare that, in certain instances, week-long childcare arrangements were available for the children of shiftworkers.

Participation in paid employment was a central part of the national psyche. Employment was defined in state discourses as both the right and duty of each GDR citizen. Each person expected, health permitting, to take part in paid employment up until retirement age. Full-time employment was the social 'norm' for both men and women and the full-time housewife was an anachronism in GDR society, a symbol of capitalist inequality and exploitation. Thus the economic transformation via capitalist reconstruction and privatisation that occurred after the collapse of state socialism not only refashioned the whole nature of work but also transmuted the very nature of East German society.

This chapter is concerned with women's subjective responses to the reconstruction of East Germany following the collapse of state socialism, and the strategies women developed to cope with their rapidly changing environment. The analysis focuses on the author's own interviews with thirty-two East German women held in May and June 1992. All the women interviewed had worked at TKC, the firm profiled in chapter 6, and thus two central strands of this study are brought together – the regional analysis of Land Brandenburg and the sectoral study of the textile and clothing industry. The sample was small and was not intended to be quantitatively representative of East German women. Since the Wende a considerable number of large-scale surveys (some of which will be referred to in this chapter) have been carried out to gather information on women's responses to change. Instead the primary objective of the interviews was to give the women involved the opportunity to tell their own stories of how their lives, particularly their working lives, had changed as a result of the Wende. Therefore, wherever possible, the women's own voices are woven into the text.

All the interviews were one-to-one, oral and taped. Prior to the interviews each woman was given a short written questionnaire to complete which provided background information on her employment record, age, marital status, qualifications, partner's employment situation and number of children. In addition, the women were requested in the questionnaire to answer questions relating to their current employment situation and that of three years before. They were asked to express their degree of satisfaction on issues relating to work conditions, costs of childcare and employment opportunities. The interviews were semi-structured in that certain topics were covered in each interview, although individual questions varied from interview to interview. In respect of confidentiality the women have been given an interviewee number and are not identified by name in the text.

The Possibilities and Limitations of Qualitative Research

The use of qualitative rather than quantitative research – for example, one-to-one interviewing and the use of individuals' own voices in texts – enables the exploration of the contradictory, multiple and dynamic nature of individual subjectivity. Attention to individual subjectivity also facilitates the exploration of individual agency in social change. By exploring how the individual makes sense of the outside world and how external events are internalised, a fuller understanding can be gained of why individuals act either to maintain social relations as they stand or to invoke social change.

However, there are problems as well as possibilities involved in this form of research, as with all research methodologies. Although the women's own words are presented within the text, the power over the selection and ordering of the interview extracts lies solely with the author. There is, for instance, considerable scope for the author/interviewer to appropriate the texts for her own use and to substantiate her own theoretical position (Opie 1992). Additionally, in the interview process itself the potential to distort and misguide the interviewees' responses already exists. For example, the phrasing and ordering of questions can sway the answers given. Furthermore, the interviewee's responses may be consciously or subconsciously influenced by certain attributes of the interviewer, including gender. Kane and Macauley (1993: 1) argue, for example, that:

> While many items do not show statistically significant gender-of-interviewer effects, we document significant effects across a variety of items. When such effects are evident, they tend to involve both male and female respondents expressing more egalitarian gender-related attitudes or greater criticism of existing gender inequalities to female interviewers. Male respondents offer significantly different responses to male and female interviewers on questions dealing with gender inequality in employment. For female respondents interviewer-gender effects are evident for items addressing gender-related collective action, policy and group interests.

In different social situations women (and men) may act and behave in different forms. Their answers may conform to what they believe is expected of them in any given situation. As Weedon (1987: 86) suggests

> Many women acknowledge the feeling of being a different person in different social situations which call for different qualities and modes of femininity. The range of ways of being a woman open to each of us at a particular time is extremely wide but we know or feel what is expected of us in particular situations.

The interview situation is no different. The reader must at least bear in mind the impact of the interview situation, the characteristics of the interviewer and the types of questions being asked on the responses given.

In addition to gender, other characteristics of the interviewer, such as nationality, ethnicity or age may also influence answers given by the interviewee. As a British woman exploring issues relating to gender, not only my own gender (as well as the gender of the interviewees) but also other factors such as my nationality and my age may have influenced the women's responses. How did the women perceive me? Would the nationality difference influence their responses? What difference did it make that I was neither West German nor East German and that I was conducting the interviews in my second language? My background did become a topic of conversation in many of the interviews. Some of the women being interviewed were especially interested in finding out more about women in Britain. They were keen to learn about women's experiences of capitalism and liberal democracy outside West Germany, to find out if the West German 'way of doing things' was replicated elsewhere or specific to West Germany.

Thus, when reading the extracts from the interviews one must bear in mind the constraints as well as the benefits of qualitative research. As Opie (1992: 58) argues, there has been unwillingness on the part of researchers to recognise the limitations of their own research. Many writers, she suggests, are intent on presenting their results as the absolute truth rather than as an interpretation of events. As she stresses,

> all representations are 'implicated, intertwined, embedded, interwoven with a great many other things besides the "truth" which is itself a representation', being embedded first in the language and then in the culture, institutions and political ambience of the representer.
>
> Yet to present one's research outcomes as contingent and incomplete goes against very strong Western notions of objectivity and truth and raises questions about the authority of texts and modes of writing in which limitations are overtly acknowledged.

Whilst the focus of this chapter is on the women's interview responses, it also includes my own analysis of the women's responses which I make in light of the questions raised and the conclusions drawn in this and previous chapters. My comments are based upon my interpretations of the interviews and do not therefore constitute or intend to masquerade as the 'absolute truth'. However, where relevant, the women's responses are compared to the results of other quantitative and qualitative surveys, in order to determine to some extent both the similarities and divergences of the women's answers to other data sources.

All of the interviews took place in German and were recorded on tape. Thus, although the women's own words are used in the text, their responses have already been translated into English. The translation of texts constitutes another possible avenue to distort or misrepresent the women's responses. Whilst care has been taken to produce an accurate representation of the women's answers, the reader should be aware that as the women's words are not presented in their original form they are instead an interpretation of the original words used.

Profile of the Women Interviewed

In total, thirty-two women were interviewed. Twenty-seven of the women were midway through a two-year retraining course in office skills at *EWA Management Berufliche Aus- und Weiterbildung GmbH*, a further education establishment in Cottbus. Three women were unemployed and two were still working at TKC but had already received their redundancy notices at the point of interview. The women taking part in the interviews were united by one common factor – they had all worked at TKC before the Wende. This aside, their ages, family backgrounds, occupational histories and qualification levels were varied. Just under a quarter of the women interviewed had worked in the garment manufacturing at TKC (two as department heads, one had trained the apprentices and four had been employed on the shop floor), over half of the women had worked in textile production (one as a quality controller, one as a shift leader, one as an instructor and fourteen as production workers). Two women had worked in the rationalisation department – one as an engineer, the other as an electrician. The remaining women had been employed as office and administrative workers. All the women were qualified to at least the *Facharbeiter* level. Three had a higher *Meister* qualification, one had an engineering qualification and two had both a *Meister* and an engineering qualification.

Overall, 40 percent of people taking part in re-training programmes in the city of Cottbus were under 30 years of age and a further 35 percent were between 30 and 40 years of age in the first half of 1992. Fewer than 8 percent of participants were over 50 years of age. At the EWA retraining programme almost two-thirds of the women taking part in the interviews were under 30 years old, significantly younger than both the average of retrainees in Cottbus and the average age of women who remained employed in clothing production at the TKC site (see chapter 6). Of the five women who were either unemployed or awaiting redundancy at the time of the interviews, four were between 40 and 49 years of age and one was between 30 and 39 years old.

Interviewee 20, at 53 years of age, was the oldest woman interviewed. She was taking part in the retraining programme but had gained her place on the course only after an enormous battle with the relevant authorities. In the GDR she had worked as a department leader in the clothing branch of TKC. After being made redundant she had been unable to find re-employment and had decided to retrain. She explained why she had chosen the retraining programme and the problems she had faced trying to secure financial support for her studies.

> I will learn what is necessary today – computer technology, bookkeeping. It does not really matter what I do. I just do not want to sit at home. I enjoy it [the retraining] but I know that I haven't got a chance of getting a job again. May be I will be lucky... I know that the chances are low. Anyhow, I'm willing. I am still healthy. I have experience [...] Because of my age they didn't even want to let me do retraining. But I knew that there wasn't a law anywhere that bans a woman over 50 years of age from doing a retraining course. I knew that, but the Labour Office tried to stop me anyway.

Interviewee 20 was exceptional amongst the women interviewed in that she had been employed at the Cottbus plant for thirty years before she was made redundant. Seventy percent of the women in the retraining programme had worked at TKC for less than ten years before losing their jobs; three had only just completed their apprenticeships before leaving TKC. A further five women interviewed had been employed at TKC for over fifteen years.

Of the thirty-two women interviewed almost three-quarters were either married or cohabiting. Twenty-three of the women had children. Just over a third of the entire sample and 40 percent of the women in the retraining programme had a preschool-age child. Just one mother of a preschool-age child and two mothers of school-age children were single parents. The partners of the women who were either married or cohabiting had an above average rate of employment. In June 1992 the male unemployment quota stood at 7.9 per cent. Almost 80 percent of the interviewees' partners were in full-time employment. Less than 5 percent were unemployed.

Looking Back: Working at TKC

Part of the interviews was spent talking about the women's experiences working at TKC in the state socialist period. The majority of the women interviewed gave generally positive accounts of their employment at TKC. Interviewee 4 was 21 years old. She had worked in textile production at TKC since leaving school and was currently retraining in office skills.

> I enjoyed working at TKC. I was happy that I had money. I wanted to carry on working in the textile industry. I'd already been there for five years and I knew my way around. It wasn't bad at all.

Interviewee 28 had worked as a clothing worker at TKC for eighteen years. Before that she had worked in the clothing industry in Saxony. When she married and moved to Cottbus she transferred to TKC. She was married with one grown-up son.

> I really liked going to work. I earned good money. This was a large firm. At home [in Saxony] I earned less money. It was a smaller firm and there was more manual work. Here [at TKC] there was already a lot of machine work. Here everything was bigger, nicer, and newer really. I had good bunch of colleagues.

But some of the women had reservations about work at TKC. Former blue-collar workers in textile production were the most likely to complain about the working conditions within the factory. In the pre-interview questionnaire almost 40 percent of the women stated that they had been dissatisfied with working conditions at TKC. Two-thirds of the women voicing their discontent were women who had worked on the shop floor in the textile production at TKC. Interviewee 12 was a single mother who lived with her own mother, just outside Cottbus. She had worked in the textile production, but had changed departments when she was pregnant.

> Where I worked before we had to stack the spools on top and below. They said because I had to stretch it was not good for a pregnant woman and that I should not do it. It was forbidden. The nightwork ended as well. In the new department I just had to work two shifts, but even so it was still a very heavy job for a pregnant woman. There was a slippery floor covered in oil and heavy carts to pull. Many women had miscarriages and they used to say women who worked there for a long time did not get pregnant anymore. I don't know if that was true or not.

I did not like working night shifts – one week early, one week late and one week nights – I used to get headaches and could not sleep. I would have preferred working in one shift.

Interviewee 6 had also worked as a shift worker in the production of textiles. She too complained about the safety of the work environment at TKC.

The work conditions were bad at TKC. Oil was often spilled and you would fall over. But no one was interested. It was dirty. You got used to it but it was not nice.

Interviewee 9 had worked in textile production for seven years before being made redundant.

For women it was a fairly heavy job. We had to take the material on and off the machines. The reels were fairly heavy. Men worked there as well, but it was about 90 percent women, a few men, but it was just a small group […]In the six months before the firm closed the work group was very small. But despite that we had to attend all the machines. That was even more difficult. The men lifted the heavy spools and the women just worked at the machines. For us that was easier physically.

The women's stories of life working in textile production at TKC point to a sexual division of labour on the factory floor despite the predominance of women overall. Yet clearly the work for both men and women alike was heavy, dirty and demanding. Blue-collar workers were also required to work shifts. Research undertaken in the GDR suggested that women were more resistant to shiftwork (especially shift-systems that required night working) than their male colleagues (see chapter 2). A survey of women in the mining industry conducted by the energy and mining union, the IGBE, after the Wende indicated that the six out of every ten women objected to working night shifts. However, the majority of women who spoke out against night working were white-collar workers. Over half of the production workers surveyed said they were willing to work nights (IGBE 1992: 12). Amongst the former TKC women the attitudes to shift working were quite mixed. Interviewee 8 had worked in the carpet yarn production at TKC for five years and had disliked her job, particularly the shift system.

I did not like the work so much. I did not work in the department I wanted. I did not like working the three shifts. I did not like night shifts.

> To be truthful I wanted to do something else... It really was quite a physical job and the night shift, the late shift, was not so good.

Interviewee 21, on the other hand, spoke much more positively of her experiences working shifts. She had worked at TKC for fourteen years and for the last six years prior to the Wende had been employed as a shift leader. After the collapse of the GDR she was moved to the position of quality controller, where she worked up until her redundancy. When asked whether she had enjoyed working in shifts she replied:

> On the whole. The only problem was that at the beginning we did not always have weekends free. But later on they found out three shifts were just as productive [as four]. I really liked working three shifts. I'm not the type of person who generally likes getting up early all the time. I had a different order of events. I looked forward to each new week, because it was always something different. One week I had evenings free. Another I could do things in the morning. I really liked it.

Although many of the women moved from blue-collar shiftwork to working in a single shift in white-collar employment after the birth of children, some of the women continued to work in a shift system even with young children. Interviewee 9 was married with a 3-year-old son:

> I must say it [working shifts] really was not a problem. I am married and my child went to the crèche then and it really was better. He did not need to spend as much time there as if I had been working normal shifts.

Interviewee 11 had worked in three shifts in the production. After the birth of her second child she moved to office work and had to just work one shift.

> I actually preferred working in three shifts as I had more time with the children. The early shift was from six until two. The night shift was from ten until six. You had more time. When I did the normal shift I had to start at seven in the morning and I finished at four o'clock. I did not get home until five and the whole day was gone.

It was clear from the interviews that not all women with young children disliked working in shifts. The comprehensive system of childcare made shiftworking a viable option for some women at TKC. Indeed as the two women above suggest, working in a rotating shift system, in some instances at least, enabled working mothers to spend more time with their children than if they had worked in a normal day shift.

Redundancy

In the city of Cottbus where the women had been employed more than nine out of every ten textile workers had lost their jobs (Buttler et al. 1993). At the time of the interviews female unemployment in the area was over double that of male unemployment. All of the women interviewed had involuntarily given up work after unification. Prior to receiving their notices of redundancy most of them had been on the threshold of unemployment for some time, either working shorter hours or no hours whatsoever (*Kurzarbeit Null*). As a result the women had known for some time that redundancy was likely although some still recounted feelings of shock and despair when the redundancy papers finally arrived.

Two of the women interviewed were still working, but had just received their redundancy notices and were preparing to leave the firm. Their responses to their imminent job loss contrasted sharply. Interviewee 32 looked quite optimistically to the future. She had worked at TKC for twenty-two years in various jobs. Since 1978 she had been employed as a secretary. Her husband had worked in the army (NVA) before the Wende, but since the collapse of the GDR had been employed in a civilian job. Interviewee 31, on the other hand, showed clear signs of distress. During the interview she broke down in tears when she spoke of the changes that happened to her and her family since the collapse of socialism. Not only was she about to lose her job but, as an ardent socialist, she felt that she had lost everything in which she had believed. She had worked at TKC for sixteen years training apprentices in the clothing production. Before that she had worked in the nearby town of Lübben in a knitwear factory. Her husband had also worked in the army before the Wende and they had moved to Cottbus when her husband had been posted there. Her husband was currently involved in a work-creation scheme but was about to finish and had no permanent job to go to afterwards. She had two children. The younger one was still at school. The eldest had worked as a kindergarten teacher but had been made redundant and was unemployed.

Then, my husband was in the army, an officer in the NVA and we were moved to Cottbus. Before we were in Lübben. I got a job here in this firm

164

straightaway, also in the training department, although there was a big difference between working there in Lübben because that was underwear and here the garments are outerwear. I had to learn it all myself [...] During this time I had the opportunity to do a correspondence course in Berlin to gain further qualifications. So job, family, children and study [*She counts them up on her fingers*]. I was given leave from work, two or three days a week or two days to study on my own. In the GDR the firm was very generous towards women who did correspondence courses. It was very accommodating. [Afterwards] I stayed in the training department and that's what I've been doing ever since but now the firm's got smaller not so many trainers are needed. Everything's being cut back. I will have to look for another job. In the past [...] [*She starts to cry and motions to me to switch off the Dictaphone. After a pause she says she is willing to continue and I switch the recorder back on*]. You were safe. You were secure. You did everything for the firm [*Voice wavers*]. You felt good, and, as a woman, you were appreciated. As a woman you were proud of your progress – housewife, study, family – that is always a problem... but women in the GDR were proud of their development. You were something as a woman. I was in the Party, in the FDJ and all of that was enjoyable, it was fun. You were there for the GDR, perhaps it's hard for some people to understand nowadays [*Voice wavers again*].... My husband has finished with the NVA. He was in the NVA for years... And he can't suddenly accept the laws of the FRG – not with his conscience. He was a fighter for the GDR and he couldn't suddenly be another fighter, you can't do that if you've been so loyal before. For him it's all over and says now for something different. Not that he did not get on with the people from the *Bundeswehr*[...]but you can't simply turn yourself around. So he said 'now I must look for something else'. But he hasn't found a job. In his applications it says 'Officer with the NVA' and some people think, O yes the Stasi, although the two were completely different areas. Both he and I had absolutely nothing to do with the Stasi. But just being in the NVA causes problems. He's had an ABM place for a year but that's ending. He's finishing in August and I'm finishing in June. My daughter also studied as a kindergarten teacher [...] In the GDR a kindergarten teacher was an important job. She studied for three years. We all made things and collected things for her job. In the GDR there was not so many things for children so you had to make a lot yourself. We all helped out... But she has also been made redundant. She worked in the kindergarten for four years. She's had to apply for *Sozialhilfe*. With the rent and all the other costs she's only got DM 200 left a month... You can say three members of the family unemployed and another child at home. It's a big strain on the family. The rents have gone up. We have a four-room apartment. We pay more than DM 500 and with all the other costs about DM 1,200 [...] we needed a car, and so we bought one but the repayments cost DM 300 every month. To look for work you need a car [...] it's a real problem... In the GDR we earned a good amount but we were not a family that saved

a lot. We did not hoard any money [...] you could live well but you could-
n't live it up. We always went on holiday. We always needed a lot of money
for that even though it was just in the GDR. And the Trabant cost money.
But we had enough. We were satisfied. We bought things that we needed...
We had a few savings but not enough to say that we had a lot of money.

Retraining

One possibility for interviewee 31 would be to retrain if she did not
find a job after leaving TKC. Women made up over half of participants
in retraining programmes in Brandenburg. However, the allocation of
retraining places tended to be gender-specific. Whilst women were
guided en masse into office-based learning programmes, men were
more likely to update existing skills or learn new skills in construction
and technical-related areas. It soon became clear from speaking to the
women in the retraining programme that many had signed up to the
course because of a lack of alternative options and, given the choice,
would have preferred to stay in blue-collar work or retrain in another
field. Interviewee 12, a textile worker, explained how she had come to
join the retraining programme at EWA.

> TKC told us that we had to do a course, a preparatory course. If we did
> not we would not get any more Kurzarbeit money. The course lasted
> from May to June 1991, two months. We learnt about computers and
> how to fill in application forms. Afterwards I was offered a place here.
> You get more money than unemployment benefit [...] I really do not
> want to work in an office, but I did not find anything else. I would have
> preferred to work in production [...] I never really wanted to work in an
> office and I do not really like it here. I wanted to go to agricultural col-
> lege and train in environmental technology. But I could not get on the
> course. They said that you had to have worked in agriculture before.

Interviewee 18, who had also been a textile worker, expressed similar reservations.

> I would rather not work in an office. I am more of a practical person. I
> would have preferred to do something else. At the time nothing else was
> on offer. I actually wanted to train to be a florist but there weren't any
> places left. I would have preferred to do that.

Although the women in retraining were only halfway through
the programme, many were already expressing doubts about the
marketability of their new skills, aware of the low take-up rate of

workers holding office and computer skills. Interviewee 9 was married, with one child aged 3.

> I had trained as a textile worker and TKC is the only textile place here. Apart from that there is nothing else left in Cottbus. In principle then, if I started something else I would be an unskilled worker, and I did not want that. I wanted to get a second skill. I thought with a business qualification I would be able to get on a little. I went to the Labour Office to get some advice. To begin with I wanted to work in sales but the advisor told me that there were already so many sales assistants that could not get jobs. He advised me that a lot of people were still needed in offices, so I did that [...] But not everyone can work in an office or in trade. New industry needs to be brought into Cottbus.

Interviewee 8 had worked as a textile worker at TKC for five years but had wanted to change jobs.

> First of all, I found out about other jobs. I could have taken a job as a sales assistant but I would not have earned much. I would have to work from early until late in the evening for little money. It would not have been worth it. So I decided to retrain, as I am still young. But a lot of people are training in office skills, but I only know that with hindsight [...] The Labour Office in Cottbus tries to get everyone who is unemployed or working shortened hours to do retraining, and they haven't got it under control at all. Almost everyone learns office and business skills.

The women's fears were not unfounded. Although specific data was not available on the employment situation of the interviewees after retraining, overall only around 40 percent of the total participants completing the programme at the EWA further education institute were able to find employment (Interview, College Director, EWA, Cottbus, 7.4.94). Although the women involved in the retraining programme displayed a readiness to adapt to the changing needs of the economy, the acquisition of new skills did not ensure re-entry into the workforce. The supply of workers with office skills available for employment exceeded the demand for office labour. As women were pigeon-holed into certain occupational groups their employment chances were linked closely to the scope for re-employment within these groups.

Unemployment/ Nonemployment

The mass exodus of women from paid employment that occurred after the Wende was, to the most part, involuntary. Despite the pressures many women faced having to combine the dual roles of mother and worker, most women with children, contrary to the proclamations of the Federal government that East German women would seize the opportunity to retreat from the 'bind' of full-time employment (see chapter 4), were reluctant to withdraw from the workforce. A survey conducted by INFAS in 1990 suggested that 65 percent of women would work even if they did not need the money. Nearly nine out of every ten women were also in favour of both partners working and both looking after the family and the home (INFAS 1991: 20). A survey commissioned by the Institute for Labour and Employment Research (IAB) to assess women's attitudes two years after the Wende produced similar results. Seven out of every ten women questioned wanted to be employed (Engelbrech 1993: 2). In the survey of women workers in the Lausitz mining and energy sector in 1991 over 90 percent of the women taking part said they would continue working even if their partner earned enough money (IGBE 1992).

Three of the women interviewed were currently unemployed. Two were having enormous difficulties coming to terms with their unemployment. Interviewee 30 was in her forties and single. She had worked at TKC for twenty-four years in various jobs and departments. Her final job had been in rationalisation centre. She held both a *Meister* and an engineering qualification. Whilst she was in Kurzarbeit she had undertaken a 13-month computer-based retraining course but had been unable to find work since finishing.

> I want to work with people [...] For me the contact with people is very, very important. Of course income is as well, but the crucial factor is working with people. I often go into town just to have contact with people... The collective was like my family [...]When I walk through [the firm] now I could cry to see what they have done to the firm. When you are single you dwell on things too much, probably more than when you are married and have got a family.

Interviewee 29 had two school-age children and her husband was employed. She had worked at TKC for twenty years before being made redundant at the end of 1991. Since 1973 she had worked as a trainer in the textile production.

> My priority is to work again as soon as possible [...] something with your fingers – a practical job. I'm not the type of person who would like to do office work. I've never done it and I wouldn't like to do it now. But it doesn't look very promising that I'll find something... I have looked and

am still looking intensively for a job, even when I was in Kurzarbeit [...]. I thought it won't be so bad but it's proved to be quite the opposite [...] The jobs are always filled elsewhere – either you are too old, too young, or so it seems. At the moment, I must say, I'm a bit, well, shocked how everything's unwinding [...] What I miss most [about work] is that I always had a lot of people around and now at home you're all alone [...] There are a lot of opportunities to retrain. But up until now I've worked on the premise that it will be possible to find a job somewhere... I'm not the type of person who can stay sitting. I need to move around, for it to be a bit hectic... But I think there must be something. Somewhere there must be a job. You hear about people getting jobs but at the end of the day I know you need contacts. That's how it seems [...] Sometimes I think that a little angel will come down and I'll get the chance to work [*she laughs*]... I'm not coping with the whole thing [...] you spend the whole time doing things that don't do much for you. You dwell on things [...] sometimes it's dreadful [...] Sometimes the children say, 'Isn't it about time you found a job?' The little one said 'Are you too stupid to find work?' Or 'Why don't you go to work? Look, aunt Birgit goes to work, why don't you?' She doesn't understand.

Unemployment represented not just the loss of income but also the loss of social contact. Loneliness and declining self-esteem and self-worth were for many women the by-products of unemployment. In a survey of women in Cottbus, just over half of working women and over 60 percent of unemployed women stated that work was important to them because of the contact it brought with other people (Strzodka 1992). Apart from the women who were unemployed other women who had experienced being out of work through baby leave and being employed on Kurzarbeit Null also expressed negative feelings about prolonged periods at home.

The Domestic Division of Labour

Under state socialism women did the majority of domestic labour within the home despite taking part in paid employment in near equal numbers to men. Since the Wende, research suggests, women are taking on even more domestic labour, especially if they are out of work (Engelbrech 1993: 11–12; MASGF 1993a: 98). Unemployed women are also more likely to care for their children within the home than employed women. A study conducted by the IAB noted that only a fifth of children under 4 years of age whose mothers were not employed attended crèches compared to two-thirds of those children with working mothers. At kindergarten age half of the children of nonworking mothers and three-quarters of children of working mothers were cared for in a childcare facility. But whilst female unemployment had a clear impact on family decisions on how to care for children, male unemployment did not have the same effect. There was no significantly greater chance of children being cared for at home if their father was unemployed than if he was in work (Engelbrech 1993: 11–12). Interestingly, the IPOS survey conducted in 1995 noted that whilst nonemployed East German women were much less likely to have their children in day-care than employed East Germans the reverse trend existed in West Germany. There, nonemployed women were more likely to take their children to a kindergarten than employed women (Bundesministerium für Familie, Senioren, Frauen und Jugend: Abteilung Frauenpolitik 1996: 18–19). This difference indicates the varied use of day-care in East and West Germany. Whilst childcare facilities in East Germany were still very much geared towards assisting parents combine work and family responsibilities and were used by parents with this in mind, in West Germany day-care was more frequently used on a part-time basis in addition to care provided in the home by the mother.

In East Germany the cost of childcare had a direct impact ón women's ability to take up paid work. In the GDR the cost of day-care had been subsidised by the state. As a result parental contributions to the cost of childcare had been kept at an extremely low level. Usually parents paid only for the cost of meals. In Brandenburg the state government had introduced legislation to regulate the size of parental contributions towards nursery, kindergarten or after-school care. Parents on lower incomes or with large families were to pay less towards the cost of childcare. However, at the federal level the government had not regulated the cost of childcare places (see chapter 4), therefore regional differences were in place within East Germany. The IAB study conducted in 1991 indicated that a quarter of the married women with children would give up work if childcare costs reached up to DM 100 per month. Just 6 percent stated they would carry on working regardless of the cost (Engelbrech 1993: 13–14).

One of the aims of the interviews with the former TKC workers was to establish the extent to which unemployment impacted upon the domestic division of labour. A study of unemployment and domestic labour in the Northeast of England indicated that in two-partner households the unemployed husbands of working women tended to perform more housework than in households where men were either the main breadwinners or both partners were in employment. Despite the redivision of labour within the home the

unemployed men held on to traditional notions of appropriate gender roles. Their greater involvement in housework was justified as a
specific response to material circumstances. Housework was still
regarded in the main (and in 'normal' circumstances) as women's
work (Wheelock 1990). Would similar patterns be identifiable in the
East German context?

The interviews confirmed all the established data that indicated
that women did far more work in the household than their male
partners. It was evident that male partners may 'help out' in the
house but that the vast majority of work and the general management of housework and childcare were carried out by the women.
However, in instances where the women's partners had been unemployed whilst they were still working, the men did take on more
household chores. However, as in Wheelock's study, on return to
work the division of labour reverted back to the traditional pattern
of distribution with the woman doing the bulk of domestic labour.
Interviewee 29's testament was typical. At the time of interview she
was unemployed and her husband was in full-time employment.
However, previously he had been unemployed for a short period
while she was still in work. They had two school-age children.

> At the moment as I am at home the whole time I am responsible for
> everything. My husband was unemployed for a short time, just three
> months. He took over all the housework then, he cooked, did every-
> thing...[Now] I do all the housework, so when they [the children] come
> out of school it's all been done. They are a bit spoiled not having any-
> thing to do. I do not wait until they come home and say, come on, put
> the rubbish out. I must say, it is a mistake, I know. But when you've got
> so much time at home, I think, well, I'll do it myself.

Men's involvement in domestic labour whilst unemployed was thus
usually a pragmatic response to their particular economic circumstances and did not reflect any clear-cut change in attitude towards
appropriate gender roles within the home. In instances where both
partners were working it was still usually expected that women
would bear the brunt of responsibility for domestic tasks.

Reconciliation of Work and Motherhood

In comparison with women in West Germany, East German women
had had a more continuous work profile in the state socialist system. Whilst East German women tended to combine employment

and motherhood simultaneously, West German women had a greater tendency to undertake both consecutively. Although the trend was in decline, many West German women followed the three-phase model – they studied or worked, took a break from employment to care for children and then returned to work when the children were older (see chapter 4). Although in the GDR women were still more likely than men to suspend employment because of family reasons, the majority of women did so within the parameters of state regulations. In the earlier years of state socialism, women had been encouraged to return to work a few months after childbirth, if crèche places were available. However, the later introduction of the *Babyjahr* authorised a lengthier period of paid leave after childbirth.

After the Wende were women more likely to interrupt employment for longer periods to care for children? Did they halt employment out of choice or because of a lack of social support? Had women in the GDR been happy with simultaneously working and caring for young children or had there been a latent desire for a more discontinuous work profile as in West Germany? To what extent did the extended family or informal networks of friends play a part in childcare?

The INFAS survey conducted in 1990 suggested that East German women wanted to take longer breaks from work for childcare than had been possible in the GDR. The survey indicated that nearly half of the women questioned would ideally interrupt their careers for a few years (*'für einige Jahre'*) after childbirth. Forty-six percent of the women interviewed agreed it was optimal when a 'woman interrupts work for a few years when she has children and returns later to work' (INFAS 1991: 37). Although this information was taken by some as an endorsement of the three-phase model by East German women (and a vindication of the West German model of parenting), the results of the survey have since been challenged. Kistler et al (1993) argue that the phrase 'for a few years' (*für einige Jahre*) was 'methodically inexact and inaccurate', and that its ambiguity invites misinterpretation and misunderstanding (Kistler et al. 1993: 45). They point to the results of a survey conducted by IPOS in autumn 1991, a year after the INFAS survey, which produced quite different answers. This later survey questionned East and West German men and women on how they thought it was best to combine both work and family. Should the woman take the shorter 8- to 14-week maternity leave (*Mutterschaftsurlaub*),[1] or the 3 year maternity leave (*Erziehungsurlaub*) and then return to work? Or should women take a longer career break before re-entering the labour market, or give up their careers forever? Three-quarters of East German women favoured the 3-year *Erziehungsurlaub*. Just 12 percent said that a woman should take a longer career break and only one in every hundred believed a woman should give up employment permanently. In stark contrast, women in West Germany favoured a more discontinuous work pattern. Whilst 44 percent advocated the three year break, a further 41 percent supported taking an even longer break from work after childbirth (Kistler et al. 1993: 45–46). A repeat survey by IPOS four years later in 1995 indicated a slight shift in the attitudes of East Germans to the issue of childcare. Fourteen percent of women thought the Mutterschaftsurlaub allowed an appropriate period away from employment after childbirth, 63 percent favoured the 3-year Erziehungsurlaub, but 20 percent (8 percent more than in 1991) thought that a longer period away from work was best. Only 3 percent thought that women should give up their jobs for good. However, stark difference still existed between East and West. Forty-three percent of West German women advocated a longer pause from employment than the Erziehungsurlaub allowed (Bundesministerium für Familie, Senioren, Frauen und Jugend: Abteilung Frauenpolitik 1996: 45–46).

In 1991 over 60 percent of West Germans thought that care outside the family was harmful to the young child. By contrast the majority of East German men and women believed that it did not harm children of kindergarten age to be cared for outside the home (Kistler et al. 1993: 46). The IPOS survey of 1995 still indicated similar results (Bundesministerium für Familie, Senioren, Frauen und Jugend: Abteilung Frauenpolitik 1996: 25). Sixty-two percent of West Germans thought the care of young children outside the family was harmful; 55 percent of East Germans fully supported the care of young children outside the home. Whilst the 1995 survey indicates an emerging decrease in support for kindergarten care in East Germany, East Germans still had a much greater tendency to support community-based childcare arrangements than West Germans.

In the pre-interview questionnaire given to the former TKC workers, the women who had preschool-age children in 1989 and the women who currently had children under school age were asked their opinions on the cost, opening hours and standard of care in the childcare facilities. Virtually all of the women who had had children attending day-care before the Wende had been satisfied with the cost of childcare, the standard of care, and the opening hours. Most of those women with children still in childcare continued to be satisfied with the standard of care and the opening times of childcare facilities. However, only a third were still happy with the cost of childcare.

During the interviews all the women were asked their thoughts on how best to combine working with childcare. The overwhelming majority supported nursery care; many of the women believed that one of the parents should stay at home when the child was very young. None thought that a woman should give up her job for good. Interviewee 7, for example, took a year's leave from work after the birth of her child but welcomed the opportunity to return to work at the end of the year.

> I did not want to stay at home any longer. I was happy that I had a crèche place because I think it's better when the child grows up with other children of the same age, rather than spend three years hanging off your apron strings. I was very happy to go back to work.

Interviewee 11 had two children aged 3 and 4.

> I recommend at least one year at home... because in the first year a child develops so much and you are able to see it... but then go back to work.

Interviewee 10 was 19 years old and had no children. When asked what she considered to be the optimal form of childcare she replied:

> In the first few years the mother should stay at home, or the father, it does not matter... then the child should go to kindergarten. Then the children are with other children and learn everything more quickly than when you teach them at home.

Interviewee 17 was married with two children aged 16 and 10.

> [In the GDR] you knew that you would have a kindergarten place and that your children would be slowly prepared for school... People say that a child should grow up with its mother... But from my experience, in the kindergarten the children are occupied in a way that they cannot be at home. What woman who is at home and has housework to do and has food to cook is able to sit down and make things, play and do everything like that... They should create jobs for women that are six hours a day so they can combine it [work] with the family better... But it's good for the children to go to kindergarten... they learn to be independent, to tie their shoe laces, to comb their hair... And they learn to be in groups and to help others and that's what I do not like about the new system. It's not like that anymore.

Interviewee 12 had a daughter aged 3. She stated that:

> I noticed that when I was at home with my child when I wanted to do the housework she would have no one to play with. I think it is better to go to the nursery during the day, even if it is just a half-day.

Some of the women with children enlisted help from their own mothers, other relatives or friends in the care of their children. Interviewee 26 was 18 years old when she had her child. Instead of her taking baby leave herself her mother and the father's mother had shared the baby year between them. Interviewee 7 also had help from her mother in the care of her child. Her mother sometimes picked up her child from kindergarten. Interviewee 9 said she sometimes left her child with her mother-in-law while she did her housework. Interviewee 15 was a grandmother herself. She helped her daughter-in-law with the care of her child. As the mother of her grandchild worked full-time and did not get home until six in the evening, interviewee 15 often looked after her grandchild in the early evening. Jobs were so scarce that many women were reluctant to take too much time off work to care for sick children and relied instead on family and friends to look after their children when they were ill and unable to go to school or to nursery. Under state socialism generous leave to care for sick children at home, together with a comprehensive network of crèches, kindergartens and after-school centres, had cut back on the need for extended family and friends to take an active part in childcare. Indeed, the rate of employment was so high it was likely that friends and relatives would also be in full-time work. Yet in the immediate post-Wende period cutbacks in certain social provisions, such as leave to care for ill children or after-school places, together with high unemployment, particularly amongst older women, had led to the growing use of family and friendship networks in childcare. Interviewee 1 lived with her partner and had a 3-year-old child who attended a kindergarten. Her mother was no longer at work. She was asked what she did with her son when he was ill. She replied, 'Thank God, I have my mum and she can look after him'. Interviewee 29 was unemployed. Both her children were at school.

> My niece is employed…. She has to think of something when her child is ill. The child is two, or almost two, and I've often looked after her when she is ill, so her mother could go to work.

In East Germany the level of (full-time) childcare provision remains significantly higher than in West Germany, despite some cutbacks in places available and increases in the cost of care borne by the parents. The 1995 IPOS poll indicated, for example, that 58 percent of West German respondents and 70 percent of East German respondents with preschool-age children had their children in day-care (Bundesministerium für Familie, Senioren, Frauen und Jugend: Abteilung Frauenpolitik 1996: II). This aside, a considerable and rising amount of childcare was still performed by women within the domestic unit on an unpaid basis, not always by the mothers of the children, but instead by relatives or friends. In certain cases the carer may be male but in the majority of instances the informal care is provided by another woman. In the post-Wende period, whilst there is still widespread support amongst East German women for community-based childcare arrangements for preschool-age children (much more so than in West Germany where the majority favour family-based care for young children), there has been a shift towards the use and support of family-based care for young children, sometimes because of unemployment, limited childcare options but also because of changes in attitudes towards childcare.

Looking Forward: Work Hours

In the GDR the full-time housewife role had been eradicated for women of working age. Even after the Wende women still overwhelmingly rejected the option of completely withdrawing from the workforce (INFAS 1991: 19). But, whilst the majority of East German women maintained a desire to take part in paid employment, not all women wanted to work full-time hours or supported the continuous work model that had existed in the GDR. Although the INFAS and the IAB surveys conducted after the Wende revealed that the majority of women wanted to continue working, they also indicated that a significant proportion of East German women favoured a partial retreat from the workforce through part-time hours. The IAB study undertaken in 1991, for example, suggests that a quarter of the East German women wanted to work part-time hours (Engelbrech 1993). The IPOS survey carried out four years later in 1995 suggested that by this point as many as 40 percent of East German women would prefer part-time hours (Bundesministerium für Familie, Senioren, Frauen und Jugend: Abteilung Frauenpolitik 1996: 42). Women's desire for part-time labour was closely linked to motherhood. Women with young children had an above-average desire to work reduced hours; the younger a woman's children the more likely she was to seek part-time employment (Engelbrech 1993: 3; Bundesministerium für Familie, Senioren, Frauen und Jugend: Abteilung Frauenpolitik 1996).

Although the women who had worked at TKC shared the common factor of wanting to work, their thoughts on the type and form of work varied. All of the women apart from one had worked full-time at TKC. Over a third of the former TKC workers who were interviewed and four out of every ten women who were taking part in retraining had children under school age. Five of the women were looking specifically for part-time work. Significantly, all of these women had at least one child under school age. In fact almost half of the women with preschool-age children were looking solely for part-time work. In line with the results of survey data (Engelbrech 1993; Bundesministerium für Familie, Senioren, Frauen und Jugend: Abteilung Frauenpolitik 1996) the women with preschool-age children were more likely to opt for part-time employment than women with older children or no children at all.

But the question of work hours was not a clear-cut issue. Some of the women had mixed feelings about part-time work and would only consider reducing their hours of employment under certain conditions. As one woman remarked; 'I would rather work part-time than not at all'. The loss of income, however, often acted as a disincentive to part-time work. Interviewee 2 had worked in textile production at TKC for nine years. She was married with a 4-year-old daughter.

> If I got a job I would want to work full-time because we need the money. But when I could choose the ideal job I would work just six hours a day because my daughter goes to the kindergarten at 6.30 in the morning and does not get home until 4 o'clock or 4.30 in the afternoon. I don't get anything from her [during the week], just at weekends.

But not all the women wanting part-time employment were women with young children. Interviewee 24, for example, was in her forties with three older children, only two of whom were still at home.

> I would prefer part-time work. Then I would have more time with the family. But if you lose your job you only get part-time unemployment benefit. That's the down side.

Looking Forward: Re-employment

The women interviewed tended to see the current labour situation either as the result of the inefficiencies of the socialist system and therefore an unavoidable corollary of political and economic change, or as the consequence of the West German political management of the transformation process. Only when asked directly about their employment chances in direct contrast to male workers did women comment upon men's relatively better chances within the post-unification labour market. Even then they did not tend to see their current labour situation to be the effect of male endeavours to marginalise women during a period of labour shortage.

In the interviews the women were asked how they thought their employment chances compared to men's. Did men have better prospects? Interviewee 3 was a single mother. She had been employed in office work at TKC prior to her redundancy. She replied:

> I think so. When you look at who is left in the firms it is for the most part men. In the apartment block where I live it is the women who are at home.

Interviewee 4, a former textile worker, answered:

> Yes, because, firstly, men can work in three shifts. Secondly, men are more in demand because women have children. If the child is ill we have to stay at home. And, thirdly, men can do heavier work.

Interviewee 9 had worked in textile production at TKC for seven years. She said:

> There's more for men here in Cottbus than for women. What can women do apart from being a sales assistant or working in an office? There isn't anything else here. Previously only women were sales assistants but now there are a lot of men too. Nowadays you go into the shops and men are working there too. They can do it just as well. On the other hand, I saw a woman working as an electrician, and she was not doing a bad job either. People should do what interests them.

Interviewee 8 had worked shifts in the carpet yarn production at TKC:

> Men have better prospects because they can do jobs like bricklaying and carpentry... There aren't as many women's jobs. There isn't any textile industry or at least not much.

Interviewee 24 had worked in various jobs in textile production in her seventeen years at TKC. She had three children: two were still at school.

Men are more independent. They can take on more than women can. Women always have to think about the family. A man can do overtime. But a woman has to think, what about the children?

Interviewee 17 had been in charge of a department in the garment manufacturing at TKC:

At the moment, yes. As I see it there are not so many firms or enterprises that need labour, and, on the whole, it is guaranteed that men will be preferred because they will not be absent so much. Of course, that depends on whether you have small children or not. I have older children, and perhaps that is to my advantage, we'll have to see. But, as I see it, the politicians are steering it that way, so women stay at home. All these years we have been used to going to work. At work all women, we stood alongside men. We were appreciated. We earned our own money. We could say okay, now I'll buy something for myself. That's what people miss. I would miss it to.

The Wende

After the collapse of state socialism in the GDR East German women experienced wide-ranging changes to their private as well as public lives. The abruptness of East Germany's split with its socialist past meant that East German women were suddenly faced with a massive learning-process, with the need to become rapidly accustomed to new laws and institutions, a different system of social and labour legislation, and rapidly rising unemployment. In general, survey data indicates that the majority of women felt that the status and position of women had deteriorated since the Wende. In a survey of men and women in Brandenburg carried out at the beginning of 1992 eight out of ten people believed that women's position had worsened since unification (INFAS 1992).

The women from TKC had mixed feelings about the Wende. They tended to see the gains mostly in terms of consumer benefits – the greater range of goods to purchase – and the freedom they had gained to travel. However, the thrill of greater consumer availability and the possibility of wider travel opportunities were offset by the growth of unemployment, the increased financial insecurity caused by widespread joblessness, the erosion of social protection, and rising crime levels. Interviewee 19 was married with two children. She was asked whether she was happy that the Wende had happened. She replied:

At first, yes. But now I am a bit disappointed with everything. In my circle of friends we celebrated a lot at the time. But lots of people expected that suddenly the golden door would open and it would be the same as in the west straightaway. Even then I thought to myself it won't work like that so quickly [...] I was really pleased that we were able to travel. But, as my mother pointed out, it's not so simple. You need money to travel and she was right. I couldn't afford to go to West Germany [...] I wouldn't want it back the way it was. But I can't say that I'm happy now either... It's very hard at the moment. But I wouldn't want to go back. I've never wanted that [...] Now you can just go and shop. You don't have to wait for weeks if you want to buy children's things or a wedding present. Now you can just go out and find something. It might sound stupid, but it's nice that we can now buy more fruit and vegetables.

Interviewee 8 was asked the same question. She replied:

With some things definitely. We can go away, we can travel and buy things that we couldn't before. What worries most people, though, is that it has become so dangerous. I don't like to go out in the evenings anymore. You worry that you might get broken into. Before, in the GDR, there weren't any attacks or break-ins.

Official data on crime and attacks on women were not made available in the GDR. On the one hand, crime has risen since the collapse of socialism. On the other, crime and violence are talked about more openly in the public sphere, thus alerting women to the potential dangers (Strzodka 1992: 37). Interviewee 12 also expressed concern about the rising crime since the Wende:

I regret that so much has been lost. Sometimes I worry about my daughter's future. If she does not get good qualifications... then she won't have a chance.

She was asked what advantages the Wende had brought:

Not so many. There are lots more things to buy. Before there were no bananas [*laughs*], no children's things. Nowadays you can go into a shop and buy anything.

She was asked what she missed:

The secure future. Crime is spreading. Before, when I used to come into Cottbus for the late shift, I could walk along the streets by myself, and nothing ever happened. Nowadays my mother still travels with the last bus, and each time I am worried that something will happen to her. It's got bad here. She is afraid too. Before everything was familiar. You didn't have to be afraid.

Interviewee 17 had worked up to the position of department head during her period of employment at TKC.

I am not happy or unhappy. It had to happen, but it came too quickly. Everything was so ill considered. I would have preferred right from the beginning if it had been taken step by step. Unification was good but it came about too quickly... The advantages [of the socialist system] were the social things. The disadvantages? Well, I never learnt anything else. The disadvantage was that everything was laid down. To get to my position I had to be a member of the Party. It did not work any other way. I don't know if you can understand, but I was born in 1950, so practically as long as the GDR existed, I grew up in the GDR and I did not know anything else. So from childhood onwards I accepted everything. It was not until after the Wende that I realised that this and that were so. But from the beginning [...] From school onwards, through my vocational training through into later life I never felt that it was a disadvantage or something bad. Because in my country I did not know anything else. And besides it was not as if we wanted anything radical. We lived here, we worked here, and for me things weren't going badly at all. So I never felt like my freedom was being restricted. It never felt like that to me. Of course, everyone has different interests, but I am not the type of person who has to travel around the world. For me it was enough to be on holiday and to be able to enjoy the countryside, to be able to go walking and to show my children, this is that bird and that is that little beetle [...] I do not have to travel all over the place [...] It is not so easy to say what is good, what was good, what was bad. Sometimes you cannot split it up like that.

The interview extracts detailed above are a 'snapshot' of a particular group of women, at a particular time. The women's stories were not meant to be representative of East German women as a whole but instead specific to particular individuals at a particular time. If the 'picture' had been taken of other women, elsewhere by a different person we cannot assume that it would be the same. Indeed, the IPOS surveys taken in two-yearly intervals, whilst indicating a considerable degree of continuity in the attitudes of East Germans, also point to certain shifts between 1991 and 1995. In East Germany there was still much greater support for the care of children outside the home and the majority of women still held a preference for full-time labour over part-time labour. In addition, the majority of women still did most of the domestic labour inside the home; 81 percent of East German women taking part in the 1995 survey said they alone did the cleaning, 77 percent stated that they had sole responsibility for cooking. However, survey data point increasingly to the rise in the amount of childcare undertaken within the home. Often this arises from the unemployment of mothers. Women with young children who are out of work are less likely to send their children to daycare. Increasingly women in work rely on family and friendship network to provide care to supplement nursery or school care or to replace it altogether. In addition the 1995 IPOS survey suggests that more women in East Germany are supporting longer pauses from work after childbirth than was the case immediately after the Wende, and greater numbers are showing a preference for part-time hours. Whilst these shifts are significant and revealing of a slight change in attitudes, it must be remembered that even in this poll three-quarters of the women questioned advocated women returning to work after either the Mutterschaftsurlaub or the Erziehungsurlaub. Six out of ten women still stated a preference for full-time work.

Looking at the responses of the 'TKC women', there were broad similarities in their responses and the responses detailed in the other pieces of research undertaken in the same time-frame, some of which were included in the discussion above. Much of the other research referred to in this chapter was in fact based on large-scale surveys. Whilst quantitative data is able to detail general trends, the discussions with the women who had worked at TKC revealed the complexities and the subtleties of people's reactions to change. As interviewee 17 stated above, 'It is not so easy to say what is good, what was good, what was bad. Sometimes you cannot split it up like that'. For most people it was impossible to draw up a simple dichotomy between state socialism/good and capitalism/bad, or vice versa. It is simple to ask a question like; 'did women lose or gain from the collapse of state socialism?'. To answer it is much more complex. Clearly one of the main losses for the TKC women was the loss of employment. Job loss is not just about the deprivation of income, although this is obviously very important, but also about the loss of identity, self-esteem and social contact. Many of the women, particularly those with children, also mourned the loss of the socialist welfare system. Yet interestingly none wanted to revert back to the old system. Although their lives, at the point of the interviews, were not as they would want them, they felt their lives *could* be better in the new system. Although choice was still denied to many because of economic insecurities, the potential for greater opportunities and choice existed, they felt, within the new system.

So whilst many of the women were anxious about their present situation most looked hopefully to the future.

Notes

1. Women do not have to work in the last 6 weeks of pregnancy and are forbidden to work in the first 8 weeks after childbirth. Women who have had premature or multiple births are not allowed to work in the first 12 weeks after childbirth. Women cannot be made redundant during pregnancy or in the first 4 months after childbirth (Presse- und Informationsamt der Bundesregierung, December 1991: 51; Bundeministerium für Frauen und Jugend 1991b).

8

Conclusions

In quantitative terms post-communist transformation has had a deteriorating effect on women's involvement in paid labour, quickly replacing the near full employment of the state socialist period with high levels of unemployment. Since the Wende East German women have been far more susceptible to unemployment, particularly to long-term unemployment, than their male counterparts. In the initial post-Wende period the gap between male and female rates of unemployment quickly widened. The more rapid rise of male unemployment between the end of 1995 and 1997, whilst closing the gender gap slightly, did not overturn the bias towards female unemployment. Throughout the post-Wende period women have had greater difficulties re-entering employment once out of work and have consistently formed the majority of the unemployed.

The declining rate of female employment in East Germany has been dramatic, in both its speed and its extent. By 1996 women's employment levels in East Germany, if one looked solely at employment in the 'free' market as opposed to work in state-subsidised employment schemes, had already dropped to below West German levels of female employment (MASGF Brandenburg 1997b: 16; see chapter 4). This decline is doubly significant. Firstly, the high level of female employment that existed in the GDR had always acted as a crucial marker of difference between East and West Germany during the years of division. Whilst the number of women involved in paid employment in the GDR was high by international standards, the incidence of female employment in West Germany, whilst increasing, was relatively low in comparison with many of its Western European neighbours. For the level of women's employment to have fallen so sharply and by so much thus illustrates the decisive and devastating impact of post-communist transformation on women's employment opportunities.

Secondly, the dramatic fall in female employment occurred despite the desire for employment amongst East German women remaining high in the post-Wende period. The fall in female employment did not arise in response to a plummeting demand for employment amongst women. On the whole, East German women, contrary to assertions made previously by the centre-right in West Germany, did not want to use the collapse of state socialism as an opportunity to escape the 'shackles' of employment. Whilst some women have welcomed the opportunities afforded by regime change to withdraw fully, partially or temporarily from the labour market, the vast majority of East German women wished to carry on working after the Wende, most on a full-time basis. The mass withdrawal of women from the workforce was thus involuntary. As a result a gap clearly quickly emerged between the expectations and desires of the women on one side and the reality of the employment situation on the other. For the majority of East German women participation in paid work was still an integral part of their identities, even though the political compulsion to work had been removed. As illustrated in the interviews detailed in chapter 7, employment provided not only financial remuneration but also social contact and self-fulfilment. Job loss and unemployment resulted often in loneliness and despair as well as financial hardship.

In part the disproportional exclusion of women from the workforce after the Wende can be explained by the legacy of state socialism. The persistence of sex segregation at work in the GDR meant that the process of economic restructuring had an uneven impact on male and female labour. Whilst women had gained access to many traditionally male areas of employment under state socialism the majority of women remained clustered in areas employing solely or mainly female labour. During the period of economic restructuring and employment crisis some female-dominated areas of employment, such as administrative work, were especially vulnerable to rationalisation. Even more significantly, many of the fields in which job expansion did occur, such as the construction industry, employed mainly male workers.

State socialism had failed to overturn deeply ingrained ideas on masculine and feminine difference. Although it became both socially accepted and socially expected that women would take up a place within the paid workforce, women were still generally perceived as a qualitatively different source of labour, often branded as a less reliable, less flexible and more expensive source of labour. Significantly, the mass mobilisation of female labour into the workforce under state socialism had occurred without any fundamental restructuring to the sexual division of labour within the home. Women continued to perform the majority of domestic labour within the household unit in addition to entering the workforce, whilst men with families continued to enter the workforce relatively unfettered by domestic commitments.

As the vast majority of women became mothers, usually for the first time in their early twenties, the issue of combining work and family was pertinent to most women at some point in their lives. The 'positive discrimination' of working women in state socialist legislation, which enabled women to combine work and family, actually reinforced inequalities between men and women. By targeting women in family legislation the ties between women, domestic labour and childcare were intensified, thus fortifying the sexual division of labour both within the home and at work. In practical terms working fathers were more flexible than working mothers in their relationship to the labour market. Despite state provisions to assist the employment of women with caring responsibilities, women still had to employ individual strategies to cope with the demands of combining both domestic and waged work. Working mothers in the GDR were, for example, more likely than working fathers to adapt their employment conditions to suit the needs of their family, either by changing jobs, seeking or at least desiring part-time employment or by refusing overtime or positions of responsibility whenever possible.

Symbolically, men were still widely perceived as having a more powerful claim than women to employment. Despite the near equal representation of women in the workforce under state socialism, the vital importance of women's wages for household units and the high incidence of single-parent families headed by women, the ideology of the male breadwinner still had resonance in East German society. Within the post-Wende context of economic crisis and the large-scale displacement of workers from the labour market, men were able to capitalise on their already stronger labour market position to win the competition for jobs. Thus whilst women's greater vulnerability to unemployment can be explained in part by reference to the distribution of men and women in the occupational structure and the uneven impact of economic restructuring on 'male' and 'female' jobs, the disparity between men and women's access to jobs is also clearly attributable to the relative strength of men within the labour market, their lesser involvement in the routine, daily caring aspects of family life and the persistence of traditional notions of gender difference. As illustrated in chapter 4, male workers were able to increase their presence not only in traditionally male areas of employment after the Wende, but also in certain fields where their representation had previously been low.

Whilst the transition to state socialism had engendered much change in women's working lives – the near full employment of women, their greater access to training and education and the recognised right of women to earn their own incomes – the social, economic and political changes within East Germany associated with state socialist transformation did not rupture the entire make-up of gender relations. Indeed the existence of underlining lines of continuity during the process of regime change are crucial to explaining how woman's stake within the labour market was undermined so emphatically and in such a short space of time once state socialism collapsed. Whilst state socialism transformed women's lives, particularly in terms of their education and employment possibilities, it did not deconstruct the hierarchical relationship between the sexes.

Frauenpolitik in the GDR was built upon a paradox. Whilst asserting that women could attain equality with men by doing the same as them in the public realm of employment, by entering the workforce in equal numbers, policy also retained the notion of a feminine difference; most notably that it was still primarily women's responsibility to take care of the daily needs of family members. Contradictions lay at the heart of the SED's agenda on women. Equality and parity within the workforce were to be achieved whilst maintaining difference and inequality within the private sphere. By failing to confront (indeed by reinforcing) the unequal division of labour within the domestic unit inequalities elsewhere (for example, in the labour market) were able to flourish. The persistence of such inequalities under state socialism in turn provided the foundation for women's disproportional exclusion from the sphere of employment and from its associated rewards after its collapse.

Of course, it would be misleading to explain women's post-Wende labour position only in terms of the state socialist heritage. The character of post-communist change in East Germany was equally as crucial in restructuring women's access to employment. Post-communist transformation in East Germany has been inextricably entwined with the unification process; indeed the two cannot be separated. The transition to a liberal democracy and to a market economy was guided throughout by West Germany and underpinned by the wholesale transfer of West German systems, institutions and legislation to East Germany. Both the 1:1 currency union between East and West Germany, which in effect re-evaluated the East German mark by 300–400 percent and the endeavour to raise wages in East Germany to West German levels had negative repercussions for the health of the East German economy and in turn the demand for labour. The inheritance of state socialist economic structures and systems already posed problems for East Germany's transition to capitalism and its ability to integrate successfully into the global capitalist economy. However, East Germany's fragile economic position was further weakened by the conditions of unification, thereby exacerbating the problems of system transfer. As argued above, men's relative strength within the state socialist labour market assisted their chances in the fight for jobs after the Wende. However, the initial period of economic crisis resulting from the process of system transfer was intensified by the conditions of unification, thus increasing the large-scale displacement of workers and the subsequent scramble for jobs.

For women, in particular, the terms of unification had an additional bearing on the regulation of work and family life. The one-way nature of the unification process involved the introduction of West German welfare legislation into East Germany. For East German women attempting to combine paid work with caring responsibilities the replacement of the East German welfare regime with the West German system was crucial. Whereas the state had intervened in the socialist system to provide the conditions to enable the full-time employment of women with caring responsibilities, the welfare system of West Germany prioritised the role of the family in the provision of care. In East Germany the establishment of a comprehensive system of public childcare by the state was pivotal to welfare aims. By contrast the number of public childcare places in West Germany was much more limited (confined mostly to part-time care for 3- to 6-year-olds) and those places that did exist were not regulated to assist women enter the workforce. Significantly, nonworking mothers in West Germany used kindergartens more frequently than working mothers (Bundesministerium für Familie, Senioren, Frauen und Jugend: Abteilung Frauenpolitik 1996: 19).

The one-way nature of the unification process introduced a regime of welfare provision into East Germany that was totally different to the state socialist system. The West German system emphasised the role of the family and supported state intervention into the provision of welfare only as a last resort. Since unification childcare provision in East Germany has suffered cutbacks in hours and increases in costs. In addition many entitlements made available to working mothers under state socialism, such as extensive leave to care for sick children, have either been cut back or eliminated completely. Yet, because of the previously high level of provision and the intervention of some state legislatures the number of childcare places, especially those available on a full-time basis and those opened to the under-3 age-group, still far exceeds that in the West. What has been lost, however, at the federal level at least, has been the political commitment to the provision of full-time, low-cost childcare designed to assist the needs of working parents. Under the CDU-led federal government the system of welfare provision implicitly challenged women's right to a full-time, continuous work profile. Instead the provision of welfare worked on the assumption that the best care for the young child was provided within the family unit by the mother, necessitating either the whole or partial withdrawal of women from work during the early years of childrearing. For parents wishing to withdraw from the labour market for an extended period to care for young children, the introduction of a three-year baby leave to East Germany enabled longer employment breaks. However, for parents wishing or needing to combine work with family responsibilities the lack of support from the federal government was felt most keenly in the increased price of childcare since unification, the closure of many facilities (particularly those geared towards after-school care for young schoolchildren or those open in school vacation periods), and cutbacks to parental entitlements such as leave from work to care for sick children; all of which place additional pressures on workers trying to reconcile waged employment and caring responsibilities.

As illustrated in chapter 1, the analysis of gender diversity and difference has dominated feminist writings over the past two decades. In response to the earlier partiality of second-wave feminist thought which tended to universalise the experiences of a small group of women – usually white, middle-class, heterosexual, Western women – more recent feminist analyses of gender have pointed to and explored the plurality and multiplicity of womanhood. Increasingly attempts to employ the categories 'woman' or 'women' have been lambasted for their essentialism and universalism; two of the major sins within the contemporary postmodern climate of social theory. However, the move towards the celebration and exploration of women's diversity has been greeted with trepidation by many feminist academics and activists (for example, Bordo 1990; Ransom 1993). As Ransom (1993: 126) points out, '[w]hat threatens to disappear is the hook on which to hang our feminism. Without the category "woman" or "women" how can we intervene to effect change to existing gender relations?'

The particular case of women in East Germany provides a useful context in which to explore the issues of diversity and commonality. In many ways the analysis of female experience in East Germany during the state socialist and post-communist periods underlines the diversity and plurality of women's lives and the problems of assuming commonality between different groups of women purely because of their sex. Firstly, if one looks at East Germany in an international and comparative context the particularity of women's lives under state socialism becomes apparent. Looking at the socioeconomic dimensions of femininity, clear differences stand out if one compares the two parts of Germany prior to the Wende, not only in terms of women's living and working conditions but also in terms of their expectations as women. To conform to the ideal of womanhood under state socialism was to be both worker and mother; it was the duty of each citizen regardless of their sex to take an active part in economic life throughout their adult lives. Expectations about and experiences of access to employment and education, the state's role in the regulation of both private and public spheres, the interaction of domestic and waged work were sufficiently different across the former divide to question the validity not only of the category 'German woman' but of the category 'woman' generally. Both state socialist and post-communist transformations have had a decisive impact on the social construction of womanhood, to the extent that the experience of being female varied in certain details quite considerably between Eastern and Western parts of Europe.

However, whilst recognising East–West differences and the specific implications for gender of the varying socioeconomic and political systems in both regions, what one must avoid is the construction of an East–West divide which, whilst emphasising the differences between both regions of Europe for women, assumes commonality and unity on both sides of the divide; thus forming the singular categories 'East European woman' and West European woman'. Firstly, within Eastern Europe (as in Western Europe) there is considerable diversity between the various regions in terms of social traditions, religious and political heritage, economic profile, ethnic composition and so on. Even under state socialism the region was heterogeneous in its social, economic and political formations. One cannot therefore assume a homogenous female identity or experience across Eastern Europe either in the period of state socialism or in the era of post-communist transformation. Secondly, difference within Eastern Europe is not a question merely of national variations existing; within nation-states what it is to be a woman in terms of one's relationship with socioeconomic and political spheres, for example, is both plural and diverse. Just as there is no unitary category 'East European woman', there is no singular identity of 'East German woman' or 'Polish woman'. Within each context being a woman is influenced by a whole host of factors including age, class, ethnicity, sexuality, able-bodiedness as well as by gender to produce multiple and diverse ways of being. If we look at the conclusions drawn from this study of women's employment in East Germany the diversity of women's socioeconomic roles and expectations is apparent. Women's relationship to the labour market and the ability to access employment varied according to a whole string of factors, such as qualification levels, age, locality and household position. Moreover what women wanted from the labour market was also plural and variable. Whilst the majority of East German women wished to continuing working, their reasons for seeking work and their expectations of employment varied considerably. For some it was purely financial need that drove them to seek employment; for others employment represented not just economic reward but also tremendous personal fulfilment. For some changes to welfare provisions, particularly the restructuring of provisions for working mothers, proved to be major barriers to their ability to take up work or to access certain forms of employment; for others the cessation of the obligation to work and the introduction of a three-year baby leave after the Wende opened up exciting new possibilities unavailable to them under state socialism. Indeed, whilst the collapse of state socialism removed the possibility of a job for life it also allowed some women (and men) a greater degree of self-determination in their employment and family decisions.

Yet whilst the study of East German women and work points to various levels on which the East German context can be used to explore the diversity of female experiences, it also suggests that attention to the diversity and plurality of women's lives is problematic if it is made at the expense of recognising and analysing potential and existing points of commonality. What it is to be female is variable, diverse and inherently unstable. But in certain contexts, and the East German labour market can be included here, experiences can and do differ according to one's gender position, whether one is male or female. As Soper (1991: 105–106) remarked:

> If feminism gets too fixated on not recognizing a feminine difference, it could end up not making any difference: it could end up by overlooking what are still very offensive and oppressive dimensions of reality. For there are still very many conditions of existence which are differentially experienced depending on what sex you happen to be, and in many ways these are particularly constraining on women.

As argued above, not all women's experiences of employment are the same and not all women will have fared badly during the process of economic restructuring. However, despite the diversity of women's experiences, analysis of the labour market suggests that women *as a social group* have been disadvantaged within employment during the transformation process. On an aggregate level, women have been disproportionately susceptible to unemployment and have been less well-represented amongst those members of society to gain from the transformation process. If one looks at employment in terms of age, locality or qualification level distinct gender differences still emerge, with women consistently faring worse than men of the same age, locality or level of qualification. To reuse Soper's words cited above, there have been very many conditions of existence for East Germans both before and after the Wende which have been differentially experienced depending on whether one was male or female. Whilst social inequalities cut across many axes, gender is still a fundamental divider in East German society, not least in the sphere of employment.

Potential points of commonality do not only exist within the East Germany itself. The adoption of a comparative and international perspective, whilst showing clear areas of diversity in female experience globally, also reveals possible points of shared experience. Taking an overview of the East German context it is fair to conclude that in socioeconomic terms women have been underrepresented amongst the winners and overrepresented amongst the losers during the course of transformation. Although some women have been able to capitalise on regime change to improve their socioeconomic status or to make positive changes in the organisation of their family lives, women have been more likely than men to be unemployed, to be unemployed for longer periods and have thus run an increased risk of poverty. Furthermore, both before and after the Wende women's working lives have been shaped and in many ways constrained by their family ties to a greater extent than men's working lives. In this context at least clear comparisons can be drawn between the experiences of East German women and other groups of women living in areas of major economic and political change in both the post-communist and the developing world (see Aslanbeigui 1994 and discussion in chapter 1) as well as between East German women and women living in the advanced capitalist West. Recent research in Britain and Europe indicates, for example, that despite women's greater involvement in paid work outside the home and a growing acceptance of women's employment throughout the European Union, in most households the majority of domestic and caring work is still undertaken by women (*British – and European – Social Attitudes: how Britain differs*, 1998, Ashgate Publishing cited in *The Guardian*, 1.12.98). Of course, global differences, in particular the uneven distribution of wealth internationally and its impact on both men and women's life chances, must be acknowledged and explored. The chances of dying in pregnancy and childbirth vary so much internationally that whilst a woman in Britain has a one in 5,100 chance of dying in this way, in Sierra Leone one in seven women die in childbirth or during pregnancy. But whilst the implications of being female vary cross-culturally and within a particular cultural context according to a multitude of factors apart from gender, certain overarching patterns of gender relations are still identifiable internationally, with women more likely to undertake unpaid domestic and caring work, to perform different tasks within the paid labour force, to be employed at lower levels and to command lower rates of pay across the world.

At a political level there are clearly potential losses in abandoning the category 'women' or in overemphasising the diversity of women's experiences at the cost of acknowledging also points of commonality. Whilst recognising the socially constructed nature of gender and the variability of male and female experiences, at a political level there is still much to accomplish from working with the categories 'female', 'male', 'women', 'men', even if the aim ultimately is to undermine not only the inequalities between men and women but also the binary distinction male-female. Whilst acknowledging the diversity of ways one can be male and female, the multiplicity of male and female subject positions and the various ways in which gender interacts with other social axes, the male-female gender distinction is still a key organiser and divider globally. It is thus not only useful to retain the categories 'female', and 'women' at an analytical level, to analyse, for example, the implications of socioeconomic transformations in East Germany as in this study, but it can also be politically advantageous to hold on to and operate with the categories in order to challenge the inequalities and hierarchies that surround and underpin gender difference.

If we ignore or underplay the significance of gender, the significance of being male or female, then the differential access of men and women to positions of power and resources may remain unchallenged. Across the world women are disproportionally underrepresented in positions of social and political power. Perhaps most notable is the relative absence of women from key areas of decision making within the formal economic and political arenas worldwide. Suggesting that women should be equally represented in such areas is not to suggest that women will bring something essentially different to the process of decision making or that women will represent certain shared interests. The notion of 'women's interests' is of course problematic. Defining a set of issues which is in the common interest of all women is infeasible given the heterogeneity of women's lives, experiences and positions. Nor does it mean that women who do access positions of power should or will campaign primarily on behalf of women, whatever that might mean or entail. However, women's relative exclusion from such areas and the dominance of certain elite groups of men suggests that in the process of decision making the full range of options and opinions are not addressed and included. To ensure an adequate range of opinions, information and expertise a broad base of people need to be consulted. Thus, it is not only vital that women are better represented in positions of social and institutional power, but also that women from a wide range of social backgrounds – women of different classes, ethnic and religious groups, ages, sexual orientation and physical ability – take part to ensure that the multiplicity of women's perspectives are taken into account.

Whilst some individual women in East Germany may have made gains in the public sphere as a result of the collapse of state socialism, what is evident in the post-communist period is the continuing underrepresentation of women in positions of economic and political power. In the GDR women gained entry to the workforce yet the structure of the political system denied them the space to articulate their own interests and to help define the political agenda. The collapse of state socialism has allowed the space for more active political participation. Yet the democratisation of the political sphere has not automatically empowered women. As has been well-documented elsewhere (for example, Böhm 1993; Einhorn 1991, 1993a, 1995), whilst women and women's groups were active in the protest movement that helped bring an end to the hegemonic rule of the SED, the transition to a liberal democratic form of government did not bring women into key decision-making posts in the political arena in any significant numbers. Likewise, the most influential managerial posts in the economic sphere have been filled primarily by men. Indeed, in the immediate transitional period a decrease in women's share of management posts has been noted (see chapter 4). As a result women have often found themselves outside the domains of public life where key decisions unfold and thus lacking the institutional and social power to play a central role in the general shaping of post-communist change and in the specific reconstruction of dominant discourses on gender. Unfortunately in this respect there has been no 'reversal of fortunes' for women.

Whilst this study has demonstrated by reference to the state socialist period in East Germany that women's entry to paid labour alone is not sufficient to overturn inequalities between men and women, the analysis of the post-Wende era in East German history also suggests that women's participation in the economic sphere is an integral part of creating greater gender equality. At the same time, however, it is vital that women secure more equal representation in the key decision-making areas of both the polity and the economy. A crucial step forward in the process of creating greater equality between men and women is therefore the political as well as the economic empowerment of women. It is imperative that women gain the space to debate and define not only their own interests but also to contribute towards the shaping of society more generally. The greater political mobilisation of women is thus a key stage on the road towards breaking down gendered inequalities.

Bibliography

ABM-Projekt "Frauenarbeitslosigkeit", *Fortschreibung des Arbeits-material zu Problemen der Frauenarbeitslosigkeit am Beispiel des Arbeitsamtsbezirkes Potsdam*, University of Potsdam, February, 1992.

Allen, Sheila and Wolkowitz, Carol, *Homeworking. Myths and Realities*, Basingstoke, Macmillan, 1987.

Amsden, A.H., *The Economics of Women and Work*, Harmondsworth, Penguin, 1980.

Andersen, Uwe, 'Economic Unification' in *German Unification. The Unexpected Challenge*, ed. Dieter Grosser, Oxford, Berg, 1992.

Aslanbeigui, Nahid et al., eds., *Women in the Age of Economic Transformation*, London, Routledge, 1994.

Bäcker, Gerhard et al., *Kürzer Arbeiten – mehr Beschäftigung. Vorschläge zur Verkürzung der Arbeitszeit in Ostdeutschland*, LASA-Studie Number 19, March 1994.

Barker, Diana Leonard and Allen, Sheila, eds., *Sexual divisions and society: process and change*, London, Tavistock Publications, 1976.

Barrett, Michele, *Women's Oppression Today*, London, Verso, 1988.

Barrett, Michele, 'Words and Things: Materialism and Method in Contemporary Feminist Analysis', in *Destabilizing Theory*, eds. Michele Barrett and Anne Phillips, Cambridge, Polity Press, 1992.

Barrett, Michele and Phillips, Anne, eds., *Destabilizing Theory*, Cambridge, Polity Press, 1992.

Barron, R.D. and Norris, G.M., 'Sexual divisions and the dual labour market, in *Sexual divisions and society: process and change*, eds. Diana Leonard and Sheila Allen, London, Tavistock Publications, 1976.

Baur, Michaela, *Frauen in Arbeitsfoedergesellschaften. Eine Untersuchung zur quantitativen und qualitativen Beteiligung von Frauen in neun Brandenburger Arbeitsfoedergesellschaften*, LASA-Studie Number 18, March 1994.

Bebel, August, *Woman under Socialism*, New York, Schocken Books, 1971.

Beechey, Veronica, 'Some Notes on Female Wage Labour in Capitalist Production, *Capital and Class*, No. 3, 1977.

Beechey, Veronica, 'On Patriarchy', *Feminist Review*, No.3, 1979.

Beechey, Veronica, 'What's so special about women's employment? A review of some recent studies of women's paid work', *Feminist Review*, No.15, November 1983.

Beechey, Veronica and Perkins, Tessa, *A Matter of Hours. Women, Part-Time Work and the Labour Market*, Cambridge, Polity Press, 1987.

Behrend, Hanna, *Women catapulted into a different social order*, Berlin, mimeo, 1990.

Berry, Ellen E., ed., *Postcommunism and the Body Politic*, New York, NYU Press, 1995.

Bethkenhagen, J. et al., eds., *DDR und Osteuropa*, Opladen, Leske Verlag, 1981.

Betriebsparteiorganisation des VEB Textilkombinat Cottbus-Stammbetrieb, *VEB Textilkombinat Cottbus-Stammbetrieb. Chronik. Teil I – 1968–1975*, Cottbus, 1985; *Teil II – 1976–1980*, Cottbus, 1987; *Teil III – 1981–1985*, Cottbus, 1989.

Boa, Elisabeth and Wharton, Janet, eds., *Women and the Wende: Social Effects and Cultural Reflections of the German Unification Process*, German Monitor, No.31, Amsterdam, Rodopi, 1994.

Böhm, Tatiana, 'The Women's Question as a Democratic Question: In Search of Civil Society', in *Gender, Politics and Post-Communism*, eds. Nanette Funk, and Magda Mueller, London, Routledge, 1993.

Bordo, Susan, 'Feminism, Postmodernism and Gender-Scepticism', in *Feminism/Postmodernism*, ed. Linda J. Nicholson, London, Routledge, 1990.

Brandenburgishe Landeszentral für politische Bildung Staatskanzlei, *Du und Dein Bundesland*, Potsdam, June 1992.

Breitenacher, Michael et al., *Die Textil- und Bekleidungsindustrie der neuen Bundeslaendern im Umbruch*, Munich, ifo Institut fuer Wirtschaftsforschung, ifo studien zur industriewirtschaft 41, 1991.

Bridger, Sue et al., *No More Heroines? Russia, Women and the Market*, London, Routledge, 1996.

Bruegel, Irene, 'Women as a reserve army of labour: a note on recent British experience, *Feminist Review*, Vol.3, 1979.

Bruegel, Irene, 'Sex and Race in the Labour Market', *Feminist Review*, No.32, Summer 1989.

Brunner, Hans-Peter, 'The Recreation of Eastern European Competitiveness: Neither Magic nor Mirage', *The European Journal of Development Research*, Vol.6, No.1, June 1994.

Buckley, Mary, 'Soviet Interpretations of the Woman Question', in *Soviet Sisterhood*, ed. Barbara Holland, London, Fourth Estate, 1985.

Buckley, Mary, *Women and Ideology in the Soviet Union*, Hemel Hempstead, Harvester Wheatsheaf, 1989.

Bundesanstalt für Arbeit, *Arbeitsmarktreport für Frauen 1993. Berufliche Bildung und Beschäftigung von Frauen. Situation und Tendenzen*, Nuremberg, 1994a.

Bundesanstalt für Arbeit, *Presseinformationen: Erheblicher Sozialmissbrauch aufgedeckt*, No.16/94, 10.3.1994b.

Bundesministerium für Arbeit und Sozialordnung/ Bundesanstalt füer Arbeit, *Ein Leitfaden über Arbeitsbeschaffungsmassnahmen (ABM) in den neuen Bundesländern*, Bonn/Nuremberg, April 1991.

Bundesministerium für Arbeit und Sozialordnung/ Bundesanstalt für Arbeit, *Qualifizierung jetzt*, Bonn/ Nuremberg, May 1991.

Bundesministerium für Familie, Senioren, Frauen und Jugend: Abteilung Frauenpolitik, *"Gleichberechtigung von Frauen und Männern"Wirklichkeit und Einstellungen in der Bevölkerung. Ipos Umfrage November 1995*, Bonn, January 1996.

Bundesministerium für Familie, Senioren, Frauen und Jugend, *Frauen in der Bundesrepublik Deutschland*, Bonn, March 1998.

Bundesministerium der Finanzen, *Die Tätigkeit der Treuhandanstalt*, Bonn, 31.10.1991.

Bundesministerium für Frauen und Jugend, *Beratung, Fortbildung, Umschulung und Arbeitsbeschaffung*, Bonn, 1991a.

Bundesministerium für Frauen und Jugend, *Mutterschutzgesetz. Leitfaden zum Mutterschutz*, Bonn, 1991b.

Bundesministerium für Frauen und Jugend, *Gleichberechtigung von Frauen und Männern. Materialien zur Frauenpolitik 34/1994. Wirklichkeit und Einstellungen in der Bevölkerung. Ergebnisse der zweiten repräsentativen Bevölkerungsumfrage zur Gleichberechtigung in Deutschland des Instituts für praxisorientierte Sozialforschung, IPOS, November 1993*, Bonn, January 1994.

Bundesministerium für Jugend, Familie, Frauen und Gesundheit, *Frauen in der Bundesrepublik Deutschland*, Bonn, 1989.

Bundesministerium für Wirstchaft, *Wirtschaftliche Föderung in den neuen Bundesländern*, Bonn, August 1991.

Burton, Clare, *Subordination, Feminism and Social Theory*, Sydney, Allen and Unwin, 1985.

Buttler, Friedrich et al., Der *Arbeitsmarkt in der Region Süd-Bran-denburg. Entwicklung – Stand – Perspektiven*, IAB-Werkstatt-bericht, Number 4, 1993.

Cannan, Crescy, 'Active and Inactive Citizens in Europe's Welfare States. The Legacy and Contribution of Beveridge', in *Beveridge 1942–1992*, ed. John Jacobs, London, Whiting & Birch, 1992.

Childs, David, *The GDR. Moscow's German Ally*, London, Allen & Unwin, 1988.

Childs, David, ed., *Honecker's Germany*, London, Allen & Unwin, 1985.

Clarke, Simon, 'The Crisis of Fordism or the Crisis of Social Democracy?', *Telos*, No.83, Spring 1990.

Clarke, Simon, 'New utopias for old: Fordist dreams and Post-Fordist fantasies', *Capital and Class*, No.42, Winter 1990.

Clements, Elizabeth, 'The Abortion Debate in Unified Germany', in *Women and the Wende: Social Effects and Cultural Reflections of the German Unification Process*, eds. Elizabeth Boa and Janet Wharton, Amsterdam, Rodopi, 1994.

Coole, Diana, 'Whither Feminisms?', *Political Studies*, Vol.XLII, No.1, March 1994.

Coole, Diana, 'Is class a difference that still makes a difference?', *Radical Philosophy*, No. 77, May/June 1996.

Core, Francoise, 'Women and the Restructuring of Employment', *The OECD Observer*, No.186, February/March 1994.

Cornelsen, Doris, 'Entwicklung im Ueberblick', in *DDR und Osteuropa*, eds. J. Bethkenhagen et al., Opladen, Leske Verlag, 1981.

Corrin, Chris, ed., *Superwomen and the Double Burden: Women's Experience of Change in Central and Eastern Europe and the Former Soviet Union*, London, Scarlet Press, 1992.

Coyle, Angela, 'Sex and Skill in the Organization of the Clothing Industry', in *Work, Women and the Labour Market*, ed. Jackie West, London, Routledge & Kegan Paul, 1982.

Dahlerup, Drude, 'Confusing concepts – confusing reality: a theoretical discussion of the patriarchal state', in *Women and the State*, ed. Anne Showstack Sassoon, London, Hutchinson Education, 1987.

Daune-Richard, Anne-Marie, 'Gender Relations and Female Wage Labor. A Consideration of Sociological Categories', in *Feminization of the Labour Force: Paradoxes and Promises*, eds. Jane Jenson et al., Cambridge, Polity Press, 1988.

Dauschke, Petra et al., 'Ausdauernd, selbstbewusst und (noch) optimistisch?! Zur Erwerbsteiligung alleinerziehende Frauen in Brandenburg', in *Alleinerziehende in den neuen Bundesländern. Immer noch eine Lebensform wie jede andere?* Bonn, Friedrich Ebert Stiftung, Gesprachskreis Frauenpolitik, Heft 9, September 1993.

Delmar, Rosalind, 'Looking Again at Engels' Origins of the Family Private Property and the State', in *The Rights and Wrongs of Women*, eds. Ann Oakley and Juliet Mitchell, Harmondsworth, Penguin, 1976.

Derleder, Peter, 'Die Entwicklung des deutschen Familienrechts seit 1945', *Institut Frau und Gesellschaft*, Heft 4, 1990.

Di Stefano, Christine, 'Dilemmas of Difference: Feminism, Modernity and Postmodernism', in *Feminism/Postmodernism*, ed. Linda J. Nicholson, New York/ London, Routledge, 1990.

Dölling, Irene, 'Between Hope and Helplessness: Women in the GDR after the 'Turning Point', *Feminist Review*, No.39, Winter 1991.

Dunford, Michael, 'Differential development, institutions, modes of regulation and comparative transitions to capitalism: Russia, the Commonwealth of Independent States and the former German Democratic Republic, in *Theorising Transition. The Political Economy of Post-Communist Transformations*, eds. John Pickles and Adrian Smith, London, Routledge, 1998.

Dunskus, Petra, 'Frauenbeschäftigung in Gefahr', in *Perspektiven für den Arbeitsmarkt in den neuen Bundesländern*, ed. Kurt Vogler-Ludwig, Munich, ifo-Institut für Wirtschaftsforschung, ifo studies zur arbeitsmarktforschung 7,1991.

Dyson, Kenneth and Wilks, S.R.M., *Industrial Crisis*, Oxford, Robertson, 1983.

Ebert, Teresa L., *Ludic Feminism and After. Postmodernism, Desire, and Labor in Late Capitalism*, University of Michigan Press, 1996.

Edwards, G.E., *GDR Society and Social Institutions*, London, Macmillan, 1985.

Einhorn, Barbara, 'Socialist Emancipation: The Women's Movement in the German Democratic Republic', in *Promissory Notes: Women in the Transition to Socialism*, eds. Sonia Kruks et al., New York, Monthly Review Press, 1989.

Einhorn, Barbara, 'Where Have All the Women Gone? Women and the Women's Movement in East Central Europe', *Feminist Review*, No.39, Winter 1991.

Einhorn, Barbara, 'Emancipated Women or Hardworking Mothers? Women in the Former GDR', in *Superwomen and the Double Burden*, ed. Chris Corrin, London, Scarlet Press, 1992.

Einhorn, Barbara, *Cinderella Goes To Market*, London, Verso, 1993a.

Einhorn, Barbara, 'Democratization and Women's Movements in Central and Eastern Europe: Concepts of Women's Rights', in *Democratic Reform and the Position of Women in Transitional Economies*, ed. Valentine M. Moghadam, Oxford, Clarendon Press, 1993b.

Einhorn, Barbara, 'Women in the New Federal States after the *Wende*: The Impact of Unification on Women's Employment Opportunities' in *Women and the Wende: Social Effects and Cultural Reflections of the German Unification Process*, eds. Elizabeth Boa and Janet Wharton, Amsterdam, Rodopi, 1994.

Einhorn, Barbara, 'Feminism in Crisis: The East German Women's Movement in the "New Europe"', *Australian Journal of Politics and History*, vol.41, no.1, 1995.

Eisenstein, Zillah ed., *Capitalist Patriarchy and the Case for Socialist Feminism*, New York, Monthly Review Press, 1979.

Economic Intelligence Unit, *EIU Country Profile: East Germany 1988–1989*.

Enders, Urilke, 'Kinder, Küche, Kombinat. Frauen in der DDR', *Aus Politik und Zeitgeschichte*, B6–7/86, 8 February 1986.

Engelbrech, Gerhard, 'Vom Arbeitskräftemangel zum gegenwärtigen Arbeitskräfteüberschuss: Frauen und Erwerbsarbeit in den neuen Bundesländern', *Mitteilungen aus der Arbeitsmarkt und Berufsforschung*, Nuremberg, Heft 4, 1991.

Engelbrech, Gerhard, 'Berufliche Segregation – Erklärungssätze und empirische Befunde', *WSI Mitteilungen. Schwerpunktsheft: Ein Schritt vorwärts – zwei Schritte zurück? Gleichberechtigungspolitik in Ost und West*, April 1992.

Engelbrech, Gerhard, *Zwischen Wunsch und Wirklichkeit – Einstellungen ostdeutscher Frauen zur Erwerbstätigkeit zwei Jahre nach der Wende*, IAB-Werkstattbericht 8, 1993.

Engels, Friedrich, *The Origin of the Family, Private Property and the State*, London, Lawrence & Wishart, 1972.

Erler, Gisela, 'The German Paradox. Non-feminization of the Labor Force and Post-Industrial Social Policies', in *Feminization of the Labour Force: Paradoxes and Promises*, eds. Jane Jenson et al., Cambridge, Polity Press, 1988.

Esping-Andersen, Gosta, *The Three Worlds of Welfare Capitalism*, Cambridge, Polity Press, 1990.

Evans, Mary and Ungerson, Clare, eds., *Sexual Divisions: Patterns and Processes*, London, Tavistock Publications, 1983.

Falke, Andreas, 'An Unwelcome Enlargement? The European Community and German Unification' in *German Unification: Processes and Outcomes*, eds. M. Donald Hancock and Helga A. Welsh, Boulder, Westview Press, 1994.

Feminist Anthology Collective, ed. *No Turning Back. Writings from the Women's Liberation Movement*, London, Women's Press, 1981.

Figge, Karin and Quack, Sigrid, *Frauenbeschäftigung in der bundesdeutschen Textil- und Bekleidungsindustrie. Entwicklungen und Perspektiven unter Berücksichtigung des europäischen Marktes*, Berlin, WZB Discussion Papers, December 1990.

Flockton, Christopher and Esser, Josef, 'Labour Market Problems and Labour Market Policy', in *Developments in German Politics*, eds. Gordon Smith et al., Basingstoke, Macmillan, 1992.

Fong, Monica and Paull, Gillian, 'Women's Economic Status in the Restructuring of Eastern Europe', in *Democratic Reform and the Position of Women in Transitional Economies*, ed. Valentine M. Moghadam, Oxford, Clarendon Press, 1993.

Fraser, Nancy and Nicholson, Linda J., 'Social Criticism without Philosophy: An Encounter between Feminism and Postmodernism', in *Feminism/Postmodernism*, ed. Linda J. Nicholson, London, Routledge, 1990.

Frevert, Ute, *Women in German History. From Bourgeois Emancipation to Sexual Liberation*, Oxford, Berg, 1989.

Friedrich-Ebert Stiftung, *Frauen in der Privatwirtschaft im Land Brandenburg*, Bonn, Gesprächskreis Frauenpolitik, Heft 6, August 1992.

Friedrich-Ebert Stiftung, *Frauenpolitische Forderungen für Gesamtdeutschland*, Bonn, Gesprächskreis Frauenpolitik, September 1990.

Frowen, Stephen F., 'The Economy of the German Democratic Republic', in *Honecker's Germany*, ed. David Childs, London, Allen & Unwin, 1985.

Fulbrook, Mary, 'Wir sind ein Volk? Reflections on German Unification', *Parliamentary Affairs*, Vol.44, No.3, July 1991.

Funk, Nanette and Mueller, Magda, eds., *Gender, Politics and Post-Communism*, London, Routledge, 1993.

Gamarnikow, Eva et al., eds., *Gender, Class and Work*, Aldershot, Gower, 1985.

Gardiner J., 'Women's Domestic Labour', in *Capitalist Patriarchy and the Case for Socialist Feminism*, ed. Zillah R. Eisenstein, New York, Monthly Review Press, 1979.

Gensior, Sabine et al., *Berufliche Weiterbildung für Frauen in den neuen Ländern*, Bonn, Bundeminsiterium für Bildung und Wissenschaft, 1991.

George, Vic and Manning, Nick, *Socialism, Social Welfare and the Soviet Union*, London, Routledge & Kegan Paul, 1980.

Githens, Marianne, 'Reproductive Rights and the Struggle with Change in Eastern Europe' in *Abortion Politics. Public Policy in Cross-Cultural Perspective*, eds. Marianne Githens and Dorothy McBride Stetson, London, Routledge, 1996.

Glaessner, Gert-Joachim, *The Unification Process in Germany*, London, Pinter, 1992.

Graf, William D., *The Internationalization of the German Political Economy*, Basingstoke, Macmillan, 1992.

Grant, Rebecca and Newland, Kathleen, eds., *Gender and International Relations*, Miltion Keynes, Open University Press, 1991.

Grosser, Dieter, ed. *German Unification. The Unexpected Challenge*, Oxford, Berg, 1992.

GTB (Abteilung Gewerkschaft- und Gesellschaftspolitik), *Leitfaden zum Welttextilabkommen*, Dusseldorf, 9.3.92.

Hakim, Catherine, *Occupational Segregation. A comparative study of the degree and pattern of the differentiation between men and women's work in Britain, the United States and other countries*, Department of Employment Paper No.9, November 1979.

Hall, Peter, *Governing the Economy. The Politics of State Intervention in Britain and France*, Cambridge, Polity Press, 1986.

Hancock, Donald M. and Welsh, Helga A., eds., *German Unification. Processes and Outcomes*, Boulder, Westview Press, 1994.

Harder, Barbara L., *Alleinerziehende in Deutschland, 1995/1996. Daten zur Haushaltsstruktur, zur Wohn-, Einkommens- und Erwerbssituation*, Bonn, Bundesministerium für Familie, Senioren, Frauen und Jugend, 1996.

Harrison, J., 'The Political Economy of Housework', *Bulletin of the Conference of Socialist Economists*, Winter 1973.

Harstock, Nancy, 'Foucault on Power. A Theory for Women?' in *Feminism/Postmodernism*, ed. Linda J. Nicholson, London, Routledge, 1990.

Hartmann, Heidi, 'Capitalism, Patriarchy and Job Segregation by Sex', in *Capitalist Patriarchy and the Case for Socialist Feminism*, ed. Zillah R. Eisenstein, New York, Monthly Review Press, 1979.

Haug, Frigga, 'The End of Socialism in Europe: A New Challenge for Socialist Feminism? *Feminist Review*, No.39, Winter 1991.

Heinen, Jacqueline, 'Inequalities at Work: The Gender Division of Labour in the Soviet Union and Eastern Europe', *Studies in Political Economy*, 33, Autumn 1990.

Heisenberg, Wolfgang, ed., *German Unification in European Perspective*, London, Brassey's for Centre for European Studies, 1991.

Heitlinger, Alena, *Women and State Socialism*, Basingstoke, Macmillan, 1979.

Henderson, Karen, The GDR and the East European Experience', *German Politics*, Vol.3, No.2, 1994.

Hennessy, Rosemary, *Materialist Feminism and the Politics of Discourse*, London, Routledge, 1993.

Hess, Beth B. and Ferree Myra Marx, *Analyzing Gender*, London, Sage, 1987.

Hettne, Bjorn, 'The Political Economy of Post-Communist Development', *The European Journal of Development Research*, Vol.6, No.1, June 1994.

Hewitt, Tim et al., eds., *Industrialization and Development*, London, Oxford University Press in association with Open University, 1992.

Hill, Roland J. and Zielonka, Jan, *Restructuring Eastern Europe. Towards a New European Order*, Aldershot, Elgar, 1990.

Himmelweit, S. and Mohun, S., 'Domestic Labour and Capital', *Cambridge Journal of Economics*, Vol.1, 1977.

Hofman, Michael and Rink, Dieter, 'Die Auflösung der ostdeutschen Arbeitermilieus', *Aus Politik und Zeitgeschichte*, 25 June 1993.

Holland, Barbara, *Soviet Sisterhood*, London, Fourth Estate, 1985.

Holmgren, Beth, 'Bug Inspectors and Beauty Queens: The Problems of Translating Feminism into Russian', in *Postcommunism and the Body Politic*, ed. Ellen E. Berry, New York, NYU Press, 1995.

Holt, Alix, *Selected Writings of Alexandra Kollantai*, London, Allison & Busby, 1977.

Horn, Hannelore, 'Collapse from Internal Weakness – The GDR from October 1989 to March 1990' in *German Unification. The Unexpected Challenge*, ed. Dieter Grosser, Oxford, Berg, 1992.

Hübner, Sabine, 'Women at the Turning-Point: The Socio-Economic Situation and Prospects of Women in the Former German Democratic Republic', *Politics and Society in Germany, Austria and Switzerland*, Vol.3, No.3, 1991.

IG Bergbau und Energie, *Frauen in der Bergbau- und Energiewirtschaft*, Bochum, 1991.

IG Bergbau und Energie, *Perspektiven der Frauenerwerbsarbeit. Ergebnisse einer Umfrage im Bezirk Lausitz 1991*, Bochum, April 1992.

INFAS, *Frauen in den neuen Bundesländern im Prozess der deutschen Einigung*, Bonn, INFAS, February 1991.

INFAS, *Politogramm Brandenburg. Die soziale Situation der Frauen. January/February 1992*, Bonn, INFAS, March 1992.

Infratest Sozialforschung: Bielenski, Harald and von Rosenbladt, Bernhard, eds, *Arbeitsmarkt Monitor für die neuen Bundesländer. Umfrage 11/90 – Textband*, Nuremberg, Institut für Arbeitsmarkt- und Berufsforschung der Bundesanstalt fuer Arbeit, BeitrAB148.1, 1991.

Infratest Sozialforschung: Bielenski, Harald, Enderle, Jovita and von Rosenbladt, Bernhard, eds., *Arbeitsmarkt-Monitor für die neuen Bundesländer. Umfrage 3/91 – Textband*, Nuremberg, Institut für Arbeitsmarkt- und Berufsforschung der Bundesanstalt fuer Arbeit, BeitrAB 148.2, 1991.

Ingraham, Chrys, 'The Heterosexual Imaginary: Feminist Sociology and Theories of Gender' in *Queer Theory/Sociology*, ed. Steven Seidman, Oxford, Blackwell, 1996.

IAB-Kurzbericht (intern), *Sektorstruktur der Arbeitsamtsbezirke in den neuen Bundesländern*, 28.11.1990.

IAB-Kurzbericht (intern), *Beschäftigungsabbau in Problembranchen der neuen Bundesländer. Landwirtschaft*, 30.4.1991.

IAB-Kurzbericht (intern), *Beschäftigungsabbau in Problembranchen der neuen Bundesländer. Braunkohlenbergbau*, 8.5.1991.

IAB-Kurzbericht (intern), *Beschäftigungsabbau in Problembranchen der neuen Bundesländern. Metallverarbeitende Industrie*, 13.5.1991.

IAB-Kurzbericht (intern), *Beschäftigungsabbau in Problembranchen der neuen Bundesländern. Textil- und Konfektionsindustrie*, 22.5.91.

IAW (Institut für angewandte Wirtschaft), *Landesreport Brandenburg. Die Wirtschaft*, Berlin, Verlag Die Wirtschaft Berlin GmbH, 1992.

IHK (Industrie- und Handelskammer) Dresden, *Die Textil- und Bekleidungsindustrie der Oberlausitz. Situation – Massnahmen – Perspektiven*, 31.5.92.

Institut für Soziologie und Sozialpolitik, Bereich Frau/Familie, Forschungsgruppe "Die Frau", *Sofortinformation über die Durchführung einer empirischen Analyse zu objektiven und subjektiven Bedingungen für das Vereinbaren von Berufstätigkeit und Mut-*

terschaft under den Bedingungen der Intensivierung des gesellschaftlichen Reproduktionsprozesses, Berlin, mimeo, 1984.

Institut für Soziologie und Sozialpolitik, *Zur Situation von Kindern und Jugendlichen in der DDR (Materialversammlung) im Auftrag des Volkskammerausschusses Familie und Frauen*, Berlin, August 1990.

Jackson, Stevie, 'The Amazing Disappearing Woman', *Trouble and Strife*, No.25, Winter 1992.

Jacobs, John, ed. *Beveridge 1942–1992*, London, Whiting & Birch, 1992.

Jancar, Barbara Wolfe, *Women Under Communism*, Baltimore/ London, Johns Hopkins University Press, 1978.

Jasper, Gerda, *Tendenzen der Veränderung in der Arbeitsmarkt- und Lebenslage der Frauen in den neuen Bundesländern*, Berlin, October 1991.

Jasper, Gerda, 'Die Ausgrenzung ostdeuscher Frauen aus dem Arbeitsmarkt – Stand, 'Perspektiven' und voraussichtliche soziale Folgen, in *Thesen zur Fachtagung des Frauenpolitischen Runden Tisches 'Frauenarmut im Osten Deutschlands'*, Berlin, February 1992.

Jeffrey, Charlie, 'Electoral Volatility in United Germany', in *German Reunification: A Reference Guide and Commentary*, ed. Jonathan Osmond, Harlow, Longman, 1992.

Jeffries, Ian, 'The GDR in Historical and International Perspective', in *The East German Economy*, eds. Ian Jeffries and Manfred Melzer, London, Croom Helm, 1987.

Jeffries, Ian, 'The impact of reunification on the east German economy', in *German Reunification: A Reference Guide and Commentary*, ed. Jonathan Osmond, Harlow, Longman, 1992.

Jeffries, Ian and Melzer, Manfred eds., *The East German Economy*, London, Croom Helm, 1987.

Jenson, Jane, 'The Limits of 'and the' Discourse. French Women as Marginal Workers', in *Feminization of the Labour Force: Paradoxes and Promises*, eds. Jane Jenson, et al., Cambridge, Polity Press, 1988.

Jenson, Jane, 'The talents of women, the skills of men: flexible specialization and women, in *The Transformation of Work?*, ed. Stephen Wood, London, Unwin and Hyman, 1989.

Jenson, Jane et al., *Feminization of the Labour Force: Paradoxes and Promises*, Cambridge, Polity Press, 1988.

Jones, Kathleen B. and Jonasdottir Anna G., eds., *The Political Interests of Gender: Developing Theory and Research with a Feminist Face*, London, Sage, 1988.

Kane, Emily W. and Macauley Laura J., 'Interviewer Gender and Gender Attitudes', *Public Opinion Quarterly*, Vol.57, 1993.

Kielmannsegg, Peter Graf, 'Germany – A Future with Two Pasts' in *German Unification. The Unexpected Challenge*, ed. Dieter Grosser, Oxford, Berg, 1992.

Kirkpatrick, Clifford, *Woman in Nazi Germany*, London, Jarrolds, 1939.

Kistler, Ernst et al., '"Die Wiedervereinigung der deutschen Maenner braucht keine Frauen.." Frauen als Wendeverliererinnen', *Aus Politik und Zeitgeschichte*, 5 February 1993.

Klammer, Ute, 'Wieder einmal auf der Verlierer(innen)seite – Zur arbeitsmarkt- und socialpolitischen Situation von Frauen im Zeitalter der "Sparpakete"', *WSI Mitteilungen*, 1/1997.

Klein, Renate D. and Steinberg, Deborah Lynne, eds., *Radical Voices. A Decade of Feminist Resistance from Women's Studies International Forum*, Oxford, Pergamon Press, 1989.

Kolinsky, Eva, 'Women in the New Germany', *Politics and Society in Germany, Austria and Switzerland*, Vol.3, No.3, 1991a.

Kolinsky, Eva, 'Political Participation and Parliamentary Careers: Women's Quotas in West Germany', *West European Politics*, Vol.14, No.1., January 1991b.

Kolinsky, Eva, 'Women in the New Germany: The East-West Divide', in *Developments in German Politics*, ed. Gordon Smith, Basingstoke, Macmillan, 1992.

Kolinsky, Eva, *Women in Contemporary Germany*, Oxford, Berg, 1993.

Koonz, Claudia, *Mothers in the Fatherland*, London, Methuen, 1988.

Kruks, Sonia et al., eds. *Promissory Notes. Women in the Transition to Socialism*, New York, Monthly Review Press, 1989.

Kühl, Jürgen et al., 'Beschaftigungsperspektiven von Treuhandunternehmen, *Mitteilungen aus der Arbeitsmarkt- und Berufsforschung* 3, 1991.

Kuhn, Annette and Wolpe, AnnMarie, eds., *Feminism and Materialism*, London, Routledge & Kegan Paul, 1978.

Kuhrig, Herta and Speigner, Wulfram, *Wie emanzipiert sind die Frauen in der DDR?: Beruf, Bildung und Familie*, Cologne, Pahl Rugenstein, 1979.

Kurz-Scherf, I., 'Geschlechterkampf am Arbeitsmarkt? – Frauenperspektiven in Deutschland', *WSI Mitteilingen. Schwerpunktheft: Ein Schritt vorwärts – zwei Schritte zuück? Gleichberectigungspolitik in Ost und West*, April 1992.

Kuusinen, O., ed., *Fundamentals of Marxism-Leninism*, London, Lawrence & Wishart, 1961.

Landes, Joan B., 'Marxism and the 'Woman Question', in *Promissory Notes. Women in the Transition to Socialism*, eds. Sonia Kruks et al., New York, Monthly Review Press, 1989.

Landesarbeitsamt Berlin-Brandenburg, *Illegale Beschaeftigung*, Berlin, 14.1.94.

Landesarbeitsamt Berlin-Brandenburg. Referat für Frauenbelange, *Jahresbericht über die Situation der Frauen am Berliner und Brandenburger Arbeitsmarkt 1996*, Berlin, 1997.

Landesamt für Datenverarbeitung und Statistik Brandenburg, *Statistische Berichte: Bevölkerung und Erwerbsleben im Land Brandenburg 1991. Ergebnisse des Mikrozensus*, Potsdam, 1993a.

Landesamt für Datenverarbeitung und Statistik Brandenburg, *Statistische Berichte: Bevölkerung und Erwerbsleben im Land Brandenburg 1992. Ergebnisse des Mikrozensus*, Potsdam, 1993b.

Lane, Christel, 'Gender and the labour market in Europe: Britain, Germany and France compared', *The Sociological Review*, Vol.41, No.2, May 1993.

Lane, David, *Leninism: A Sociological Interpretation*, Cambridge, Cambridge University Press, 1981.

Langan, Mary and Ostner, Ilona, 'Gender and Welfare. Towards a Comparative Framework', in *Towards a European Welfare State?*, ed. Graham Room, Bristol, SAUS, 1991.

Lees, Charles, 'A Watershed Election: The Berlin State and District Elections of 22 October 1995', *Regional and Federal Studies*, Vol.6, No.1, Spring 1996.

Lehmbruch, Gerhard, 'Die improvisierte Vereinigung: Die Dritte Deutsche Republik', *Leviathan*, Vol.18, Part 4, 1990.

Lehmbruch, Gerhard, 'Die deutsche Vereinigung: Strukturen und Strategien', *Politische Vierteljahresschrift*, Vol.4, December 1991.

Lenin, Vladimir Ilyich, *On the Emancipation of Women*, New York, International Publishers, 1966.

Management Partner GmbH, *Ergebnisse Umfrage Textilindustrie Sacshen/Thüringen*, Stuggart/Chemnitz, May 1992.

March, James G. and Olsen, Johan P., 'The New Institutionalism: Organizational Factors in Political Life', *American Political Science Review*, Vol.78, No.3, Sept. 1984.

Marschall, Dieter, *Bekämpfung illegaler Beschäftigung*, Munich, Verlag C.H.Beck, 1983.

Marsh, David, *The Bundesbank: The Bank That Rules Europe*, London, Mandarin, 1993.

Marx Ferree, Myra, 'The Rise and Fall of 'Mommy Politics':
Feminism and Unification in (East) Germany', *Feminist Studies*,
19, no.1, 1993.

Massey, Doreen, *Space, Place and Gender*, Cambridge, Polity Press,
1994.

McAdams, A. James, 'Towards a New Germany? – Problems of
Unification, *Government and Opposition*, Vol.25, No.3, Summer
1990.

McDonough, Roisin and Harrison, Rachel, 'Patriarchy and Rela-
tions of Production' in *Feminism and Materialism*, eds. Annette
Kuhn and AnnMarie Wolpe, London, Routledge & Kegan
Paul, 1978.

Menschik, Jutta and Leopold, Evelyn, *Gretchens rote Schwestern.
Frauen in der DDR*, Frankfurt, Fischer Taschenbuch, 1974.

Miall, Hugh, *Shaping the New Europe*, London, Pinter, 1993.

Millard, Frances, 'Women in Poland: The Impact of Post-Communist Transformation', *Journal of Area Studies*, Number 6,
Spring 1995.

MASGF (Ministerium für Arbeit, Soziales, Gesundheit und
Frauen) Brandenburg, *Richtlinie über die Gewährung von
Zuschüssen zu den Betriebskosten von Kindergärten und Kinderkrip-
pen*, Potsdam, 15.12.1991.

MASGF Brandenburg, *Ratgeber für Alleinerziehende*, Potsdam,
December 1992.

MASGF Brandenburg, *1.Frauenreport Land Brandenburg*, Potsdam, 1993a.

MASGF Brandenburg (Abteilung Arbeit), *Informationsblatt zum
$249h AFG*, Potsdam, August 1993b.

MASGF Brandenburg, *Wege aus der Arbeitslosigkeit. Teil 1: Projekte
für Frauen*, Potsdam, October, 1993c.

MASGF Brandenburg, *Landesprogramm 'Qualifizierung und Arbeit
für Brandenburg'. Stand 1.March 1994*, Potsdam, February 1994.

MASGF Brandenburg, *Arbeitsmarktbericht für das Land Brandenburg 1956*, Potsdam, 1996.

MASGF Brandenburg, *Arbeitsmarktbericht für das Land Brandenburg 1996*, Potsdam, 1997a.

MASGF Brandenburg, *IAB-Betriebspanel. Länderbericht Brandenburg – Ergebnisse der ersten Welle 1996*, Potsdam, 1997b.

Ministerium für Bildung, Jugend und Sport (MBJS) Brandenburg, *Kitagesetz für das Land Brandenburg*, 1992.

MWMT (Ministerium für Wirtschaft, Mittelstand und Technolo-
gie) Brandenburg, *Konferenz: Zukunft der Braunkohle in Bran-*

denburg. Bericht zur Konferenz am 8. und 9. Juli 1991, Potsdam, 1991.

MWMT Brandenburg, Aussenreferat Cottbus, *Situation, Probleme und Entwicklungsvorstellungen der Textilindustrie in der Region der Niederlausitz*, Cottbus, 13.3.92.

MWMT Brandenburg, *Jahreswirtschaftsbericht Brandenburg 1992*, Potsdam, 1993.

MWMT Brandenburg, *Jahreswirtschaftsbericht Brandenburg 1993*, Potsdam, 1994.

Moghadam, Valentine M., *Gender and Restructuring: Perestroika, the 1989 Revolutions and Women*, Helsinki, WIDER, November 1990.

Moghadam, Valentine M., 'Bringing the Third World In: A Comparative Analysis of Gender and Restructuring' in *Democratic Reform and the Position of Women in Transitional Economies*, ed. V.M. Moghadam, Oxford, Clarendon Press, 1993.

Moghadam, Valentine M. ed., *Democratic Reform and the Position of Women in Transitional Economies*, Oxford, Clarendon Press, 1993.

Molyneux, Maxine, 'Beyond the Domestic Labour Debate', *New Left Review*, No.116, July-August 1979.

Molyneux, Maxine, 'Women in Socialist Societies. Problems of Theory and Practice', in *Of Marriage and the Market*, eds Kate Young et al., London, CSE, 1981.

Molyneux, Maxine, 'The Woman Question in the Age of Perestroika', *New Left Review*, 183, Sept/Oct 1990.

Molyneux, Maxine, 'Marxism, feminism and the demise of the Soviet model' in *Gender and International Relations*, eds. Rebecca Grant and Kathleen Newland, Milton Keynes, Open University Press, 1991.

Nash, June and Fernandez-Kelly, Maria Patricia, eds., *Women, Men and the International Division of Labour*, Albany, State University of New York Press, 1983.

Nicholson, Linda J., ed., *Feminism/Postmodernism*, London, Routledge, 1990.

Oakley, Ann, *Sex, Gender and Society*, London, Temple Smith, 1972.

Oakley, Ann, *Housewife*, Harmondsworth, Penguin, 1974.

Oakley, Ann and Mitchell, Juliet, *The Rights and Wrongs of Women*, Harmondsworth, Penguin, 1976.

OECD, OECD *Economic Surveys. Germany 1991/1992*, Paris, OECD, 1992.

Opie, Ann, 'Qualitative Research, Appropriation of the 'Other' and Empowerment', *Feminist Review*, No.40. Spring 1992.

Osmond, Jonathan, ed., *German Reunification: A Reference Guide and Commentary*, Harlow, Longman, 1992.

Paraskewopoulos, Spiridon, Employment Problems in the GDR during the Transition to a Market Economy, *Aussenpolitik* (English Edition), Vol.41, 1990.

Paterson, William E. and Smith, Gordon, 'German Unity', in *Developments in German Politics*, eds. Gordon Smith et al., Basingstoke, Macmillan, 1992.

PDS/Linke Liste AK Feminisierung der Gesellchaft, *Zur Lage der Frauen in den neuen Bundesländern*, Bonn, February 1992.

Pearson, Ruth, 'Gender Issues in Industrialization' in *Industrialization and Development*, eds. Tim Hewitt et al., London, Oxford University Press in association with Open University, 1992.

Penrose, Virginia, 'Vierzig Jahre SED-Frauenpolitik: Ziele, Strategien und Ergebnisse', *Institut Frau und Gesellschaft*, Heft 4, 1990.

Phillips, Anne, 'Universal Pretensions in Political Thought', in *Destabilizing Theory*, eds. Michele Barrett and Anne Phillips, Cambridge, Polity Press, 1992.

Pickles, John and Smith, Adrian, *Theorising Transition. The Political Economy of Post-Communist Transformations*, London, Routledge, 1998.

Pollert, Anna, 'Women, Gender Relations and Wage Labour', in *Gender, Class and Work*, eds. Eva Garmanikow, Aldershot, Gower, 1985.

Presse- und Informationsamt der Bundesregierung, *Politik für die Familie*, Bonn, 1.1.1991.

Presse- und Informationsamt der Bundesregierung, *Politik für Frauen*, Bonn, 1.12.1991.

Presse- und Informationsamt der Bundesregierung, *Unsere Wirtschaft – gestern – heute – morgen*, Bonn, January 1992.

Pringle, Rosemary and Watson, Sophie, ''Women's Interests and the Post-Structuralist State', in *Destabilizing Theory*, eds. Michele Barrett and Anne Phillips, Cambridge, Polity Press, 1992.

Raasch, Sibylle and Wahnschaffe, Phillip, 'The Integration of the West German Textile and Clothing Industry into the New International Division of Labour', in *The Internationalisation of the German Political Economy*, ed William D. Graf, Basingstoke, Macmillan, 1992.

Ramazanoglu, Caroline, ed., *Up Against Foucault*, London, Routledge, 1993.

Ransom, Janet, 'Feminism, difference and discourse: the limits of discursive analysis for feminism', in *Up Against Foucault*, ed. Caroline Ramazanoglu, , London, Routledge, 1993.

Redclift, Nanneka and Sinclair, M.Thea, *Working Women: International Perspectives*, London, Routledge, 1991.

Robert, Annette, 'The Effects of the International Division of Labour on Female Workers in the Textile and Clothing Industries', *Development and Change*, Vol.14, 1983.

Roberts, B., Finnegan D. and Gallie, D., eds., *New Approaches to Economic Life*, Manchester, Manchester University Press, 1985.

Roberts, Geoffrey K., 'Emigrants in their own Country. German Reunification and its Political Consequences.' *Parliamentary Affairs*, Vol.44, No.3, July 1991.

Room, Graham, ed., *Towards a European Welfare State?* Bristol, SAUS, 1991.

Rose, Richard and Page Edward C., '*German Responses to Regime Change: Culture, Class, Economy or Context?*'*West European Politics*, Vol.19, No.1, January 1996.

Röth, Ute, *Zur Vereinbarkeit von Berufstätigkeit und Mutterschaft als gesellscaftlichem Problem und gegenwärtige Entwicklungstendenzen bei besonderer Berücksichtigung sozialstruktureller Aspekte der Nutzung des Qualifikationsniveaus von berufstätigen Müttern unter den Bedingungen der Intensivierung in der Industrie,*Thesen zur Dissertation A, Berlin, 1988.

Rowbotham, Sheila, 'The trouble with 'patriarchy'', in *No Turning Back. Writings from the Women's Liberation Movement*, ed. Feminist Anthology Collective, London, The Women's Press, 1981.

Rubery, Jill, 'Structured Labour Markets, Worker Organization and Low Pay', in *The Economics of Women and Work*, ed. A.H. Amsden, Harmondsworth, Penguin, 1980.

Rubery, Jill, ed., *Women and Recession*, London, Routledge & Kegan Paul, 1988.

Rudolph, Hedwig, 'Brot und Rosen zu DM-Preisen? Frauenarbeit im wirtschaftlichen Umbruch', *Institut Frau und Gesellschaft*, Heft4, 1990a.

Rudolph, Helmut, 'Beschäftigungsstrukturen in der DDR vor der Wende. Eine Typisierung von Kreisen und Arbeitsämtern', *Mitteilungen aus der Arbeitsmarkt- und Berufsforschung (Schwerpunktheft Gesamtdeutscher Arbeitsmarkt)* 4, 1990b.

Rueschemeyer, Dietrich et al., *Capitalist Development and Democracy*, Cambridge, Polity Press, 1992.

Rueschemeyer, Marilyn, 'Women in East Germany: From State Socialism to Capitalist Welfare State', in *Democratic Reform and the Position of Women in Transitional Economies*, ed. Valentine M. Moghadam, Oxford, Clarendon Press, 1993.

Rzhanitsina, L., *Female Labour under Socialism: The Socio-Economic Facts*, Moscow, Progress Publishers, 1983.

Schindler, Christiane, *Alleinerziehend – eine Lebensalternative? (eine lebbare Alternative)*, Berlin, October 1991.

Schuldt, Karsten, *Sozio-ökonomische Aspekte der Gestaltung der Lebensarbeitszeit in der DDR bis 1989*, Nuremberg, Institut für Arbeitsmarkt- und Berufsforschung der Bundesanstalt fuer Arbeit, BeitrAB 141, 1991.

Schuldt, Karsten, *Arbeitspendler im Land Brandenburg*, LASA-Studie Number 17, October 1993.

Schütte, Ilse and Minx, Bärbel, *Bergbau – nur eine Männersache*, Dortmund, Sozialforschungsstelle (sfs), 1993.

Scott, Hilda, *Women and Socialism: experiences from eastern Europe*, London, Allison & Busby, 1976.

Senatsverwaltung fuer Arbeit und Frauen Berlin, *arbeitslos, über 40, weiblich*, Berlin, January 1992.

Showstack Sassoon, Anne, ed., *Women and the State*, London, Hutchinson Education, 1987.

Sinclair, M. Thea, 'Women, work and skill', in *Working Women. International Perspectives*, eds. Nanneke Redclift and Thea M. Sinclair, London, Routledge, 1991.

Smart, Carol, 'Patriarchal relations and law: an examination of family law and sexual equality in the 1950s, in *Sexual Divisions: Patterns and Processes*, eds. Mary Evans and Clare Ungerson, London, Tavistock Publications, 1983.

Smith, Adrian and Pickles, John, ' Introduction: theorising transition and the political economy of transformation' in *Theorising Transition. The Political Economy of Post-Communist Transformations*, eds. John Pickles and Adrian Smith, London, Routledge, 1998.

Smith, Gordon, 'The Nature of the Unified State', in *Developments in German Politics*, eds. Gordon Smith et al., Basingstoke, Macmillan, 1992.

Smith, Gordon et al., eds. *Developments in German Politics*, Basingstoke, Macmillan, 1992.

Soper, Kate, 'Postmodernism and its Discontents', *Feminist Review*, No. 39, Winter 1991.

Stacey, Jackie, 'Untangling Feminist Theory' in *Introducing Women's Studies*, eds. Diane Richardson and Victoria Robinson, Basingstoke, Macmillan, 1993.

Strzodka, Ursula, *Studie zur Situation von Frauen in Cottbus*, Cottbus, mimeo, 1992.

Teschner, Julia, '*Demokratischer Frauenbund Deutschlands*: Socialist Mass Organisation and Western Charity? in *Women and the Wende: Social Effects and Cultural Reflections of the German Unification Process*, eds. Elizabeth Boa and Janet Wharton, Amsterdam, Rodopi, 1994.

THA Direktorat Textil/Bekleidung/Leder, *Bericht über die Textil- und Bekleidungsindustrie in Sachsen (Schwerpunkt: zentralbetreute THA-Unternehmen)*, Berlin, 17.8.92.

Timmins, Graham, 'Trade Unions: The Social Dimension', in *German Reunification: A Reference Guide and Commentary*, ed. Jonathan Osmond, Harlow, Longman, 1992.

Tischer, Ute and Doering, Gabriele, *Arbeitsmarkt für Frauen. Aktuelle Entwicklungen und Tendenzen im Überblick*, Nuremberg, Bundesanstalt für Arbeit, 1998.

Trostman, Heinz, 'Berufstätigkeit, Mutterschaft und berufliche Weiterbildung', *Informationen des wissenschaftlichen Rates 'Die Frau in der sozialistischen Gesellschaft*, Heft 2, 1988.

Veen, Hans-Joachim and Zelle Carsten, 'National Identity and Political Priorities in Eastern and Western Germany', *German Politics*, Vol.4, No.1, April 1995.

Vogelheim, Elisabeth, 'Women in a Changing Workplace. The Case of the Federal Republic of Germany' in *Feminization of the Labour Force: Paradoxes and Promises*, eds. Jane Jenson et al., Cambridge, Polity Press, 1988.

Vogler-Ludwig, Kurt, *Perspektiven für den Arbeitsmarkt in den neuen Bundesländern*, Munich, ifo Institut fuer Wirtschaftsforschung, ifo studien zur arbeitsmarktforschung 7, 1991.

Völkel, Brigitte, 'Zu regionalen Aspekten des Arbeitmarktes am Beispiel Dresden dargestellt', in *Perspektiven für den Arbeitsmarkt in den neuen Bundesländern*, ed Kurt Vogler-Ludwig, Munich, ifo Institut fuer Wirtschaftsforschung, ifo studien zur arbeitsmarktforschung 7, 1991.

von Beyme, Klaus, 'Transition to Democracy – or Anschluss? The Two Germanies and Europe, *Government and Opposition*, Vol.25, No.2, Spring 1990.

von Beyme, Klaus, 'The Effects of Reunification on German Democracy: A Preliminary Evaluation of a Great Social Experiment', *Government and Opposition*, Vol.27, No.2, Spring 1992.

Wagner Gert et al., eds. *An der Schwelle zur Sozialen Marktwirtschaft. Ergebnisse aus des Basiserhebung des Sozio-oekonomischen Panels in der DDR im Juni 1990*, Nuremberg, Institut für Arbeitsmarkt- und Berufsforschung der Bundesanstalt fuer Arbeit, BeitrAB 143, 1991.

Walby, Sylvia, 'Patriarchal Structures: The Case of Unemployment', in *Gender, Class and Work*, eds. Eva Gamarnikow et al., Aldershot, Gower, 1985.

Walby, Sylvia, 'Flexibility and the changing sexual division of labour', in *The Transformation of Work*, ed. Stephen Wood, London, Unwin and Hyman, 1989.

Walby, Sylvia, *Theorizing Patriarchy*, Oxford, Basil Blackwell, 1990.

Walby, Sylvia, 'Post-Post Modernism? Theorizing Social Complexity', in *Destabilizing Theory*, eds. Michele Barrett and Anne Phillips, Cambridge, Polity Press, 1992.

Walby, Sylvia, *Gender Transformations,* London, Routledge, 1997.

Walby, Sylvia, ed., *Gender Segregation at Work*, Milton Keynes, Open University Press, 1988.

Walker, Rachel, 'The Relevance of Ideology' in *Restructuring Eastern Europe. Towards a New European Order*, eds. Roland J. Hilland and Jan Zielonka, Aldershot, Elgar, 1990.

Waller, Peter P., 'Towards a Comprehensive Development Cooperation with the Transformation Countries in Eastern Europe', *The European Journal of Development Research*, Vol.6, No.1, June 1994.

Weedon, Chris, *Feminist Practice and Poststructuralist Theory,* Oxford, Basil Blackwell, 1987.

Wegner, Manfred, Systemstransformation und Beschäftigungsaussichten', in *Perspektiven für den Arbeitsmarkt in den neuen Bundesländern*, ed Kurt Vogler-Ludwig, Munich, ifo-Institut für Wirtschaftsforschung, ifo studien zur arbeitsmarktforschung 7, 1991.

Welsh, Helga A., 'The Collapse of Communism in Eastern Europe and the GDR: Evolution, Revolution, and Diffusion' in *German Unification. Processes and Outcomes*, eds Donald M. Hancock, and Helga A. Welsh, Boulder, Westview Press, 1994.

Wheelock, Jane, 'Capital restructuring and the domestic economy: Family self-respect and the irrelevance of the 'rational economic man'', *Capital and Class*, No.41, Summer 1990.

Wilson, Elizabeth, *Women and the Welfare State*, London, Tavistock Publications, 1977.

Winkler, Gunnar, ed., *Frauenreport '90*, Berlin, Verlag Die Wirtschaft GmbH, 1990.

Wood, Stephen ed. *The Transformation of Work?*, London, Unwin and Hyman, 1989.

Woods, Roger, 'The Significance of East German Intellectuals in Opposition', in *Honecker's Germany*, ed. David Childs, London, Allen & Unwin, 1985.

Young, Kate et al., *Of Marriage and the Market. Women's subordination internationally and its lessons*, London, CSE, 1981.

Zimmer, Katherine, *Das Leben vor der Geburt*, Bundesministerium für Familie und Senioren, Bonn, 1991.

Index

U.W.E.L. LEARNING RESOURCES